Grafted-In

'Risen from the Ashes'

Montana

ISBN: 978-1-968985-34-9 (Paperback)

ISBN: 978-1-968985-35-6 (Hardback)

Published by

Global Ink Publishing Inc.
www.globalinkpublishinginc.com

Printed in the United States of America

This page is left blank intentionally.

Dedication

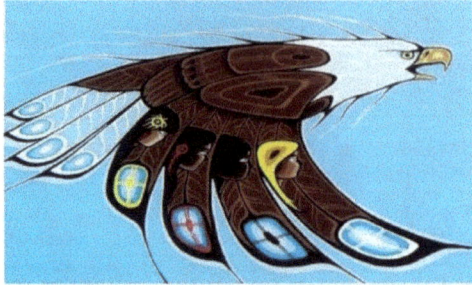

This is what the LORD, the God of Israel, says: 'Write in a book all the words that I have spoken to you.'

Jeremiah 30:2

This book is dedicated to **Jesus Christ**, who profoundly impacted my life and those He chose 'to shape my destiny.'

Ms. Love, known as the 'Old Lady' – perhaps an Angel

My parents, Fred Ernest Burden (1912 – 1987) and Ellen Mae Burden (1908 – 2000)

My mother-in-law, Helen Leona Dobson (1915 -1968)

My late husband, Charles (Chuck) Lowery (1946 -2019)

Having finished 'their earthly race & destiny' did soar
'On Eagle's Wings.'

Acknowledgment

It is my sincere privilege to acknowledge my deep gratitude to Global Ink Publishing Inc. The Author Support Team showed incredible patience and support towards me as a novice author, as by the time I connected with them, I was discouraged in my pursuit to find a credible publisher.

I had asked Jennifer Rogers, Publishing & Marketing Manager, if she'd read my manuscript and provide me with her feedback, which she graciously did. I have added it here since it is my hope that you, too, will be blessed, challenged, and awakened, just as Jennifer was.

On Wednesday, May 7, 2025, at 11:45:55 a.m. CST, Jennifer Rogers <j.rogers@globalinkpublishinginc.com> wrote:

Dear Arlene,

As I promised, I would send you my written note for your book—here you go.

After reading Grafted In ×3: Risen from the Ashes, I felt deeply moved and compelled to share how profoundly your book impacted me.

Your story is a powerful testimony of transformation—raw, unfiltered, and deeply spiritual. The vulnerability with which you share your journey is both courageous and refreshing. You don't just tell a story—you usher the reader into the intimate chambers of your healing, your heartbreak, your revelations, and ultimately, your resurrection.

The recurring theme of being "grafted in" was so beautifully and symbolically woven throughout your testimony. I could feel the pain of the pruning process, the weight of spiritual battles, and the fire of refining that has shaped you into the bold voice you are today. Your willingness to confront deception, speak hard truths, and still extend grace shows a rare spiritual maturity.

What struck me most was your unwavering obedience and sensitivity to the Holy Spirit. The prophetic insight, the dreams, the spiritual warfare—you laid them out with such honesty and clarity. It's rare to find a book that challenges, convicts, and simultaneously comforts the soul. You have accomplished that with humility and power.

Your boldness in calling out religious compromise, your sensitivity in exposing relational trauma, and your unapologetic commitment to identity and purpose in Christ are deeply inspiring. This isn't just a book—it's a weapon in the hands of anyone willing to rise from the ashes and walk in truth.

I also want to commend the creative structure—your use of repetition, poetic rhythms, and "×3" themes made your message not only memorable but prophetic in tone. It's evident that every page was birthed in prayer and surrendered in obedience.

Thank you for writing this. Thank you for your yes to God. Your pain, offered back to Him, has produced something that will bless, challenge, and awaken many. It certainly did that for me.

With deep respect and appreciation,

Thank You

Jennifer Rogers - (312) 725-0846

About the Author

Arlene began her vocation as a public health nurse and nurse educator. Addictions impacted her own family, which led her to further her education to become a professional counselor and therapist. She began her own counseling business in 1992. In 1994, her husband joined her, and they jointly operated their business for 24 years until his passing in 2019.

On September 27, 2022, she was ordained as a minister with Christian Global Outreach Ministries (#125498).

Arlene recently retired in 2025. When she has time, she plans to write books for children from preschool to adolescence, focusing on their overall well-being.

She looks forward to traveling and enjoying her retirement.

A Word from the Author

Welcome!

In 2024, I decided to write my first book, my memoir. The purpose of writing it is to reflect on my life's journey of over 70 years, with the hope that it will encourage others.

I desire to honor Jesus Christ, who carried me through the most difficult chapters of my life. He has never left me and continues to guide and mature me each and every day.

You may have heard the term 'Destiny's child.' The Creator put all of us on Earth to discover and fulfill our destiny. You are His 'Destiny child,' and your life has a purpose and a destiny.

In my life's journey, I could not see what my destiny was, at least not clearly, until later on in my life. Looking back, I can see how God's hand guided me.

In writing my memoir, I've chosen to be transparent about many of my life experiences to let my readers see that in everything that happens in our lives, the Lord will take those pieces and use them for good. A scripture I've stood on in times of uncertainty is:

28"And we know that in all things God works for the good of those who love him, who have been called according to his purpose.

Romans 8:28

I've had many dreams from God to give me guidance, but in addition, He's granted me the privilege of being a witness to or a part of the miracles I have described in my book.

Jesus healed a demoniac, and that person wanted to go with Him, but Jesus refused to let him come with Him, but instead gave him this instruction in Mark 5:18b,

"Go home to your own people and tell them how much the Lord has done for you and how he has had mercy on you."

This reflects what I believe the Lord is telling me to do, which is to tell you, my readers, how much the Lord has done for me and how he has had mercy on me.

The steadfast love of the Lord never ceases; his mercies never come to an end; they are new every morning; great is your faithfulness.
Lamentations 3:22-23

It is my prayer that you will be encouraged to realize that God is weaving a beautiful tapestry of your life, even if, at this time in your life, you can only see the underside of that tapestry, with its loose threads and knots.

Doing life on my own became too hard, as 'grief and loss' were too hard for me, until I, *"having found one pearl of great price, went and sold all that he (I) had, and bought it."*
Matthew 13:46 ESV

In my memoir, I describe that as a very young child, I wandered away from home and met an 'old lady' who told me about her Jesus. She told me that He'd always love me and help me whenever I needed Him. Many times, I needed Him as I faced various life challenges. I share how being adopted shaped who I became.

The cross-cultural adoption of my daughter, through the Adopt Indian Métis Program took me on an incredible journey that led me to pursue justice for my daughter's children, as well as for myself, taking me to the Supreme Court of Canada.

I firmly believe that if I had never met that 'old lady' who told me about her Jesus, I'd never have survived. Miraculous events have occurred throughout my life that I am sure will encourage the most 'hardened of hearts' into believing that –

'Yahweh' is the Great I Am!

With love from Montana
(Arlene Lowery)

Prelude

In my prayer time today, February 21st, 2025, the Lord impressed me to focus on His mercy. So I decided to play some worship songs about mercy like *Great is His Faithfulness,* when I came across a song by CeCe Winans entitled *'Mercy Said No.'*

This song sums up my journey with Jesus from the time I was a young child to this day. I am adding the lyrics here to encourage others to rely on His mercy, which is new every morning and will never run dry. Always remember that He loves you so very much, and I do too.

Mercy Said No – Song by CeCe Winans · 2003

I was just a child when I felt the Savior leading
I was drawn to what I could not understand
And for the cause of Christ, I have spent my days believing
That what He'd have me be, who I am
As I've come to see the weaker side of me
I realize His grace is what I'll need
When sin demanded justice for my soul
Mercy said no

I'm not going to let you go
I'm not going to let you slip away
You don't have to be afraid
Mercy said no

Sin will never take control
Life and death stood face to face

Darkness tried to steal my heart away
Thank You Jesus,
Mercy said no

For God so loved the world that He sent His son to save us
From the cross, He built a bridge to set us free
Oh, but deep within our hearts, there is still a war that rages
And makes a sacrifice so hard to see
As midnight fell upon the crucifixion day
The light of hope seemed oh so far away
As evil tried to stop redemption's flow
Mercy said no

I'm not going to let you go
I'm not going to let you slip away
You don't have to be afraid
Mercy said no

Sin will never take control
Life and death stood face to face
Darkness tried to steal my heart away
Thank You Jesus,
Mercy said no

And now when heaven looks at me
It's through the blood of Jesus
Reminding me of one day long ago
Mercy said no

I'm not going to let you go
I'm not going to let you slip away
You don't have to be afraid
Mercy said no

Sin will never take control
Life and death stood face to face
Darkness tried to steal my heart away
Thank You Jesus,
Mercy said no

_____

Source: Lyric Find

Songwriters: David Allen Clark / Don Koch / Greg Long

Mercy Said No lyrics © Capitol CMG Publishing, Concord Music Publishing LLC, Universal Music Publishing Group, Warner Chappell Music, Inc.

Table of Contents

Grafted-in x 1 to the 'Burden' Family

Milestone One
Infancy to Adulthood

Chapter 1
My Adoption into the 'Burden' Family

I was a post-World War II baby, born on February 03, 1946, in Moose Jaw, Saskatchewan, Canada, to a single unwed mother. Before I was one year old, Fred and May Burden adopted me. I came to live with my parents in Regina, Saskatchewan. My brother, Gordon, was four years older than I and was adopted a few years earlier.

Gordon holding me after I was adopted.

I later learned that I could not be adopted right away because I had to have surgeries on my back and my right thigh. Apparently, I had two hemangiomas, which are superficial growths that are raised collections of blood vessels.

The scar on my back is neat and linear, but the scar on my right thigh must have been large as the contour of my thigh was rather disfiguring.

As a child, I decided that when I got married, I would also adopt a child who needed a home like I did. Another promise I'd made myself was that I would find my birth mother for sure.

We begin my story when I was three years of age, as anything before that time is not clear in my memory. It is now known as childhood amnesia, before we have actual memories.

The study of the interplay between our mind and our body and the effects of trauma on our memories is such an important area of study for mental health workers.

Me at about one year of age.

A fascinating field of knowledge for me is the neuroscience of body memories and how our brain retains memories both prenatally and before we actually have cognitive memories. Mom told me stories of my early childhood that I don't recall. I found one of them particularly funny.

Apparently, I was a thumb sucker, and to break the habit, Mom pinned wool mittens onto my pajama sleeves, figuring that my getting wool in my mouth would surely break the habit. After a few days, she removed the mitts, and I cried, wanting them back on.

One of my earliest memories is of me putting a spoon in an electrical socket in the kitchen, seeing a flame shooting up from it, and turning the wall black above it.

That was the first of many reprimands and choruses of 'dos and don'ts.'

Collecting Odd Things

I was around three years old when, one day, I heard Mom scream my name from the basement. She was washing clothes and was upset with me because there were collections of worms and grasshoppers I'd stuffed in my jeans pockets floating in her wash water.

After a rain, I recall collecting earthworms from the sidewalk. I'd sometimes cut them in half to watch if one half would wiggle one way and the other would wiggle the other way. I guess I was trying to make two out of one. I must have thought they were like pets and stuffed them in my pockets. Obviously, I was also intrigued by grasshoppers.

One day, I was out playing and discovered foxtails. I found them to be very soft and silky, so soft that I harvested many of them without anyone knowing. I took them home and lined my bed with them, thinking it would be like sleeping on a fluffy cloud. I could hardly wait to go to bed. Certainly, Mom didn't know of this.

Sure enough, it was not like sleeping on a cloud as I woke up crying and hollering. Mom came in and found my 'foxtail-lined bed.' She said, "Arlene, what have you done now?"

Mom told me that foxtails are weeds and not soft enough to lie on. She was right. They are very prickly. I recall her showing me that if you stroked them upward, they felt soft, but the opposite way, they were prickly. Well, so much for that experiment.

My Parents

My parents were middle-class earners who knew how to work hard and did so all their lives. During the war, Dad served in the Canadian Air Force as a ham radio operator in Prince George, British Columbia, Canada.

Mom was raised on a farm near Rocanville, Saskatchewan. She told me she was her dad's 'right-hand man' and helped him with the farming.

She also told me that once she grew up, she left the farm and came to Regina, where she worked for wealthy and important people as a maid, cooking and cleaning.

While my parents were raising Gordon and me, Mom worked at Simpsons Sears and later at the Saskatchewan Legislative Building at Queen's Printers. Dad worked at the Post Office for over 30 years, sorting mail by hand.

Looking back, I know we had an average home nestled in a middle-class neighborhood. The area is now one of the worst, run-down areas in Regina, Saskatchewan, Canada, and has a very high crime rate.

Back then, our home was immaculate, inside and out, and homes around us were much like ours. This was the first home they'd owned. Mom insisted everything was to be clean and nothing was to be out of place. One of her famous sayings was, 'Cleanliness is next to godliness!' I am certain I never believed this.

My grandparents originated from England. At an early age, I learned that Mom was born in Canada and that Dad was born in

England in Nottingham Forest, where Robin Hood lived. Mom's maiden name was Bond, you know, like 'James Bond!'

I concluded that Dad knew Robin Hood and Mom was related to James Bond, which immediately gave me notoriety. Since I established that I must be rather famous, I often told others about my fame. Later in my life, I realized that the English thought they were the 'upper-crust' of society and somehow thought they were better than the average person.

Mom had seven siblings. She was one of six girls and two brothers. Three of the girls, Mom being one of them, could not have children, so they all adopted their children.

Dad and Mom were married during the war. I never saw them being very affectionate with one another, and I don't recall them hugging or kissing one another or hearing them tell one another, "I love you!" This was likely an English thing, and it was done privately.

They were indeed dedicated to one another. I was sure they must like one another since they slept together and seemed friendly. I never witnessed arguments or fights. Dad was often a 'yes man!' He'd do anything for Mom.

I looked at photos to add to my memoir, and I found one when they were younger. I am not certain if they had adopted Gordon or me, but I think not, as I don't have this picture in my mind. I noted that in this photo, they looked happy, and Dad had his arm around Mom.

I do not recall either of them telling Gordon and me that they loved us. I do remember that every night, I was expected to kiss them goodnight. However, it felt more like a ritual, like my duty to show my appreciation to them for something. Spontaneous hugs or telling me they loved me did not occur.

Gordon and I were never to go into their bedroom. I recall one Christmas morning when I was able to sit in their bed to open my Christmas stocking. That was very special.

There were always lots of 'do this and don't do that.' Therefore, I rarely asked for permission to do anything; I just did it.

I don't recall the day I was told that I was adopted and what that meant. I was told very early and very often, "Arlene, your dad and I got you to give you a chance in life," and "Your mother was young and had you 'out of wedlock,' and she couldn't take care of you."

I knew I was a part of this family, and in time, I realized that being adopted was like being 'grafted-in' because I was not born into this family or genetically connected.

Surgery at 4 Years of Age

I first had surgery after being born for the removal of two hemangiomas. Of course, I have no cognitive memory of that, but I am sure there would be stored memories.

I cannot recall when I first wore glasses, but I was told that I began wearing those ugly wire-rimmed glasses at 18 months. At around three years old, I recall being frequently seen by the eye doctor. I had to wear a patch over the better eye so I would use what was the weaker eye.

Apparently, that didn't work very well because when I was four years old, Mom told me I needed to have an eye operation. I had no fear but just knew that the doctor would fix my eyes. Later, I came to learn that my condition was called *strabismus*, known as crossed-eyes.

I was told it was done in the Grey Nuns' Hospital in Regina, Saskatchewan. When I woke up from the surgery, I recall there were bandages wrapped around my head, covering my eyes.

I distinctly recall two nuns coming into my room and asking me if I could see through the bandages. I knew I was not to be seeing through them. There was a tiny slit, though, that I could see through. I lied, telling them I couldn't see anything.

One of the nuns came up to my bed and took the soft rubber ball Mom and Dad had bought for me, walked back to the other nun, and without saying a word, threw it towards me. Of course, I raised my arms to try and catch it, and I was caught in my lie.

Soon after that, those nasty nuns came back and taped my slit shut, plunging me into total darkness.

Curious Beyond Borders – *Finding The 'Old Lady'*

At around four years, I would just take off and go exploring in the neighborhood.

I found an 'old lady' who lived a little farther from my home. I was walking down an alley when I discovered her working in her backyard. I stopped to talk with her and found her to be quite friendly.

She was like a grandma and was the first person who had an impact on my life in coming to know Jesus Christ in a personal way. She'd take me into her house, play the piano, sing hymns like "Jesus Loves Me," and tell me Bible stories.

She told me that Jesus loved me very much and that I was very special to him. I remember feeling loved and accepted by her and also by this Jesus she knew.

She was very special to me as she really seemed to like me and took an interest in me. I was thrilled that she was playing her piano just for me.

Perhaps she nicely told me to go home at some point because I know I didn't want to. So I would find my way home, only to hurry back the next day.

I can't be sure how many times she played her piano and sang to me, but it was quite a few times. I loved that 'old lady,' and I knew she loved me. I also knew she loved Jesus, and if she was certain that Jesus loved me, then I was convinced that this had to be true.

One day I went there, but I couldn't find her. I'd knock on her door, but there was never an answer. I couldn't find her in her yard. I checked this out a few times, but she was gone. I was so sad that she wasn't there anymore. Finally, I realized that she was never coming back and that life had to go on without her.

Today, I am fully aware of the huge impact this dear elderly woman had on me in my coming to know her Jesus and in my finding a personal relationship with Him. Perhaps she was an angel.

My Adventures with the Milkman

One of my other adventures at this early age was catching rides with the milkman on his horse-drawn milk wagon, like the one shown below. I loved that, and he would take me a block or two and then tell me to go home until the next time he came around.

He, too, was pleasant. I am sure I talked his ear off, as I know I talked a lot. In the 1950s, they stopped using them.

Time for Kindergarten

I was now five years old, and kindergarten began for me at Herchmer School. I remember nap times there, and I liked them the most. I spotted a girl who was wearing the same dress as me. Since we were twinning with our dresses, we became friends as I thought she must be like me or like a sister. Her name was Carol. I soon found out she lived down the back lane from me at the end of the next block. She was an only child, and her parents were very nice to me.

Chapter 2
1952 to 1956 – Ages 6 to 10 years

Family Adventures

We used to travel to Whitewood to Mom's side of the family on special occasions. Aunt Lily and Uncle Roy lived on a farm owned by wealthy farmers. Uncle Roy was their hired hand, and they lived in one of their very modest homes.

I loved spending holidays there in the summer. Mom and Dad left me in the care of Aunt Lily and Uncle Roy, which was wonderful.

They had four children, and the youngest was just a year or two older than me, so we hung out and enjoyed one another's company.

Uncle Roy was the hired hand for a cattle producer and wheat farmer who were very well off. I soon realized that my aunt and uncle were not well off, but they were happy, caring, and always very good to me.

My cousins were a lot of fun, particularly Dale, who was just two years older than me. We'd go for horseback rides to the nearby sloughs to swim. We'd make diving boards out of I'm not sure what, but we'd jump or dive off of them until they broke.

It was a lot of fun, but looking back, I don't think we knew how deep those sloughs were, but we lived to see another day.

Aunt Lily always made homemade bread, and I'd toast a thick slice of it on an iron rack over the wood-burning stove and then plaster it with the homemade butter Uncle Roy had made and the homemade jam that Aunt Lily had made. My mouth is watering as I am writing this.

When it started to get dark, Uncle Roy would pump the kerosene lamps and light them to hang up on hooks from the ceiling. So cool!

Saturdays were special. We would bathe in the afternoon before getting ready for a trip to town (Whitewood). The galvanized tub was put on the kitchen floor, and Aunt Lily filled it with warm water that was heated on their wood stove. Each of us had our baths. So cool!

I'd pick berries with my aunt and cousins. We'd pick pin cherries that made the best jelly, choke cherries, Saskatoon berries, and gooseberries.

I'd go to the barn to see Uncle Roy milk his cows and then put the milk in a separator and bottle it. They had a fruit cellar where it was cooler to store preserves, root foods, and the like. It was only a dirt floor below their wooden floor. They had a pulley system to put things down there.

I am so grateful for that family and my cousins since they treated me like I was one of them. I knew by now that I had been 'grafted-in' to my adopted family and now to this extended family. I never actually felt 'grafted-in' with this family because I was 'just in!'

I would also spend a shorter time of my holidays at my maternal Uncle Ed and Aunt Dot's farm, which was not far from theirs. They had two children, a boy and a girl, who were closer to my age.

They owned their farm, and their home was more modern, with electricity and an indoor bathroom. I enjoyed these cousins, too. We'd take lunches out to the field for Uncle Ed during harvest time. That was fun and interesting. I got to ride horses and ride on their tractor.

I had fun there, too, but Aunty Dot was stricter than Aunt Lily; perhaps she reminded me of my mom a bit. Yet, she was still nice.

If I had to choose only one farm to go to during the summer holidays, it would have been Aunt Lily and Uncle Roy's farm, 'hands down.' What I experienced there was that you didn't need a lot of fancy things to be loved and happy.

It was a simple but profound lesson that I now feel privileged to have experienced. They reflected unconditional love and acceptance, which I had not experienced in my own home.

Who Am I? – *Rejection and Insecurities*

Mom often told me, "Arlene, we got you to give you a chance in life!"

She would tell me that she tried to make me look nice, but, for some reason, she'd never succeed. I felt responsible for her disappointed feelings.

I remember visiting Mom's parents in Whitewood and walking with my grandpa. I recall that I was so happy to hold his hand and walk with him, but upon returning home, he complained to Mom that I pulled on his arm, and he was so glad to have gotten home with me.

I felt crushed as the last thing I wanted to do was disappoint my grandpa, but it was obvious I had. He hadn't enjoyed the walk as much as I had. Mom adored her dad. Perhaps he had a lot of 'dos and don'ts' like Mom, which she abided by, which pleased him.

Mom always dressed nicely, and she was a rather nice-looking woman. She was three years older than Dad. Back then, I thought that was strange and that it should be the other way around.

I never saw much emotion from Mom as she always acted very stoic. Yet, going through the photo albums, I would see they had their arms around each other for photos. In 1954, when I was around eight years old, I found Mom crying. She said Grandpa had died.

I wanted to comfort her but didn't know how, so I went to a couple of strangers' homes in the neighborhood, telling them my grandpa had died and Mom was crying. I don't recall what they said to me, but I found my way home feeling helpless in helping Mom.

My Pet Cat – *A Source of Comfort*

We had a cat, and she gave me some comfort. Her name was Dinkelpuss. I haven't a clue how we ever got that name. One day, she had a litter of kittens. They were so cute.

A little while later, I noticed that the kittens were not there anymore, and I thought they must have been adopted like I was. Around then, I overheard Dad telling Mom how he had drowned them in Wascana Lake. I thought this was horrible and never said anything because I thought that it had to be a family secret, because it was so bad. They didn't know I knew.

Soon after that, Dinkelpuss was gone, and I was told she'd run away like she had one other time. This time, she never came back. We never had another pet except for a goldfish.

OMG – *I'm the Ugly Duckling in that Story!*

At around eight years old, I was told I had flat feet and no arches. I saw an orthopedic doctor who gave me exercises to strengthen the muscles in my feet, like picking up marbles with my toes and rolling my feet over a pop bottle.

Then there were the ugly brown boots I had to wear. Every morning, I put those ugly things on and laced them up to go to school.

I was far-sighted and had to wear glasses, which were very thick. They seemed like coke bottle glasses in wire-rimmed frames. I found out that I began wearing these ugly glasses at 18 months of age. I never did like my ugly glasses or those ugly brown boots.

Below is a photo of Gordon and me.

I'm wearing those ugly glasses and brown boots.

Me at 4 years old and Gordon at 8 years old

One day, it dawned on me, "Oh my gosh, Mom was right! She wasn't able to ever make me look nice because I am so ugly." I actually began to feel sorry for Mom.

When I heard the story of 'The Ugly Duckling,' I immediately related to that ugly duckling. It actually became my favorite childhood story because of its' happy ending. The poor, ugly duckling, sad and rejected, turned into 'A Beautiful Swan.'

My feeling ugly gave me hope that someday, somehow, I'd turn into that 'beautiful swan' just like the ugly duckling did.

Time-Outs Were a Blessing

I know now that I carried a lot of stress, which is anxiety. Supper was always at the table. I don't recall if we said grace, but I do recall that if we had company, it would have been said for sure. Almost everything was for show.

Mom had a 'perfectionist script.' I knew I could never measure up to that. I felt exhausted thinking about it, so I did not try. I felt a lot of tension at the kitchen table since I'd get in trouble if I talked with my mouth full, made too much noise chewing my food, or slurped when I drank.

I often did all three of these and 'acted out' at the supper table on purpose, so they'd make me eat my supper on the basement steps. At least they put my supper on the step because I did love food. Further, I loved being by myself on the steps.

I'd sit down on the steps and look up to the top of the stairs, where the light shone under the basement door. I had enough light to give me some ambiance while I ate in peace. I liked my company.

In our family, we all knew if mom was happy, we'd all likely be happy, or at least happier.

Boys and Men – *I Don't Think I Like Them Much*

Of course, the two main men in my family were my dad and my brother.

As I mentioned, Gordon was four years older than I, and he was busy doing his guy things. We did not interact too much except on holidays.

Dad played the accordion and started to teach Gordon how to play it. Gordon got so good at playing it that he got to play in the Lions' A band. As a teenager, he taught music lessons at The Arcade Music Centre. Gordon was no dummy!

A photo of Gordon playing at Mom's parents 'Golden Wedding Anniversary.'

Dad tried to teach me the accordion, too. I got as far as the Lion's B Band but hated playing the accordion. Dad and I were not very close during this time in my life.

My Dad – *The Upside and the Downside*:

The upside was when Dad got our first family car, a 1954 Pontiac, and we had short trips. We were one of the last families to get a car, or so I thought. This is a photo of our family:

The best and the worst times with Dad were when Mom visited her mom in Whitewood, SK; that would be around 1954, after her dad died.

Others had black and white televisions, which I wanted. When Mom went to visit her mom in Whitewood, Dad would rent a television for us. I don't think he ever told Mom.

Dad enjoyed watching wrestling, but it came on late in the evening. He told us if we went to sleep, he'd wake us up to watch it with him. I don't know if Gordon fell asleep, but I recall Dad waking me up to watch it. That was special, and I felt included.

The downside was being sure that I'd get the strap while Mom was away. Even though I tried not to get in trouble and make Dad upset during that time, I knew he'd find something to get mad about, and out would come the strap from behind the bread box. The strap was an old leather belt. My parents were nice enough to cut the buckle off of it.

Knowing I was about to get the strap, I was always prepared. I would run upstairs to my bedroom and shove a skinny booklet down my underwear before he got to my bedroom. Before the strap hit my bottom, I'd already be hollering 'bloody murder.'

I should have won an Oscar for my performance. When it was all over, and Dad went downstairs again, I would remove the booklet with a big grin. I believe I even had a good laugh.

If this happened today, Child Protection would definitely have shown up. Back then, the motto was 'spare the rod, spoil the child.'

In those days, the strap was even given at school. My parents warned me that if I got the strap at school, I'd get another one as soon as I got home. Thank God I never did get the strap at school.

I cannot recall Gordon ever getting the strap, and to this day, I have never asked him if he did. I likely got enough of them for both of us.

My Brother and the Neighbor Boys

I think I annoyed my brother. I wanted him to like me, and I think he did.

I recall one time when we were on holiday as a family when Dad stopped for gas, and I went to the bathroom. When I came out, I saw our car gone. I soon realized they'd left me behind, but I didn't panic. In fact, it reminded me of when I was alone on the basement steps.

Soon, they showed up. I was told that Gordon finally said, "You know Arlene isn't in the car?" I know he tolerated me, but I don't think it ever really bothered me.

Gordon was to be minding me before Mom and Dad got home from work, but instead, he'd stage these wrestling matches in our living room, using me as the scapegoat.

Neighborhood kids would come into the living room as an audience, and the bets were placed on who would win. I'd get whipped every time with these older boys laughing at me. That was humiliating!

Around that time, the same kids were in the front yard of the neighbor's house. I was in gymnastics, so the boys told me they wanted to lift me up and do a gymnastic act with me. Since I was good at doing gymnastics, I thought this was my time to shine, and so I was eager to follow their directions.

Below is a photo of Gordon (in the lighter colored coat) with the neighbor boys.

Just as one of them was going to lift me up, that boy pulled my pants down. Of course, everyone began laughing. I was embarrassed. I pulled my pants up and went home crying.

Once again, I was totally humiliated and concluded that boys really didn't like me, and I was certainly starting to dislike them.

I never told Mom or Dad about the wrestling matches or that prank of my 'pants being pulled down.'

Shortly after that, Gordon was to be minding me one evening while Mom and Dad went somewhere. Those same boys, his buddies, came over when I was already in bed, asleep.

I was awakened by these boys standing over me in my bedroom, shining a flashlight in the dark, but aimed at me.

I figured I was around nine years old, and my brother about 13. The older boys were about 15 or 16 years of age. With their flashlight on me, one of them nicely asked me to take my pajama bottoms off. Being hardly awake, I complied.

With my pajama bottoms off and this flashlight shining on my privates, they began to coax me to do something, which now had me fully awake. I became so upset that I got up and screamed at them, saying they were bad and that all of them were going to be in a lot of trouble when I told Mom and Dad. They immediately took off.

Thank God I was a scrappy enough kid and had the guts to stick up for myself and get myself out of that situation. I now think my brother was trying to please his older peers, who pressured him into doing something he lost control of.

We never discussed it, and that was the end of all those pranks. I never did tell my parents about any of them.

Flight or Fight – *Bob and Fred*

So, with my experiences with boys, I had to figure out how to balance things out and 'take my power back' so as to never be humiliated again.

That decision resulted in my challenging the boys at school to fight me after school. I was in grade four.

I met my opponent on the playground and managed to win those fights until one day, I challenged Bob Wolf to fight me after school. I knew he'd be a challenge because he was a little older and bigger than me, but I figured I could still 'clean his clock.'

There was always an audience for these scraps, and that day was no different. Well, Bob 'cleaned my clock,' and that day, upon walking home, I decided that I would not be a 'tomboy' any longer and reluctantly decided I would need to be a girl.

That wasn't quite the end since there was one more altercation with a boy named Fred. We were in grade five. That altercation was not planned but spontaneous and occurred right in the classroom, with the class going on.

I had just started to develop breasts, and that was somewhat earlier than most of the girls. Fred must have noticed. He was a 'pain in the butt' and always bugging me. He sat across the aisle from me to my right.

On this day, he leaned over and whispered to me, "Heh, Arlene, are your tits tender?" With absolutely no emotional regulation, I stood up on the seat of my desk and jumped over the side of it, wrestling him to the floor and directing a few choice words at him.

Of course, I had to see the principal and the teacher. I did tell them what Fred said to me. Of course, we both got into trouble. The principal or teacher never involved my parents, thank God!

If these incidents with boys had happened today, I may have had gender confusion and decided that I didn't like my gender and become a lesbian, which would be the male role, of course.

I have seen kids in my counseling practice who have that confusion and are supported at home for the gender switch. That topic is likely for another book in the future.

Miracle # 1: 'The Faith of A Child' – Carol walks!

1954 was a year to remember. Grandpa died, and Mom cried. Remember Carol, who wore the same dress as me in kindergarten? She got polio that year and couldn't walk anymore. She was now in a wheelchair, and she'd never walk again. Knowing this made me profoundly sad.

I was over at her house a lot. Her parents were older and very nice. I remember they both worked for the government. Her mom worked at SaskTel. I particularly noticed that they both drank liquor and smoked, which were both taboo in our home.

When we were around nine years old, her parents would order us a taxi on a Saturday afternoon to get us downtown to go and see a movie. They must have needed a break. We were okay with this. They'd give us money for these adventures and call a cab for us to get there and back from the movie.

There was often a lineup to get into the theatre, so I'd tell Carol that I'd get us in without waiting in line. I would tell her to just watch me. Then I'd holler out, "Make way for the cripple. She needs to get upfront to get in!" as I pushed her wheelchair past the line. Once we were in through the door, we'd have a good laugh, get our popcorn and drinks, and enjoy the movie.

My parents often let me have sleepovers at her home, which was fun, too.

Obviously, I felt very bad for my friend Carol. I was determined to make her life as good as possible. I was a kid, and I thought the best way to do that was to 'spice it up!' So I decided we should steal a couple of her parents' cigarettes and matches, too, of course. Carol thought that would be great fun, so we took two cigarettes and went off.

I'd push her about two and a half blocks to the grounds of the nearby high school called Scott Collegiate, where there were caragana bushes that we could hide in and enjoy those cigarettes.

I don't recall how we managed to light those cigarettes, but we did. I recall that we didn't enjoy them at all as we hadn't a clue how to smoke them. After trying to smoke them and gagging, we butted them out and headed home. I never did smoke after that, so perhaps that saved us both from that bad habit.

Remember the 'old lady' who told me about Jesus? She must have told me about his miracles and told me He could do those miracles today. I'd go to Sunday school every Sunday at the United Church, but I don't recall being told that Jesus did miracles today.

Back then, I had the 'faith of a child,' and I knew Jesus could make her walk again. I was positive that Jesus did not want her to stay in that wheelchair.

So, I told Carol about Jesus, that He had done miracles and He'd make her walk again. She believed like I did, and we joined our faith as children can do, believing Carol would walk again.

Neither of us thought to be cautious about it as we had faith that it absolutely would work.

So that day, when we were in her kitchen and with her wheelchair parked between the sink and their table, I told her that I would help her stand up using the sink as a prop, and then I would back up from her, and she'd walk towards me.

So, with my help, she stood straight up with one hand on the kitchen sink counter.

I then backed away. I wasn't close to her to catch her in case she fell because there was no way she'd fall as today she'd be walking, and of course, we had asked Jesus to do this.

I was several feet from her and said, "Carol, now walk over to me." She then took one step, two steps, three, four, and a few more.

I was thrilled to see her walking. But I wasn't really surprised since, after all, both of us still had the simple faith of a child. Carol was focused as she carefully took these steps, holding on to nothing.

Right about then, her mother came around the corner and witnessed her in the middle of the kitchen floor. Seeing her standing on her own and possibly taking a step, she screamed, "Carol!"

Immediately, she collapsed on the floor. That was the end of that, and Carol never did walk again.

Sadly, her parents died rather young, but her Aunt Molly and Uncle Dan finished raising her. God bless their souls.

Carol never returned to our school and had to go to a special school for kids like her. I stayed in touch with her. As an adult, she moved to Ontario, but years later, we briefly reconnected when she visited Regina. She had acquired Post-polio Syndrome (PPS).

What I experienced with her taking those steps on her own was 'the power of God,' and realized that miracles can happen with 'the faith of a child.'

Of course, I didn't put that altogether back then. But what I witnessed was Jesus performing a miracle before my eyes, which was the first of many more miracles that I'd witnessed throughout my life and which I continue to witness.

I'm thankful that Mom and Dad took us to church every Sunday. They baptized me as an infant, and at thirteen, I did a 'confession of faith,' which is called a confirmation.

I suppose I was to have accepted Jesus as my Lord and Savior when I was confirmed, promising to follow Him. Truthfully, it didn't mean much to me back then.

I don't remember much about going to Sunday school back then, but I do recall one incident when I asked my teacher to sign my autograph book.

Everyone had an autograph book back then. For fun, we'd ask people to write something in it and then see what they'd write. This teacher wrote in my autograph book, "Good better best, never let it rest until the good be better and the better be best!"

Reading that, I recall having a visceral reaction. Later in my life, I understood why. I knew that if the better ever became the best, it still wouldn't be good enough. Therefore, I could never rest. This vicious cycle would be exhausting; it was, as I lived it growing up.

Around my preteen years, my mom enrolled me in dance lessons at Veronica Dance Studio, which was a few blocks from our place. She also enrolled me in gymnastics at the YWCA. One year, I won the Group A competition for my age group in our province. I was told I was double-jointed. Maybe I was, as I could bend myself 'into a pretzel.'

Chapter 3
1956 to 1960 – Ages 10 to 14

Medical Concerns

Just a few days before my 11th birthday, Mom gave me a booklet about the 'birds and the bees' entitled, 'Becoming A Young Lady Now.' The information was all news to me. I don't know how I was so naïve. Nowadays, with social media, kids know a lot and likely too much too early.

Bleeding out blood from your privates sounded disgusting to me, so I recall saying to Mom, "I am absolutely not going to have to do this every month as it says here! I am going to do what Dad and you did and adopt my kids!" Hearing this, Mom welled up with sadness and tears and said, "Oh, no, Arlene, your Dad and I would have loved to have had our own baby, so don't ever say that."

Well, I did feel sorry for Mom in that moment, but at the same time, she did not reassure me that having adopted me was a blessing, that she was so glad to be able to have adopted me, or that I was good enough when she could not have their own child. Was I really 'grafted-in' to this family, or was it really 'just to give me a chance in life' like she often said? I felt that I was just not good enough as an adopted kid, but rather a 'fill-in.' Looking back, I know I was a very anxious child. My hands and feet would get sweaty, and dealing with that was a nuisance. Just thinking of it would cause my hands and feet to sweat. It was quite annoying!

Mom told me that my hair would be soaking wet when I woke up as a baby. Our doctor said that this was caused by my having an overactive sympathetic nervous system, but there was no help for this. How did it become so overactive?

When I turned 11 years old, I began complaining about back pain. My back kept hurting a lot, and Mom took me to the doctor, who sent me to an orthopedic doctor. He told us that my spine was crooked and that I had scoliosis, and that my diagnosis was guarded since, as an adult, I may have what is called a Dowager's Hump or Curve. There was discussion about putting me into a body cast, but I think Mom decided against it.

I was very glad I never went into one. Mom was determined that this Dowager's Hump was not going to happen, so I did stand up as straight as possible, even though I often felt discomfort or pain. Mom would always say to me, "Arlene, stand up straight, shoulders back!" This got on my nerves, but I knew she was doing that for my own good so I wouldn't live a life dealing with problems.

Yet, I was very thankful I never had gotten polio like Carol and had to be in a wheelchair. That helped me not dwell on these problems or feel sorry for myself.

The Love of Family

Mom was an exceptional cook and housekeeper. She never taught me how to cook or bake, but I watched her carefully, and as an adult, I also became good at those things.

She taught me how to set the table properly and ironing. I hated ironing, particularly her underpants and the pillowcases, which had to be folded perfectly.

As I mentioned, Mom was a maid to 'well-to-do people' when she came to Regina, so she learned these meticulous habits. She was determined to pass those onto me, which I'm sure she didn't like. Our parents wanted the best for us and did the best they knew how to, as most parents do.

Besides accordion lessons, dance lessons, and gymnastics, they enrolled me in art and vocal lessons. I am thankful that they provided me with these opportunities, which helped me overcome some of my insecurities and build self-esteem.

Mom had a lot of interesting sayings that I'm sure she passed on from her mom. They still are with me today, like:

- It's up to a woman to keep her doorstep clean (remain a virgin until marriage).
- Why buy the cow when you get the milk free (why would a man marry you if you give him sex before marriage?)?
- If you let someone go and they come back to you, then it was meant to be. If they don't, then that was also meant to be.
- Cleanliness is next to godliness.
- 'The road to hell' is paved with good intentions.
- It'll all come out in the wash (meaning you will always get found out if you are hiding anything).
- The hens will come home to roost-they always do!

Uncle Charlie – *One of the Family Secrets*

One summer, when Gordon and I were on a family trip to Waskesui, we were told that Dad had a brother who lived on his own in the bush near Waskesui whom he had never met. We were about to visit him.

Dad's parents lived on Lulu Island near Vancouver, British Columbia. As the story goes, Dad's parents had Charlie out of wedlock and gave him to the paternal parents until they were married, and then they'd take him back. The grandparents, worried that one day they'd take him from them, fled all the way to northern Saskatchewan, hiding him away in the bush. There, they raised him. Those grandparents had already died when we met Uncle Charlie.

Gordon and I were intrigued by this story, so finding Dad's long-lost brother and getting an uncle for us was like getting an early Christmas present.

We pulled up to his house. He lived his whole life in that one-bedroom shack made out of logs and plaster.

After he died, I painted this picture below from a photo we had taken.

I will never forget that first meeting. I was sitting on a chair, and a mouse came out of a hole in the floor, running across it. There was a trail of mini pink mice running behind their mom. His cat was in hot pursuit, gobbling the babies up like candy. Uncle Charlie never batted an eye.

He worked for years as a hired hand for a well-to-do family, the Handsons, on their nearby farm. Yet, there was no doubt in my mind that he was a very poor bachelor who lived in the bush with no family of his own.

He was poorly socialized beyond those immediately around him, but he seemed to love our family, and we loved him.

Below is a photo of Gordon and me having a wiener roast with Uncle Charlie.

As we grew up, he'd spend summer holidays with us at Waskesui. Every Christmas, he would drive his truck to Regina to stay at our home for a couple of weeks.

He was a hunter. Every year, he'd bring us wild meat, usually moose meat. We came to love it, and Mom cooked it perfectly with all of the trimmings.

His arrival on Christmas was more exciting to us than when we believed Santa Claus was coming. Dad and he acted like long-lost brothers, which was great to see.

Gordon and I loved him as he showed love and acceptance towards us as we did to him.

During one of the Christmases that he came, Dad and Uncle Charlie took Gordon and me tobogganing in the Lumsden Valley hills. Gordon was on the back of the toboggan, and I was on the front.

As we went over the first hill, we both saw the second hill and heavy bushes awaiting us at the end of it. Gordon said, "Jump off!" I couldn't. My foot was caught on the side rope.

As Gordon jumped off, I went even faster and yelled out, "I'll see you in heaven, Gordon!" When I think of that incident, I can still feel the branches hitting my face. At least my big brother was looking out for me and telling me to jump off.

My face was a mess for about three weeks, with lacerations and bruises. Mom gave Dad and Uncle Charlie heck for not being careful where they took us, but I don't recall getting any tender loving care from anyone.

Uncle Charlie was a bright spot in the life of our family. He was always respectful and a gentleman. There was one time I questioned that when I was in grade six, and he happened to open my bedroom door and saw me standing in my bra.

He reached out to touch my breast, and I simply said, "Don't!" He came out of what seemed to be like a 'deer in the headlights' moment and immediately left my room.

Later, I concluded that he likely had come into my room by accident and had never seen a breast before. I dismissed it as an indiscretion. Except for that one incident, I have wonderful memories of my Uncle Charlie, and I know he loved Gordon and me as if we were his own kids because he never had a wife or kids.

I was an adult when he was sick and dying. I remember praying with him, and he accepted Jesus. I know I will see him again when I go to be with Jesus. When he died, he left everything to Gordon and me. Surprisingly, he had a fair amount of money.

He told Mom and Dad he was leaving everything to Gordon and me, but our parents talked him into leaving it in their care until they died. At least they told us his wishes.

Grade 6 – *Miss. Hitsman – No Wonder No One Married Her!*

Miss. Hitsman, rest her soul, was stricter than Mom, being over the top with her 'dos and don'ts.' I used to think, 'No wonder she's not married because she's so cranky!'

I gave her a lot of resistance, or I thought, but she would give anyone who wouldn't get their work done or talk in class so many lines to write of 'The quick brown fox jumped over the lazy dog.' This had to be done at home and brought back the next day.

If you didn't learn the first time, she'd double up the lines the next time. I was a slow learner, as I know I filled up a lot of those scribblers.

During that year, I became more aware of my appearance. I still hated my glasses and how I looked in them. So I would stick them under our back steps and go to school without them. When

I got home, I'd 'fish them out' and put them on before going into the house.

Grade 8 – *Mr. Pickard*

For some reason, I have little recollection of grade seven, but grade eight came along, and it stands out for me. I was now a teenager. I was a talkative student in the class and often cut jokes to get others to laugh.

Mr. Pickard, the principal, was a bachelor nearing retirement. I carried on so much that he put me in the row, butting up to the front of his desk. For some reason, he took an interest in me. Every time I looked up at him, he'd wink at me, and I immediately dropped my gaze.

I am now certain that I had Attention-Deficit Hyperactivity Disorder (ADHD), but back then, it wasn't being diagnosed like now. Like many others, I adapted to manage life and learning.

I did like school. I liked the challenge of learning and enjoyed being able to debate my opponent, particularly guys, and win, of course! We'd have classmates in the auditorium as an audience to vote for the winner. I won all of the time, not like when I fought them on the playground.

Boys were now becoming more interesting. There were school dances in grade eight, and I really liked one boy, Johnny. I wasn't sure if he even noticed me, but I hoped he did.

At the one and only school dance that I attended, Johnny came over to ask me to dance a waltz. Right in the middle of the dance, my hands started to sweat, and I became so embarrassed that I said I had to go home early. I left before the dance was over and went home upset. I went right to my room and cried my heart out.

Grade Eight Graduation

I was the valedictorian in eighth grade, which I thought was very cool. I didn't shy away from public speaking, so I guess that's why I was chosen.

I still remember my graduation dress. I was sure that I had the nicest dress there since I loved it so much. Mom and Dad did not scrimp when it came to providing for us, even though they would have been financially at the lower end of the middle class.

By the time I started high school, Gordon had joined the Canadian Air Force and was stationed in Goose Bay, Labrador. I was sad to see him go. But in my heart, I knew he needed to leave home.

Chapter 4
1960 to 1964–Ages 14 to 18

Snotty Girls! – *Dr. Bean's Wisdom*

When I began high school, I noticed that there were cliques. Those were the popular girls. I never really wanted to be one of them, but I did feel somewhat left out. I recall telling my family doctor at my annual checkup about how I felt that I didn't fit in at school.

He told me, "Arlene, in your lifetime, if you can count five people on your hand who will love you and care about you no matter what, you will be very fortunate. Hopefully, that will be both your parents, your husband, and a couple of others. Know this: all the others will come and go in your life and only be acquaintances."

Then he told me about Jesus and the disciples and about how He was rejected by Judas, concluding that He was 'God with us' and that this even happened to Him. He said Jesus loved me and would never reject me.

This reminded me of the dear old lady I met around age four, who told me the same thing. Being reassured, I now had the courage to face high school.

When Dr. Bean retired, I painted him a picture. He was so moved by it that he got emotional and had tears in his eyes. He was a special doctor throughout my childhood.

What's With Men?

Gordon's bedroom was upstairs, across from mine. Since it was now empty, it became the guest room. That year, my maternal uncle, who was visiting from out of province, was given this guest room. It was a known fact that he was an alcoholic. He'd been drinking the night before and during that night, when I was sleeping, he came into my room and got into bed with me.

It wasn't long before his wandering hands woke me up. Having already experienced dealing with those neighbor boys at an early age and being older, I handled this very well and kicked him out, threatening him that I'd tell my parents if he didn't get moving. He quickly went to his room. That incident was also kept a secret, well, until now.

Humor – *A Relief – A Smoke-Screen – A Gift*

I discovered before high school that I could make people laugh, and so I utilized this gift to connect with my peers in high school. I was still very awkward around guys.

At school dances, when I was asked to dance, I would become so anxious that my hands would begin sweating.

One time, to avoid being embarrassed, I offered to play Santa Claus at the Christmas dance. This way, I could have the boys sitting on my lap, telling me what they wanted for Christmas, and I'd crack some funnies. This was fun and masked my huge insecurities and my somewhat low self-esteem. I could still have a connection with the guys and feel accepted.

I also had a somewhat rebellious or cheeky nature and was often sent to the detention hall. I kind of loved it, as it reminded me of when I was put on the basement steps.

Now, as a mental health practitioner for over thirty years, I have come to realize that I was actually emotionally regulating myself.

As mentioned, I self-diagnosed as having ADHD, and I now realize that both my brother and I would have suffered from what is known as Childhood Emotional Neglect (CEN), having two working parents and not being told we were loved.

In high school, I enjoyed playing basketball and softball, and loved sports. I also joined the drama club and really loved it, singing and acting in various performances. We had one performance in the auditorium, and I don't remember what the theme was, but I did a skit to the song 'I'm A Woman' where I went out on stage and began singing the song and belting out "Cuz I'm a Woman- W-O-M-A-N, and *I'll Say It Again and Again and Again!'* while at the same time whipping off my wrap-around skirt and continuing to sing. I was wearing shorts and tights under the skirt.

The students were bent over laughing hilariously. I enjoyed doing that and thought that day that maybe I'd become a comedian like "I Love Lucy," a popular television show back then. I must have thought I could really do this, as I seriously entertained the idea of going to drama school in Ontario, and then I'd go and make lots of money doing something I knew I'd love to do.

I am sure I realized by then that there was a lot of sadness in the world and that I could help others find relief by laughing. Underneath, I had a lot of sadness, too, but I was not aware of that until much later. My high school years were relatively enjoyable.

Grade 12 – *My First Boyfriend*

Mom and Dad told me to never drink alcohol, as it could get me in trouble because I wouldn't know what I was doing.

I disobeyed them and had my first couple of drinks one summer night between grades 11 and 12 when a couple of my girlfriends got some alcohol to consume.

I don't recall how we got out to this dance pavilion on the highway outside of Regina, but I do recall that I was feeling the alcohol and very relaxed. For the first time, my hands weren't sweating, and I was dancing the night away like a pro, so I thought, and I felt 'on top of the world!'

I decided that my parents misled me about not knowing what I was doing because I was sure I knew what I was doing. I had all my faculties. Alcohol was like a gift to me.

I met Robert that evening, and he called me the next day. I was surprised to know that his parents ran a farm near Uncle Roy and Aunt Lily's farm near Whitewood, SK.

His parents were well-off, like the people my Uncle Roy worked for. In fact, Robert's dad was the brother of Uncle Roy's boss.

Robert had a younger sister still at home. After Robert finished grade 12, he left the farm as he had asthma and was unable to farm alongside his dad. This was a huge disappointment for both of them. He came to Regina and worked at a high-end men's clothing store.

I thought he was too well-dressed for me, always wearing classy men's clothing, but I got used to it. I would go on the odd weekend or on holidays to his parents' farm. I enjoyed going there as the area was familiar to me from my days of going to my relatives' farms.

I was still in high school, and my girlfriends on my block already had boyfriends. We were all growing up, for sure. I still, on occasion, drank alcohol as I still liked the relaxed feeling it gave me and how it masked my insecurities.

At the end of grade 12, Robert and I decided that we loved one another and we'd get married. After that decision, Robert 'didn't have to buy the cow,' as Mom put it, because 'he got the milk free.' I'd concluded that although it was drilled into me to remain a virgin until marriage, cheating ahead of time didn't matter so much because we'd be getting married.

It looks like I did disobey my parents, as I drank alcohol and, well, you know the rest.

Time To Launch My Career Path

Grade 12 was almost over, and it was time to launch my career path. Mom and Dad indicated that I needed to become a nurse, and they gave me an engraved nurse's watch as a grade 12 graduation gift. I guess I couldn't follow my dreams of becoming a comedian and making lots of money.

Grade 12 graduation photo: June, 1964

Since I was going to marry Robert, my plans would need to change anyway. I also didn't need to use comedy as much anymore to cover up my massive insecurities with men, because I had found my man and alcohol a perfect combination.

Milestone Two
Adulthood to Mid-life

Chapter 5
1964 to 1972 – Ages 18 to 26

Launching My Career

In the fall of 1964, I entered the three-year nursing program at the Regina General Hospital (RGH), Saskatchewan. I had also applied at the Regina Grey Nuns' Hospital and was accepted there too. However, I chose RGH since their third year was called an internship, where we'd have more responsibilities with direct care. We were also paid a modest monthly amount of money.

There were over 100 nursing students enrolled in my first year, but about 15 percent either quit or were asked to leave during that first year.

We all had a roommate, except for the odd single room available for some of us in our third year when we had to work shifts.

The experience of hanging out with all these girls was wonderful, and we became a sisterhood. We often gathered in each other's rooms and gabbed about our boyfriends, family, work experiences, and the patients we cared for.

I remember one time when the girls were trying to have a séance with a Ouija Board in one of the girls' rooms, and I became spooked. I sensed a dark entity or entities in the room and left before the others.

In the summer, we'd go up to the roof of the residence, which was tar and gravel, where we spread baby oil all over ourselves and lay on that not-so-soft roof, trying to see who could get the best tan.

We literally baked in the sun with no concern about harmful UV rays and getting skin cancer or becoming wrinkled prematurely.

The Wedding's Off!

After my first year of nursing school, Robert and I were still together. He picked me up one evening in a brand new, very swanky car. I thought it was very nice too. He wanted to really show it off and would get into drag races on Albert Street by Wascana Park.

I thought this was somewhat reckless and immature, and asked him to please not do this when I was with him. He kept it up, and I said, "If you do that again, you'll have to take me home." That weekend, I was staying at my parents' place, so he did it again, and I asked him to promptly take me home.

I had not seen that side of Robert until that day. Less than a week later, my childhood girlfriend asked me, "Did you know that Robert took out Aimee?"

I knew Aimee from high school, but I was not close to her.

The next time he called me, I told him what I knew about his taking out Aimee, and I simply told him that we were over. At that point, we'd gone out for two years without a break-up, but surprisingly, I was not too upset knowing that our wedding plans had just tanked.

Learning and Experiencing

Nursing school was challenging, and we were learning a lot. I studied hard and did well. Physically and emotionally, it was often very taxing for me.

In the residence, there is a tub room. There were about ten claw-foot tubs separated by partial walls and doors. There were no showers, but soaking in a tub after a hard day was a treat.

It was during the winter in my third year when I fell asleep in one of those tubs. When I woke up, the water was cold, and it had gotten dark outside.

Once in my room, I saw that it was almost 7:30. I was supposed to be in the ward in the hospital by 7:00 a.m. Panicking, I hurried into my uniform and ran through the underground tunnel that led to the main hospital area.

As I arrived at the ward, the head nurse asked, "Burden, what are you doing here?" It soon became apparent to me, as it did to them, that it was 7:30 p.m. and not a.m. We had a good laugh, and I headed back to the residence to crawl into bed.

I recall the first time I had to give a man a complete bed bath. He'd be somewhere in his forties. I was so stressed that I'm sure I never looked at him. If I could have done his bath with my eyes closed, I'd have done it. I managed to get it done.

There were always new experiences and certainly challenging situations to attend to. We had to grow up fast, as we often faced life-and-death situations that most of us had never encountered.

I had to face death for the first time. I had only known about death at eight years old when I found Mom crying when her dad died.

I had never seen a dead person until my second year when, one morning, the head nurse told me Mrs. Jones had died in the night, and I was to help another nurse prepare her for the morgue. She was elderly, and it was still difficult to participate in this, but I soon adjusted.

In my third year of training, our internship year, I was in charge of nights on a medical ward. This was just before the Intensive Care Unit was put in place at RGH.

That particular evening, we had a 16-year-old girl in our medical ward. She had injured her leg badly while doing track and field. That night, she had a heart attack. I began Cardiopulmonary Resuscitation (CPR) on her until the crisis medical team arrived. They continued to work on her, shocking her heart several times, but she was gone. When the night shift was over, and I was walking through the tunnel back to the nurses' residence, I was deep in thought, realizing that this teen who should have had her whole life ahead of her had passed through that celestial tunnel to heaven and was with Jesus.

I thought of her parents and family, who would be in shock and heartbroken at losing her. Life didn't seem fair at all. I asked Jesus, "Where were you tonight? I know I was praying to him in my spirit, calling out to him to help us bring her back, but nothing!" We had to stop working on her. I just felt numb and didn't even cry.

We later learned that she had a blood clot that had moved from her injured area, which led to her having a massive heart attack.

There were other tragedies that I witnessed that year, and some were quite overwhelming.

I realized that life can be over just like that, and I determined that we should love and live our best lives. Yet, I wasn't quite sure how to do that. God, please don't leave me.

Life had become serious now, and the sense of humor that brought me relief was often stifled. Yet, I still managed to have fun and let loose at times, but it was usually when we girls got together.

The Love of My Life – *Reflections of Joy and Grief!*

After Robert, I had a couple of dates in my second year of nursing school. One of those dates was when my friend lined me up with a blind date along with her and her date. It wasn't much of a date as we drove around until we ended up at the parents' home of her date.

His parents soon came home. Shortly after, a friend of these two guys showed up. His name was Wayne Dobson. I certainly noticed him because I thought he was very good-looking with a flashing white smile. He was very charismatic and had a sense of humor.

I had consumed a couple of drinks that evening, but I reminded my date that I needed to get back to the nurses' residence as I had a curfew and had work the next day.

Once in the car, Wayne came outside, hung his head through the car window, and asked me for my phone number. I found this quite rude, as I was out with his buddy.

He must have gotten my phone number from the other guy as he called me the next day, asking me for a date. I accepted.

I was only 19 years of age at the time, and he was 24 years old. For the first date, he took me to a bar in Regina. I told him I had to be 21 years old to get into a pub, and he told me not to worry that if anyone asked for my identification, he would handle it.

Once a month, we got a weekend pass from the nurses' residence to go home if we wanted to. The date night was on one such weekend, and I was staying with my parents. They knew I was out on a date with someone new and waited up to see that I'd be home when I said I would.

As was the case when I was out with any guy and went home, they ensured I didn't stay in the car too long. If I went over by ten minutes, they'd turn the outside front door light off and on repeatedly until I came in. We had a good laugh.

Stand Me Up and You're Out!

On one of those dates, he stood me up, so I told him that was it for him. Apparently, he'd been drinking with a buddy, and he forgot, but that was not a good enough excuse.

He was persistent and promised it would never happen again. I gave him another chance. At that time, Robert called me, but I reassured him that I had moved on, and that was the last time I spoke to him.

Meeting Our Parents

Mom and Dad met Wayne when they invited him for supper. When he was in the presence of my parents, he was noticeably uncomfortable and had a tic with his lip making a slight sucking sound.

For the first time, I realized he was not as confident or sure of himself as he tried to make himself out to be in front of his friends.

Soon, I met his mom and dad and his younger teenage brother, Jim. They lived at Buena Vista, which was next to Regina Beach. He also had two younger sisters, one married and one not.

Getting to Know You

Wayne worked for the Saskatchewan Department of Highways and was posted in northern Saskatchewan. Dating was sporadic, but I was still in my second year of nursing school, so that was fine by me.

Early in our dating, he sent me a letter that he had carefully carved with a pocketknife on a large strip of birch bark. I was very impressed by this, as I knew that this would have taken him some time to do. The words weren't gushy, but he was letting me know he really cared about me.

I tried coordinating my days off for when he'd be home. One weekend, he paid for me to travel up north on the Greyhound bus to where he was working.

He supervised a crew of guys, but he made a place for me to bunk in, in this Department of Highways trailer. Soon, one big party began with him and those he was to be supervising.

I was now 20 years old. I had no clue what addiction looked like, or rather, I did not know the warning signs if someone was getting in trouble with it.

Soon, Wayne quit the highways and was home, starting up his own construction business at Regina Beach, Saskatchewan.

I got to know his mom and dad very well because I spent most of my off time out there. I became especially fond of his mom, Helen. She was the most loving and humble woman I had ever met, and it didn't take long for me to love her.

Helen Leona Dobson

Looking back, I now recognize that she carried herself with a certain grace that I had not experienced before. It drew me to her, falling in love.

Falling in Love

I loved it when Wayne picked me up from the nurses' residence to go to the beach for the weekend. We'd do a lot of interesting things there, which was new and exciting for me and a relief from nursing school.

Early in our relationship, he asked me if I'd like to go waterskiing. Of course, he asked me if I had ever done that before. I told him, "Yes, I've water-skied before, and I'd love to go."

Well, I didn't lie about waterskiing because when I was on a trip in my teens with my friend Jennifer and her family, I did water ski. I tried to water-ski. I didn't tell him that I had a lot of trouble getting up on the skis. In fact, as I recall, it was pretty much a disaster.

Off we went with his friend Dr. So & So, who was single and a much older friend to Wayne. The good doctor was single and a Player and Entertainer. He thought he was pretty much God's gift to the universe, and I think he wanted Wayne to model after him since he took great interest in him.

He did have a lovely boat and skis. I knew I needed to do well at water-skiing as I wanted to impress Wayne. Like a lot of us, we pray just when we need help. I was praying because I sure needed help and wanted all to go well.

Unsurprisingly, it didn't go well! I'd momentarily get up on the skis, and then I'd fall backwards. After the second failed try, Dr. So & So became impatient and said, "Wayne, get her in the boat! It's obvious she can't ski!"

I thought, 'How rude and ignorant of the doc.'

Luckily, Wayne showed compassion towards me and said to him, "Let her try one more time!" He jumped into the water and showed me what I was doing wrong, which was not pulling the tow rope over my head to give the boat time to speed up.

I was successful the third time, all thanks to God and Wayne. I noticed that Wayne had patience and compassion towards me. He was not only handsome but strong. I was told he'd even swim across the lake, having done that on more than one occasion.

I was most definitely attracted to him in every way and wondered why he was attracted to me, as I thought he could get anyone.

My 'self-image' of being an 'ugly duckling' still lingered with me. I guess I was still hoping that someone would let me know that I'd become that beautiful swan. I likely wouldn't have believed it anyway because my insecurities still ran deep.

Yet I still had hope that one day I'd become that beautiful swan. Of course, I did realize that beauty comes from within, but that was not my concern; rather, how I looked to others.

Mom had taught me that. She told me to always have clean (and likely ironed) underwear on at all times in case I was ever in an accident and had to be hospitalized. She stressed that you wouldn't want those admitting you to see you had dirty underwear on. Never mind if I was hurt and being in an accident, I may have involuntarily dirtied my underpants. Yet, that was my mom!

I continued to try to always look my best, if possible. I made an effort to ignore or drown out Mom's persistent and consistent criticisms that played over in my head.

As I look back, I realize that I wished my mom were like Wayne's Mom. I knew she accepted me and was kind all the time. I always loved seeing her. I knew that Wayne was very close to her, and I'd see him tease her. I could see how deeply he loved his mom.

Enjoying Being Together – *Growing Together*

Wayne and I did enjoy going for swims at Buena Vista Beach when it was dark and raining. The beach was just a block from his home, and we usually had it all to ourselves. When it rained, the water felt the warmest.

I felt loved and safe with him even though he didn't tell me he loved me.

Wayne worked hard, but he also liked 'big toys' such as when he purchased a splashy motor boat and later a catamaran, which I'd never seen or been on until then.

In the winter, he did commercial fishing on the side and had what he called his *Bombardiere*. Apparently, it's called a Snow Trac. It looked somewhat like this:

Everything seemed new and exciting to me, riding in his Bombardiere, watching him set his nets under the ice to catch tullibee or white fish, depending, which season was open.

He taught me how to ice fish, as shown in the photos below. He used an auger to bore a hole in the ice to set me up to catch perch while he pulled his nets.

After setting his nets, he'd go a day or so later to pull them. If at all possible, I'd go along for the experience,

With heavy rubber gloves on, he'd squeeze the fish out of the nets and throw them on the ice. When done, he'd put them in the back of his truck to take them to the fish plant, which was towards Moose Jaw, Saskatchewan.

He also had a skidoo, and we'd go on rides, which I also loved. For a short time, he sold skidoos at the beach. I was living in a new and exciting world, and my sense of humor was even coming back because I was happy and in love. Being at the beach was a relief from the city, which was often the sadder side of life in the hospital.

Getting to Know Him More

I came to know him better as I began to know his mother more. She talked about Wayne contracting tuberculosis (TB) and how she and Cork had to take him to Fort Sanatorium near Fort Qu'Appelle to have him admitted. She said it was so hard to leave him there.

Wayne was 11 years old when he was admitted there. When he turned 12 years old, his parents came to attend his yearly medical review to determine if he could be discharged and finally go home.

She shared how her heart broke when they were told that there were still spots on his lungs and he couldn't go home. Obviously, this was a black hole in his parents' lives, but even more so for Wayne, who spent another year there. When he turned 13 years old, he was given the green light to go home.

I asked him what it was like there, and he reluctantly managed to tell me a few things. He said the pills they had to take were like horse pills. He described how he and the other guys made slingshots and used their pills to take aim at the birds in the trees outside their windows.

Perhaps this led to his TB not getting cleared up more quickly. Those boys, being young like him, were likely bored and restless, having to be bedridden, and found this as a way to entertain themselves.

He told me that he'd get to know the patients there and that when he heard the wheels of the gurney (stretcher) rolling down the hall in the middle of the night, he knew someone had died. The gurney was going to the morgue. In the morning, he'd hear who had passed away in the night.

I recognized how difficult it must have been for him to live away from his parents and siblings and never know if he'd see them again because he knew when he was there that he was sick, and that could be him on that gurney in the middle of the night.

He told me about the 'dirty nurses' aides,' as he put it. He told me that they'd climb into bed with him at night and feel him up. My reaction was that of shock, "Wow! That's crazy that they'd do something like that!"

I recall thinking that was disgusting, but I never asked for details or thought at the time that he was sexually abused because this was not discussed much back then, and I was still 19 years old.

I realized much later on that I, too, had experienced sexual interference. Further, I realized and appreciated that there were several significant variables as to how sexual abuse impacts one.

The adverse effects that one can be left with are related to the victim's developmental age at the time, the length of time the abuse went on, their temperament, and their ability to cope with the assault or if they were able to have it stop.

The first line of support can come from parents, a trusted family member, or a counselor to ensure it stops and a safe environment is established. Yet, that was not available to him.

What happened to Wayne happened to so many Indigenous young people who were sent to residential schools and suffered abuse from authority figures. There was an entrapment, and they could not walk away and tell someone. The perpetrators were authority figures doing this. Often, there is a 'no talk rule,' and the silence is marred in shame, guilt, and threats.

As a professional therapist, counseling for over thirty years, I know personally and professionally the devastating effects of trauma on us and what results from it.

Addictions most often become coping strategies, which, if not checked, have devastating outcomes. That's why it is so important to heal and arrest addictions as soon as possible.

Addictions are a cancer on the individual and their family, having DEATH written all over them! In the two years that Wayne spent at Fort San, he never received counseling, nor did he get it after being discharged. He never spoke about his stay there again, as I am sure he wanted to forget that dark period in his life.

At 13 years old, he was back living at his home in Buena Vista, Saskatchewan, and would need to refocus in trying to adjust back to a normal life.

The Name 'Dobson'

The name Dobson was well-known around there. His dad's nickname was Cork or Corky, which was short for Claire. Cork owned a lot of land around Buena Vista adjacent to Regina Beach. To this day, I don't know how he acquired the land.

Cork farmed some of that land and also had a small business of fixing things in his oversized garage at the back of their home. Everyone knew him around there. He was jovial and outgoing.

The Saskatchewan Government had a ribbon cutting ceremony at Buena Vista, Saskatchewan, naming a small regional area The Dobson Heritage Park, of course, after the Dobson family name.

Cork's elderly parents lived at Regina Beach in a cute little house off the main street. Wayne and I would go visit them, and they were very kind and humble.

Claire, as his parents called him, was an only child. You knew from interacting with them that they thought that 'the sun rose and set' on their son. I am sure he was catered to and spoiled.

I found Wayne's dad to be somewhat emotionally immature. He really liked to be babied. And I noted his wife Helen did that to some extent. They did work together with the farming and slept together, so I concluded that they must have gotten along.

Cork was pleasant with me, and we managed small talk. Witnessing Wayne and his dad interacting, I could see their relationship was not a warm father-son relationship. They made small talk whenever I heard them, appearing to be emotionally detached from one another.

Dore the Dog

They had a family dog called Dore. He was more Wayne's mom's dog. Cork tells the story that when he was up north fishing and hunting, he found Dore (near Dore Lake) in a wolf's den and brought him home. He claimed he was a cross between a wolf and a husky dog.

You didn't mess around with Dore. He was a protector, and he did have some wild blood in him for sure. I painted Dore for Wayne's mom, but I have no idea where it is now.

Dore became a hero for Wayne and his mom.

After lunch one day, Wayne's mom drove their hired hand back to the tractor to work. When she stopped the truck to let him off, he attempted to rape her.

Fortunately, Dore was in the back of the truck. She managed to open the door of the truck, and Dore attacked him.

As the story goes, she called Dore off of him and put Dore in the front of the truck, leaving the hired hand behind. She told Cork what happened, and he found the hired hand and had words with him, but the attack was never reported to the RCMP. They never saw him again.

The shocking part of this was that this man had worked for the Dobsons for a considerable amount of time, eating meals with them. They trusted him. He lived on a nearby reserve and did this in broad daylight and hadn't been drinking. Dore was now a hero!

Addictions and Trauma

Dr. So & So, the one who was so impatient with me getting up on water-skis, well, I thought he likely was an alcoholic because he loved his booze and was always having fancy parties. He loved having Wayne over for supper and an evening of entertaining. I was often with Wayne. I think I was still a 'thorn in his side.'

After Wayne was home from Fort San, he soon began drinking with the doc. I now think he was grooming Wayne, as later on, he had a male partner who was an extra good friend. He lived with him up until doc passed away.

Wayne was very personable and had a lot of friends in Regina as well as at the beach. It seemed they all liked to party, and of course, the beach was a resort, and lots of city people came to their cabins and partied.

Wayne would throw the odd party or attend them. If I weren't working in the hospital, I'd be right there with him.

Towards the end of every August, Wayne would have a 'corn roast' on the beach that was Dobson's land. There were lots of people at it, and the liquor was flowing. I had to be back at the residence by midnight, and calling in with an excuse would not look good.

Wayne promised to get me back in time, but I saw him getting plastered, or I should say drunk. I kept going to him and saying I need you to get me back to the residence. He said, "I will. Just wait," Then he continued on while I appealed to him repeatedly. He stood there with a dumb smile on his face, which I decided to wipe off. I slapped him across the face.

With that, his drunk friend stepped in and said, "Heh, you don't hit my friend like that!" I responded, "If you want to take over for your friend, then you will get just what he got." And I slapped him across the face.

He replied, "If you weren't my friend's girlfriend, I'd give it back to you." Thank God I didn't start a brawl. I did call into the residence, telling the supervisor I was sick,

I narrate this incident because it was then that I first began to realize that Wayne was in trouble with alcohol. Yet, life turned back to normal, and as is the case with alcoholism, denial is a huge defense mechanism in not coming to terms with it.

Hindsight is 20/20, and so at some rudimentary level at age 21 years, I knew that Wayne and I both had childhood trauma and Wayne was self-medicating with alcohol. I figured I better be careful, or I wouldn't be far behind.

The Dream!

Wayne would talk about us getting married. He walked me down to the far end of Buena Vista to show me what was called the peninsula on his dad's land. The peninsula was a beautiful, scenic, and serene spot.

He had a great imagination, and when we would get there, he'd tell me what a beautiful home he was going to build there for us and how it would overlook the lake, and we'd have our children Bobby and Susie. He'd paint a picture of them playing there and our going fishing and boating.

I knew he loved me, but I had not heard him say it to me. Mom and Dad never said it to me, either. I did tell him that I loved him because I was in love with him. Of course, I wanted the dream home and to have his children.

Do You Love Me?

When I would ask him, "Wayne, do you love me?" he'd reply, "Arlene, if I change my mind, I'll let you know!"

Then we'd laugh, as I was to assume from that response that he did love me but also that he could stop loving me, which wasn't a secure feeling at all.

I realize now that his response was unacceptable, but why did I accept it? After all, we need to know and hear from the one who loves us that they, in fact, do love us. We need to know that this person is committed to us. They won't just get up one day and realize they no longer love you. I was likely making excuses for him that he'd not heard it either.

Perhaps it was because I never recall my parents telling me that they loved me even though I knew they did. Perhaps it was because I still thought I was an ugly duckling striving to become a beautiful swan and shouldn't expect anything better.

My ignorance about what was happening and my insecurities kept me from seeing the 'red flags' in this man, his incapability to love me the way I knew one should. It, however, wasn't yet a 'big enough red flag' for me to leave.

Over the Top Humor

Wayne had a very sporty car. He liked to live it up, and when drinking, he was somewhat on the wild side but was never nasty or abusive to me.

His buddies nicknamed him 'Slew Foot.' I never liked that name, but I wasn't sure why. After I became a Christian, I found that name is a Southern slang term for the Devil or Lucifer, Satan, etcetera, and so I knew then why I didn't like it.

Wayne, at times, had a wicked sense of humor and loved getting a reaction out of me. One such time was when we were driving to the beach on the old #54 highway, and he just nonchalantly pulled the steering wheel off and tossed it in the back seat.

I hollered, "What are you doing?" as I leaned in the back seat, grabbing the steering wheel for him to put back on. He put it back on with a smile and kept driving while I was still mortified.

Another day, driving down that same road, I noted a car wheel rolling along the ditch beside me. I said, "Look at that wheel rolling along in the ditch!"

Smiling nonchalantly, he said, "Yup, that's my wheel," as we were coming to a definite stop.

He wanted to deny death or laugh in its face since he bought an old hearse and drove that thing around. I never drove with him in that toy because it 'creeped me out.' Perhaps he did that, seeing so many friends died of tuberculosis when he spent two years in the sanatorium. No longer would he fear death but flaunt it!

He'd Take Care of Me

On the other hand, Wayne also had a calming effect on me. When there was a problem, I felt safe that he could fix it.

Onetime, he was heading to the beach on the same #54 highway when his truck just came to a stop. It was the middle of winter and below forty degrees. The truck was not going to move.

No one was going to come down the road this late at night. We had to walk to his parents' place in Buena Vista. I was beginning to panic since I was not dressed well enough to walk.

I told him that this would be impossible as we'd have to walk several miles from there. He calmed my fears and said that he had two Skidoo suits behind the seat. He also had heavy boots and mitts, so we both put them on.

I looked like the abominable snowman because my outfit was definitely oversized. I was warm, but I wondered how I'd ever walk that far in this.

He held my gloved hand and walked beside me, talking about random things. It kept my mind occupied from worrying about the distance we had to go or whether we'd even make it. Yet, I knew with him that we'd make it, and it seemed that in no time at all, we arrived at his parents' place.

When we got home, we lay on the couch and cuddled until we fell asleep. We definitely bonded with each other, and I know we cared deeply, one for the other, but he did not communicate that in words.

I absolutely knew that I loved him deeply. This was the first time that I'd actually fallen in love, and he definitely was my 'first love.'

His two sisters, Wilma and Lydia, came to their parents' place for holidays. They were only two and three years older than me. Wilma was the oldest, and her husband, Dale, had two adorable children under the age of five, Joey and Jane. Lydia was not yet married.

I tried to get close to his sisters, but I found it somewhat difficult to engage in any meaningful conversation with them. They'd enjoy poking fun at me at times, enjoying a laugh at my expense, like when I went to do a 'mom thing' and strained the gravy that I'd made for supper. That struck them so funny, and they were laughing with no concern for how I might feel.

That was not the only time that they'd ridicule what I did or how I did it. Since their making fun of me was at my expense, I was guarded around them. I concluded that they were like those 'snotty girls' in high school.

Wayne's mom taught Sunday school and summer Vocational Bible School at the United Church in Regina Beach, often hosting the visiting intern pastors who were posted there.

She rarely had a social drink, but she was a smoker, as were too many people back then. I knew that she loved children. We definitely had that in common, our love for children, and also our love for Wayne. To me, she was just a very loving woman.

Graduation from Nursing School – *June 1967*

Wayne was invited to my graduation ceremony, but he had some reason why he could not attend. Yet, when I got home to my parents, he picked me up to go out to the lake.

As time went on, I realized that he never really wanted to be around events that pertained to me or even be around my friends or my parents. He seemed somewhat anxious and uncomfortable in their presence, and I didn't understand why. In my third year of nursing school, I decided that I would not want to work on a hospital ward taking direct care of patients. Although my back issues when I was younger were much improved, they still were an issue for me when working directly with patients, lifting them, and doing other heavy physical work.

I also wanted to teach and become a Nursing Instructor. I didn't want to ask my parents for money to go to university as I didn't think they could afford to send me. I was determined I'd find a way to go and pay for it on my own.

A New Chapter in My Career

I decided to apply for a Saskatchewan Provincial Bursary. My marks coming out of nursing school were high enough for me to obtain a bursary.

The conditions were that the bursary would provide my tuition, books, and living expenses for three years, and in return, I promised to work in the province for three years after receiving my degree.

Once I received the bursary, my parents drove me to Saskatoon to see the University campus and to help me find a room to rent.

In walking around the expansive campus of this university, I was in awe of the layout and expanse of this academic setting. To me, it was so beautiful, with the Tyndall stone buildings and well-manicured grounds all nestled beside the Saskatchewan River. It seemed out of this world.

Photo of the College of Nursing at the U of S

In reading about these buildings made of Tyndall stone, I found out that it was a unique material found in many University of Saskatchewan (U of S) buildings, which had received international attention. Tyndall Stone is limestone that has fossil fragments in it. It can only be found in Manitoba and dates back over 400 million years.

I felt like I was in a new world. I was excited for this new venture to begin, but I felt like 'a fish out of water.' I began to experience anxiety that I'd never experienced like that before. I felt insecure about leaving my home base and being away from Wayne.

I did see a doctor and was diagnosed with anxiety and depression, and was put on an antidepressant for a while.

Finding a Place to Live

I found a rooming place a few blocks away from the University. The older woman who owned and ran the place reminded me of the stern and cranky old supervisor who ran the nurses' residence. She had some traits of my mom and grade six teacher, Miss Hitsman.

My one room was on the third floor of this very old home, but it was within walking distance of the university. It had everything that I needed in it: a bed, stove, slop pail, a table, a desk, a small fridge, and a few dishes, pots, and pans. I was used to living in one room in the nurses' residence, so I adapted there quite well.

Other students lived on the second floor in their rooms. Across from mine was a sweet old woman who had to be a hoarder. She had newspapers and books stacked to the ceiling, and she smoked. Since there was no smoke alarm, I checked if I could get out of the window onto the roof in case she lit the place on fire. I saw that I could get out, and that was some comfort.

I enjoyed my neighbor and found her to be a dear soul. She became an inspiration to me since she was taking university classes late in life, in her seventies at least, which showed me that age has no limits for one to have a zest for life and learning.

The landlady, on the other hand, was very nosy. I knew she would come into my room when I was away, and so I set a booby trap to catch her. I taped newspaper to my floor just inside my door, placing wide strips of clear sticky tape facing upwards, thinking that this was a brilliant idea so that when she came in, she'd have to step on the tape, and the paper would rip.

Sure enough, when I came back from class, it was ripped. Shortly after that, I moved into a house with other students. That didn't last too long as it was a bit crowded, and they liked to party.

Wayne rarely came to Saskatoon to see me, but did on a couple of occasions. I would travel back to visit him at the beach, but it became more like a long-distance relationship. He still had Wayne Dobson Construction, and there seemed to be lots of work for him.

Two of my childhood friends on our block, Evelyn and Lynne, were now married, and Wayne and I had fleetingly talked about doing the same, but we did not take it to the next level. I began giving him hints, which was humiliating for me.

Finally, I went on a couple of dates, but that didn't feel right. Wayne must have known that unless he did 'pop the question,' I might end up moving on, so he began to visit me more.

The Engagement

One evening in March of 1968, Wayne came up to Saskatoon to visit me. While I was doing dishes with my roommate, he said, "Arlene, I have something for you," and handed me a jewelry box that looked like a ring box. I asked what it was and he responded, "Open it and see."

I opened it, and it was empty. He was sitting there with his familiar grin. I tossed it back at him. He said, "Well, don't you want it?"

I was curious, so I said. "Let's see it, and I will see if I want it." Sure enough, it was a diamond engagement ring he was holding.

71

Although this engagement was far from romantic, and I figured he should not be playing emotional games with me with something so special, I went ahead and asked him, "Does this mean you want to marry me?"

He managed to say, "Yes," but I tried to ignore his behavior. It was demeaning. Yet, I reasoned that, after all, he must love me, or he wouldn't have bought this ring, and there was no doubt for me that I did love him.

So when was the wedding to be? That was not even discussed. I got back to completing my nursing degree while Wayne went back to Buena Vista to work in his business.

Overwhelming Grief

I was completing the first year of my three-year program and interning in the Pediatric Ward at the Saskatchewan Royal University Hospital when I was called aside by the head nurse, telling me I had to take a phone call that was important.

It was Wayne. He told me that his mom had a stroke and was in the hospital. I asked him how he was and whether she could talk to him. He said that she could. She said to him, "Wayne, you know how I stoop down to wash the floor? Well, that is when it happened."

Shortly after speaking to Wayne, he called back to say she had another stroke, and this time, they were told that it was a massive one. Wayne hurried up to get me to be with him. When we got to Bladworth, Saskatchewan, I asked him to stop at a pay phone near the highway so I could call the hospital to check on her.

I wanted to know that she was still with us, praying and wanting her to hold on so we could be there before she passed, as I knew her condition was very grave.

I went back to the truck and told Wayne that nothing had changed. We were in shock and deep grief. His mom had only turned 54 years old. She meant the world to him and many others, including me. His mom was so very special to him that I was very worried as to how he'd be able to deal with this if she should die.

When we arrived at the waiting room just outside the Intensive Care Unit of the hospital I'd graduated from, Cork was there with Jim, and they appeared numb and in shock. Jim was now in his mid-teens. To this day, I can't recall who else was there.

Wayne and I went in to see her, and I don't know what we said to her other than to say we were there. I told Wayne that she'd be hearing us as that sense remains even if you are unconscious. I don't recall that he said he loved her or anything. He seemed paralyzed in his grief, realizing the gravity of what was occurring.

The family left, and Wayne went somewhere, too, but I stayed. I walked back into her area where the curtains were drawn around her, and my nursing sister Sylvia, whom I'd graduated with, was providing her nursing care.

I looked at Sylvia and broke down for the first time, and she held me and cried with me. I'll never forget her immense act of compassion towards me.

Miracle # 2: – His Holy Spirit Descended

So there I was, alone with this woman who had impacted my life so immensely. She was so kind and loving, full of grace and strength of character, and now was at the end of her life.

She was not going to come back to us after this massive stroke. She was only 54 years old. I began to talk to her, telling her that she was not to worry about us and that we'd look out for Cork and help Jim to finish growing up. I told her how much I loved her.

I had prayed to God many times, but this time was different than any other time. I prayed deep in my spirit without words, asking for God to come and take her home. As I was by her side and holding her hand, I spoke softly to her that Jesus would come now to take her home and that it was alright for her to go with Him, assuring her that one day we'd all be together forever and we'd all be so happy.

The next thing that occurred was the presence of the Lord, perhaps an angel, who descended at an angle to the right of where I was standing. With my eyes closed, I experienced her spirit leave her body, and I felt two energies join each other and ascend out of her room.

This all happened immediately after I spoke to her and prayed for Jesus to come for her. This was not a miracle as one thinks of miracles, but for me, I'd just witnessed a second miracle. You may recall that the first miracle was when Carol walked.

As I was leaving her room, I felt a 'Holy peace' and told Sylvia, "She's gone." With that, she coded her, and the resuscitation team arrived. I knew she would not be revived, but they had to follow protocol.

I then called Wayne and told him she was gone and to please come for me.

The Funeral

The family and the community were in shock at Helen's passing. Like most families who lose a loved one, particularly if it is sudden and unexpected, they are thrown into grief. We all grieve in our own way, but it is all grief.

I learned about Charlie, who, the previous summer, had been a student intern pastor at the beach. Helen and he had a wonderful connection. The family decided they wanted him to do her service, but he was living in New Brunswick, Canada, working now as an ordained United Church minister.

Cork contacted him, and he agreed to come. Of course, his expenses were paid for. You see, regardless of race, your circumstances, or your position in life, this woman, Helen, mom to her children, a wife to Cork and a role model for her children and me, was so loved because of her gentle, caring spirit, demonstrating to those around her the love of Jesus, without fanfare.

She never told others to believe, or they'd go to hell. She lived her faith and was 'Light.' That is how our lives should be— like an 'Open Book' that when our children and others see us and read it and interact with us, that they feel the love of God coming from us.

Jesus told us when He walked among us that unless we become like these little children, we shall not enter the kingdom of God. Jesus said:

"I assure you and most solemnly say to you, unless you repent [that is, change your inner self—your old way of thinking, live changed lives] and become like children [trusting, humble, and forgiving], you will never enter the kingdom of heaven."
Matthew 18:3 Amplified Bible

That sums up Helen. She might not be perfect, and she did not want anyone thinking she was either, because she needed Jesus as her Savior too, but she displayed His gentle Spirit and love.

Soon, Charlie arrived. He was a stately large black man that exuded God's love. He was upbeat and lifted all of our spirits with his positivity and presence. He reassured everyone that we'd all be together in heaven one day, and all sorrow and tears would be wiped away.

I recall Wayne saying to him, "Pastor, Arlene is taking this so hard!"

I had been worried about Wayne, but he was concerned for me. His response was, "Wayne, it's us sensitive souls that suffer." Looking back, I may have been trying to carry Wayne's pain, too, but I certainly had enough of my own.

In my counseling practice, I sometimes recommend the book Kids Who Carry Our Pain by Dr. Robert Hemfelt and Dr. Paul Warren. They describe how one child in the family will often carry the pain of the entire family.

I don't remember much of the service, but I do remember the theme of it, which was *Joy Cometh In the Morning,* based on this scripture:

> *"Weeping may endure for a night, but joy cometh in the morning."*
>
> *Psalm 30:5*

This is the other scripture that comforted me:

> *"He will wipe away every tear from their eyes, and death shall be no more, neither shall there be mourning, nor crying, nor pain anymore, for the former things have passed away."*
>
> *Revelations 21:4*

Helen's body was laid to rest in the Regina Beach Cemetery, and her spirit is with Him.

Planning Our Wedding

With a cloud of grief still over us, we planned our wedding for September 07, 1968. Wayne and I spent a lot of time together during the summer months at the beach. Everyone was coping with what was our new normal.

That summer, Wayne's sisters spent a lot of their time at their parents' place. Cork would come and go, and we prepared meals and sometimes ate together.

As summer was ending, I realized that I did not want to return to university. But I had no choice. There were conditions of my bursary to fulfill.

I was going back and forth a lot with my parents as they were involved in planning our wedding. Wilma and Dale's children were to be at our wedding party. Jane was to be the flower girl, and Joey would be the ring bearer.

The wedding was to be at St. John's United Church, where I attended with my parents. After the wedding, the supper would be in the church basement, with the dance back at the Regina Beach Community Hall.

Should We Get Married? – *Unresolved Grief*

During those planning months, Wayne shared more about his grief about his mom and said he'd never get over her death. He also shared about a girlfriend he had before me. I had never heard about this before.

He told me that she'd come to the beach each summer with her family, and they lived in Moose Jaw, SK, and owned a business there.

He shared that she was very special to him, and then she got cancer and died. As he told me about her, I could see that he had cared deeply for her. A deep sadness came over him. He likely loved her and hadn't recovered from her death.

As it is with grief, when you have fresh grief about a loss like your mom, another unresolved grief often surfaces. He had not had time to resolve the grief from his mom's death, and it brought forth the grief of the loss of his first love. I felt incredibly sad for him.

At the same time, I began to question if he had ever gotten over her. It didn't appear so. How could he really love me and marry me? Perhaps that's why he never told me he loved me— because of her. Or perhaps he told her that he loved her, and she died after that, so he would be sure not to tell me he loved me.

Then, I thought about our relationship with his mom. I talked to Wayne about how I was feeling and my concerns about us getting married. I told him that I wondered, with his mother gone and what appeared to be unresolved grief over his girlfriend, was there really enough there to hold us together? Without hesitation, he told me that there was enough for us to get married and that we'd be okay.

I thought he must still love me because he told me that if he changed his mind, he would let me know, so the marriage plans continued.

Towards the end of August 1968, Wilma and her family, and Lydia went back to their homes and their lives. Wayne lived with Cork. Both of us would be when we were married.

With my needing to go back to university right after our wedding, I decided to do some meal prepping and clean the house after Wilma and Lydia left. I decided to go into Cork's bedroom since I knew that no one had cleaned his room or washed his bedding or clothes over the summer.

So, like my mom, I got into 'high gear' and got it done before he came home for supper.

When he walked into his bedroom, he came right back out and said, "Arlene, did you do that?"

I replied, "Yes, I did. I hope you don't mind?"

He broke down, bawling and said, "Oh, thank you so much," and went back into his bedroom.

From that day on, we developed a closer relationship. Wayne also interacted more with him.

Our Wedding

Weddings are stressful as well as being a joyful occasion. Gordon and his wife Sheila and their new daughter, Dawn, came from New Brunswick for it, and Dad's parents and his sister came too. I cannot even remember the other relatives that attended our wedding.

My bridesmaids were two of my childhood friends, Evelyn and Jennifer, and one of my nursing sisters, Cheryl. Although we do not see one another often, we are lifelong friends.

September 07, 1968, was our wedding day. Mom was involved with helping me get ready. It was very surprising to me, but she showed up in my bedroom as we were all getting dressed with a glass of orange juice for each of us spiked with vodka and said, "This will relax you, girls."

Now, to my knowledge, there was never liquor in the house, but perhaps mom was a 'closet drinker' as she knew vodka would have no smell, and she obviously got hold of some.

That song, *Get Me To The Church on Time,* resonated with me. We all arrived at the church on time. Wayne was standing there with his three best men at the front of the church. The music began, and Dad walked me down the aisle.

We exchanged our vows, but I was anxious about getting them right, as Wayne likely was, too. When he kissed the bride, me, it was all over, and the music began playing again. As we left the church to have pictures taken, he almost ran out while I hurried down the aisle, trying to keep up with him. That was a bit embarrassing.

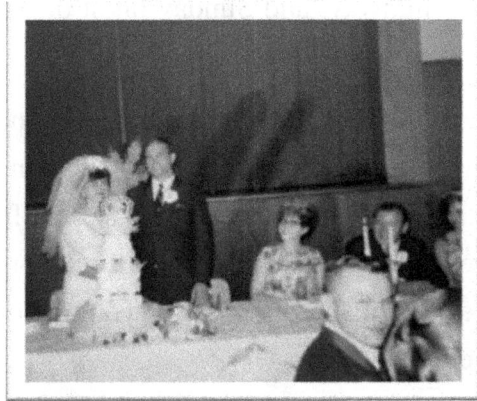

We didn't get a professional photographer, so our photographs are raw and unfiltered.

The rest of the evening was much better. We had a nice wedding supper and managed to do what was expected of us, like standing and kissing when the glasses were being clinked.

After the dance, we changed our clothes and hurried into Regina to stay in the bridal suite at the Regina Inn. After this very stressful and eventful day, Wayne went into the bathtub and I onto the couch, where we both fell asleep.

Married Life

Now, married life was underway, as was my second year of the three years of university that I had to complete.

Every weekend, I took the Greyhound bus back and forth to the beach. Wayne was always there waiting for me at the junction of Highway #11 and #54. The bus driver would drop me off along

#11 highway, and Sunday night or early Monday morning, he'd pick me up.

I worked hard in my classes, but not much studying was done on those weekends. Wayne and I soon moved out of Cork's home and rented a home in Regina Beach. It was cute, built high up so we could oversee the lake. The only problem living there was that we were just a block away from the one and only Regina Beach Hotel and Bar.

The locals and the seasonal people congregated there. It was like a small town and one that gossiped. Everyone thought they knew everyone else's business.

Wayne's drinking increased, and of course, I couldn't see what he was drinking when I was away at school. He had a lot of friends who were also married, and they loved dropping by and partying on the weekends.

I knew there was too much drinking going on, and when I mentioned my concern to him, he dismissed it, saying we're just having fun and cutting loose from working all week. My social drinking had stopped as we became pregnant very shortly after. How did that happen?

Back in university, I began to have morning sickness. It was so bad for the first three months that Wayne came to Saskatoon a few more times, as I did not feel like traveling.

I managed to stay in university that year. Wayne's brother, Jim, came to live with us as he had been staying with his sister, Wilma, and her husband, Dale and her family while finishing high school. Wayne and I were happy to have him come and live with us, and Wayne had him working with him some of the time.

We had moved again to rent a larger home across the street from the general store and post office and just a few more steps closer to the bar.

The house we moved into had been used as a restaurant, and it had a commercial gas stove with lots of burners. This home was excellent for entertaining our friends and putting on Sunday brunches 'to nurse hangovers' from a Saturday night of partying.

Called Upon as the Town Nurse

The locals knew I was a nurse, so I was frequently called upon to administer First Aid for a variety of situations, with some being very serious.

Some incidents still stand out for me. Like the neighbor who had a heart attack in his driveway, and I ran over and worked on him until the ambulance came. He was gone.

Wayne played ball at the beach, and one of his buddies who was playing had a heart attack at the ball diamond. I worked on him until the ambulance arrived, and the paramedics took over. He was never revived and was only around forty years of age.

Then, there was a huge accident after a Pow-wow at Kinookimaw, a hamlet by Little Arm next to Regina Beach. It was a quiet summer evening when we heard a loud crash. Two cars had collided head-on. We lived a block away from the accident.

Both Wayne and I rushed to the scene. When we got there, we saw eight people pulled onto the street beside their cars. Two ambulances were dispatched.

I walked to each person to assess their injuries and determine if any of them had died on impact. I began working on the others who were alive but badly injured. The two ambulances came and loaded four in each, putting the four deceased on the top.

Miracle # 3: – A Life Saved

There was this one time I was in the bar with Wayne, and one of the regulars came running in frantically, saying that I had to come with him right away as his mom had collapsed and was turning blue, and he thought she may have stopped breathing.

I went with him, and when I arrived, she was in the hallway face down and was not breathing. I managed to turn her over and got a weak pulse and then did a couple of inhalations, and I was not getting anywhere.

So, I thought I would check her airway again, and it was clear. At this point, I said, "Jesus, you are going to need to help me here, or I am going to lose her." Then I heard in my spirit, "Reach away down in her airway," which would be further than I had previously done two times already, and I did that and felt something that I knew shouldn't be there.

Luckily, I had long nails and sank them into whatever I was feeling. I pulled out of her airway a three-inch piece of fat and then proceeded to give her a couple of breaths, and she was back fully alive and fully drunk.

I found out that she had trimmed that fat off of her steak, and being drunk, she put it in her mouth, and well, you know what happened next.

I knew his mother very briefly when, months earlier, we'd attended a party at his place. She was there and drunk, and I cannot recall what the interaction was about, but she let me know she did not like me.

So her memory must have been clear since once upon her feet, she looked at me and said, "What the hell is she doing here? Get her out of here!"

The son said, "Mom, Arlene just saved your life!"

She responded, "Saved my life, my ass!"

He then said, "Mom, the ambulance will be here any minute."

"I don't need any damn ambulance!" was her reply.

Fortunately, just about then, the ambulance arrived, but she refused to go. I told her son to give her Tylenol if she began to hurt, and when she's sober tomorrow, you will need to get her into the doctor because I may have cracked a rib or two. Sure enough, she saw a doctor, and she did have a couple of broken ribs. I was always glad to help in any situation if I could.

I call this incident a miracle because when I tried clearing her airway twice, I thought I had gone deep enough. Nothing seemed to be obstructing it, so I would not have done anything further.

Yet, when I asked God to help me because I was losing her, I was instructed to go deeper down her airway with my fingers to discover this chunk of fat. It was certainly a miracle for her, or she'd not be here.

Numerous other incidents occurred in the years that I lived at the beach, related to deaths or near deaths or lifetime injuries that occurred. In most of these tragedies, alcohol was involved. It seemed like the whole town drank and drank too much! I know that's an overstatement, but there were lots who drank to excess.

We used to call Regina Beach Peyton Place. I looked up Peyton Place on Google because I forgot what I was referencing here, and this is what it said:

"Fifty years ago, the novel Peyton Place shocked America with its tale of secrets, sex, and hypocrisy in a small New Hampshire town, becoming one of the best-selling dirty books ever, a hit movie, and TV's first prime-time soap."

Regina Beach, being compared to Peyton Place, was a perfect comparison.

Planning for Our Baby's Arrival

Back then, there were no ultrasounds, so we didn't know if our baby was a boy or a girl. At my doctor's appointments, around seven months, he'd manipulate the baby's position from the breech to the head-down position.

Before I got home, the baby had kicked back to the breech position. Finally, the baby got too big, and the head finally engaged for the delivery.

I began spotting blood at almost eight months and went to hospital, but thank God it never progressed.

At home, Wayne and I were getting the second bedroom ready to bring our baby home to. The due date was October 06th, 1969. Jim would share the bedroom with the baby.

In the fall of 1969, I would be in my third and final year of university. I also would have my baby with me, so I needed to go to Saskatoon ahead of time to find a place.

I found a very nice two-bedroom basement suite to live in. The landlords were Italian. They had a wonderful big garden in their backyard. They also raised rabbits. The rabbit pens were lined along their backyard fence, which was something I'd never seen before. Of course, they ate these rabbits, and that rather grossed me out.

They obviously liked their wine, as across from my room was a huge wine vat where they made their own wine.

He told me there was another girl coming to take the other bedroom. She was a single parent with a baby girl. He knew I'd be having our baby soon, but he was just fine with bringing a second baby into their home, even though there was just a floor separating us.

I set up a crib and a changing table in my bedroom to bring the baby back with me for my second year of university. Of course, I needed a sitter when I was in classes.

That same year, Cork's mom, Lydia Dobson, passed away (1892-1969). Cork's dad was in Pioneer Village in Regina. Cork was grieving, having lost his mom a year after losing his wife.

Cork did find a lady friend, and after a while, it became obvious to the family that she was what one would describe as a 'gold digger.' They got married. Cork bought her nice things, and they went on holiday. I was glad he had someone to brighten up his life, but I never interacted with them much.

Jim began to use alcohol and often seemed like a lost soul. He did not receive as much help in his grief over the loss of his mom. We had quality family time with him, but I now realize that he'd been somewhat neglected after his mom's death.

Our Baby Arrives

Well, I was at home and now almost three weeks over the due date. So it was decided that I would be admitted to labor and delivery at RGH.

On October 24th, 1969, I was induced. So began the long labor and the much-anticipated arrival of our baby. Wayne was very anxious, but he stayed with me for almost 24 hours through this labor. I needed pain medication, hollering that I couldn't go through with this.

On October 25, 1969, we welcomed our baby boy. Unfortunately, dads were not yet able to be with moms in the delivery room. We were 'over the moon' with our new baby boy, who was perfect in every way. We tried to figure out what we would call our son because we did not have a name chosen.

Recently, we'd heard the name Lincoln, and it really stuck with us, so his first name became Lincoln. Then we needed a middle name, so we chose Dore, after our most famous dog, Dore, who was a hero.

My parents came up to the hospital to have a look at their new grandson. I was hoping Mom would offer to come and stay with me and help me with Lincoln that first week, but she didn't offer, and I never asked her to.

Chapter 6
1969 to 1983 – From 23 to 37

Home-Big Adjustments

That first week home, Wayne helped me some, but I witnessed him having a panic attack. I think he was overwhelmed thinking of the responsibility that he now had. Also, going through that birthing event had taken a lot out of him, as it had me.

Lincoln's early months were as hectic as mine, but somehow we managed. He was quite colicky the first few months, and that became poor sleep for both of us. I soon gave up trying to breastfeed him. With school and commuting, I felt emotionally drained.

Thinking back on this time is somewhat of a blur as I was going back and forth from university to the beach, taking Lincoln as an infant with me. It was hard for a new baby, too.

Wayne's drinking increased. When I was home on the weekend, many of these times were devoted to him entertaining his friends and their wives, and I thought I had to let on that I was okay with it.

Of course, they had become my friends too, but I wanted a normal life as possible, and coming from university to home with a baby and being tired, partying wasn't my thing. I had washing to do, beddings to change, and all of that, and possibly being called on to be the town nurse.

Wayne and I had a couple of heated disagreements over his drinking. Thank God there was never name-calling or belittling me or anything physical.

A Miscarriage

Wayne and I were managing, but emotionally, we didn't have enough time for ourselves. I thought Dore, our dog, got more affection from Wayne than I did, and when I saw him on the floor rubbing his tummy and playing with him, I wished I were Dore.

Obviously, we did get together that year as I got pregnant again. At around three months into the pregnancy, I miscarried. I was admitted to the Royal University Hospital in Saskatoon and had a procedure called a 'Dilatation and Curettage' known as a D&C.

After the D&C, I recall being in the recovery room and sitting up on the gurney, looking to my right and then to my left, and seeing two men who were out cold. I turned to the guy on my right and said, "Today, you will be with me in paradise."

For anyone who doesn't know where that saying comes from, it is in the Bible where Jesus, who was dying on the cross, hung between two thieves who were also being crucified. One of the thieves recognized who Jesus was and acknowledged Him, and then Jesus said to him, "Today you will be with me in paradise."

Several nurses and staff who were at the nurses' station heard me say this, and they burst out laughing. My attention was then directed at them, and I said something like, "What the f***are you laughing about? Shut your 'f******' mouths!"

They laughed all the more.

From the time I met 'the old lady,' I was trying to connect with her Jesus and God, and prayed for help. He always came through for me. I was confirmed in the United Church, so I thought I must be a Christian, but I was never quite sure.

That incident in the hospital was understandable, as I signed a piece of paper giving the hospital permission to use

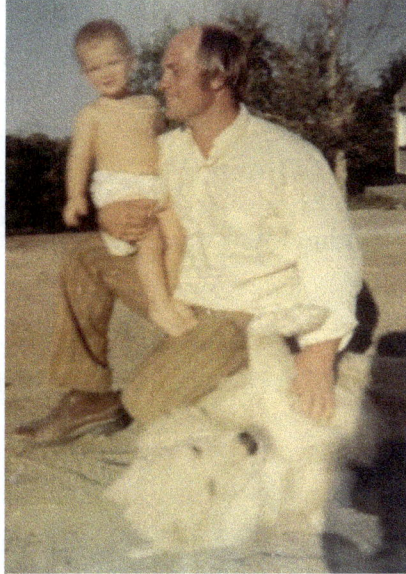

Summer of 1970-Wayne with Lincoln and Dore.

an anesthetic on me as a trial drug. A lot of research went on at this hospital, so I consented. Obviously, I was a bit delusional, and God wouldn't mind me playing the role of Jesus, would he? Yet, I was Jesus one minute and the devil the next. That anesthetic was a failure.

I was right back to the same routine. I didn't even have time to grieve our loss of what would have been another baby for us.

In the summer of 1970, we had Lincoln baptized by Rev. Morrison from the United Church in Lumsden, SK. In the summer of 1970, I became more involved with the United Church at the beach. I organized *The Women's World Day of Prayer* and asked for Rev. Morrison to come to speak at it. He sent his son, Keith Morrison, who was considering going into the ministry.

I later learned that he moved to the United States and got a career as a moderator and an interviewer for the television series Dateline.

Rape-Aborted

One lovely summer night in 1970, Wayne and I came home from a social function. After letting the babysitter go, Wayne went to bed, and I got into my nightgown and decided to watch some television before joining him. Instead, I fell asleep on the couch.

I was awakened by a very large Aboriginal man lying on top of me, who smelled of alcohol and was about to rape me. I began screaming for Wayne to come to help me, and thank God, this scared this guy off, and he ran out the door.

We never locked our doors, which was crazy considering we lived almost next door to the local pub, and there were lots of transient people at the beach.

Now, despite being in shock, I knew this was not just a bad dream. I got up and went into the kitchen, plugged in the kettle, and made myself a cup of coffee. As I was coming back into the living room to have my coffee, Wayne came out to ask me if I was calling him.

I told him that I had been calling him as some guy was trying to rape me, and your reaction time was so bad that he could have raped me already and left. I told him that my screaming for him had him run off and emphasized that we'd have to lock our doors from now on. He agreed that we should do that, locked the doors and went back to bed as I sat drinking my coffee.

No police report, nothing, and life went on as usual. Looking back on this, I realized that there was a normalizing of deviant events that went on in this town. I was also beginning to recognize the emotional disconnect between Wayne and me widening, which saddened me, but I didn't think about that for very long.

Miracle # 4: – Heaven's Instructions!

It was now the fall of 1970. Lincoln and I had started going back to university for my third and final year. He was almost a year old, and we were home for the Thanksgiving break.

There was always work that had to be done when I came home, like beds to change, washing to be done, and the like. I didn't have a washer or dryer, so I always made the trip to the Lumsden Laundromat, which was about a 10-minute drive.

That weekend, on Saturday afternoon, I asked this local teen, Paulette, who'd babysat Lincoln before, to come with me to the Laundromat. I did not have an infant or child car seat back then, so she could hold him on the drive here and back, and also help me at the Laundromat.

Wayne had gotten me a beater of a car just to get me around for short trips. I complained about the brakes in the car as they were not good and asked him to look into the issue.

He told me I was just low on brake fluid, so he topped it up again. The front passenger door still would not open, and he said he couldn't fix it then, but he'd look at it another day.

Before leaving Lumsden, I put a couple of baskets of clean clothes on the back seat and a box of clothing next to the door that wouldn't open. Paulette had Lincoln on her lap and sat between that box of laundry and me.

We were nearly home. I began to drive down Regina Beach Main Street, which had a steep decline all the way to the lake. As I began to drive down it, I applied the brakes to slow down. I immediately realized that I had no brakes.

I went into shock as this was a definite crisis. I recall saying, "Paulette, just hold onto Lincoln as tight as you can and don't say a word!" and saying to myself, "God, you need 'to take the wheel' here and help me!"

As I began to pick up speed, I kept communicating in my spirit to God, "Do I go right down to the lake?" I was thinking that I'd just do that and hit the water, and then the car would stop. I was provided an instant vision of people lined up to get into the Fowl Supper at the Community Hall on the main street, and His answer was a definite, "No!"

Then I heard in my spirit, "Go wide to the right just in front of Cope's Grocery store and then crank the wheel hard to the left and aim for the alley beside Donoval's Café. Anyone familiar with Regina Beach will know just where these landmarks are.

I did exactly as I was instructed to do, and by the grace of God, I drove onto the alley, which was on an incline, and the car came to a stop.

When it stopped, Paulette had one foot outside the passenger side of the door that had never opened before, and she did what she was asked to do, which was to hold on to Lincoln tightly.

I said we would just walk home from here.

As we began to walk, I saw my underwear and other clothes that had been in the box strewn on the ground. I quickly picked up the clothes, and tossed them back into the car, and began walking home.

When we were at the end of the alley, Lol Watson, who lived across the lake, walked up to me and said, "Arlene, I was watching you coming down the hill, and I could see you had no brakes, and I thought how is she going to get out of this situation? And you know, Arlene, you did the only thing possible!"

I agreed with him and said, "Wayne would come back for the car." And we walked solemnly back to my home. We were still absorbing what had just occurred. I got Lincoln a bottle and put him down for a nap, and then I went to the fridge and got a beer and shared it with Paulette.

I don't know if she'd ever had a beer, but she drank it with me before Wayne showed up. I told him what happened, and he immediately left the house without saying a word.

I never set eyes on that vehicle again or our clothes, as Wayne obviously did something with it. Again, life went on as usual, and this was not discussed.

I recognized this was indeed a miracle because my instinct was to panic and just ride the car right down into the lake, but I asked God to help me, and in split seconds, he gave me this vision of people on the street and instructed me as to what to do.

I did exactly what He told me to do. I give no credit to my intelligence or nurses' training in crisis situations because I know it was His Spirit speaking to mine. Absolutely, lives were spared, including ours.

Completing University for My B.Sc.N. Degree

Lincoln was growing and a very active baby. By 14 months, he had figured out how to get out of his crib. It was quite the feat to observe.

He had a stronger upper body, so while placing his hands on the rail of the crib and curling his toes on the top of it, he managed to pull himself up and turn himself around, all the while hanging onto the rail. He'd then dangle for a few seconds, and knowing how far he had to drop, he did it with precision. I put a thinner mattress in there, but he soon mastered that, too.

Lincoln – one year old

We continued to take the Greyhound bus home every weekend. Jim was still living with us but still partying, too. I used to drag him home from parties, but soon, I stopped fetching him home as he was now too old for that.

While in Saskatoon during the week, there was not much time to focus on studies. Time was taken up with getting to classes, time taking the bus, caring for Lincoln, getting groceries and then getting ready to go home to the beach every weekend.

My Italian landlords were a robust bunch, as they often had family and friends gather in the evening. As the evening progressed, the accordion music and their voices got louder. The gatherings always ended early in the morning with a family feud breaking out.

I very much enjoyed them. They were kind to me and enjoyed interacting with Lincoln. I appreciated them finding me a responsible sitter to come in when I had to be at classes.

One day, when I came home, I found sitting on my kitchen table a bowl of spaghetti with a leg of meat over it. I knew it was a rabbit leg and thigh. Being hungry, I started with the spaghetti and began picking at the meat, and before I knew it, I was looking at an empty bowl with a couple of bare bones in it. Oh, my gosh! I ate the bunny! I had to admit it tasted like chicken, and perhaps even better.

Having to Pass!

By now, I badly wanted the university to be over with. It seemed like I was going forever, and I just wanted to be at home and have a more normal life.

On Friday, I had an English class. I regularly missed it so I could head back home with Lincoln to Wayne. I left on Thursday afternoons, and Wayne would pick us up. The three-day weekends became habitual since I reasoned that if I studied enough, handed in my assignments, and passed the test, the professor could not fail me.

Then came the final English test. There were fewer than ten minutes left on the test, and I turned the page over and found another few questions, which were half of the test. I was mortified and in a panic. I madly wrote under each heading until the time was up.

I usually would not do this, but when I was back from the weekend, I got up the nerve to go and knock on this professor's door. I heard him say, "Come in," and when I was in, he was sitting behind his desk with a big grin and said, "I was waiting for you to show up."

I don't know exactly what I said, but obviously, I told him I'd missed seeing the questions on the back and was worried I had not passed his class.

He warmly smiled and said, "I saw you were missing those questions until right at the end, but I was impressed how you managed to write enough relevant information under the headings and with your work on the rest of the exam and your assignments, I was able to pass you without any problem." I thanked him, and when I left, I said, "Thank you, God!"

University is Over – *Hooray!*

In the spring of 1971, my convocation finally arrived. Mom and Dad came to it, as did Wayne. He'd broken his foot in a work accident. I was happy he came as he missed my nurses' graduation.

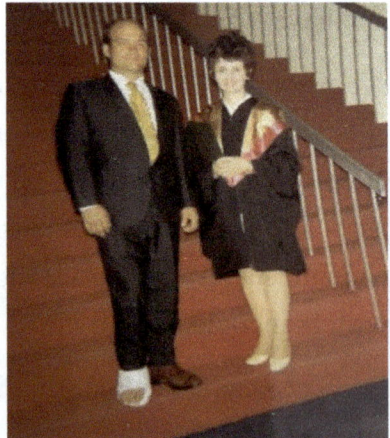

We each had rooms at the lovely Bessborough Hotel in Saskatoon, which is along the Saskatchewan riverbank. It was a memorable time.

The university was paid for and over with, and now I had to fulfill my bursary obligation and work for three years in the nursing field in Saskatchewan.

First, I was looking forward to a few months of downtime to be home as a family with Wayne and our now toddler, plus Jim and our dog, Dore. I just wanted to enjoy the summer with my family and go swimming and boating before thinking of work.

Time to Get To Work!

Job #1: At the end of the summer, I began my first job in Regina with the VON, which stands for the Victorian Order of Nurses.

I was supposed to have a license to drive one of their Beetle Volkswagens that they were famous for, but I applied without having my driver's license. I got the job and then scrambled to get lessons on a standard. I got my license just in time before my start date. Thank God again!

Job #2: In 1971, I found a job as a Regina Public Health Nurse. That meant more commuting every day, which was about a 45-minute drive there and back.

My district was near the downtown area, and I had two schools, Davin and Strathcona. My offices were next to the Principal's office.

At Strathcona School, there were always students receiving the strap for bad behavior. The area had low-income families with varied social problems.

Of course, these students were given the strap on an open, outstretched hand with the palm turned up. The slaps of the strap that I heard were very meaningful. If something like that occurred today, the principal would be charged with child abuse.

I loved working as a Public Health Nurse. The nurses were all great and friendly, and we worked well as a team when immunizing kids. I loved working with our pediatrician, Dr. Moffat, in the Well-baby Clinics held at the main office. I learned a lot from Dr. Moffat.

There were so many new experiences, like finding people who had tested positive for Sexually Transmitted Diseases (STDs), locating them in rooming houses or in downtown bars, and ensuring they knew that they were positive and that they got their medications.

I saw poverty first-hand, the underprivileged who had no hope and were affected by street drugs and alcohol, getting their hands on anything that would get them high.

My heart would go out to them because most of them were so deep into their addictions and had damaged their bodies so badly, particularly their brains, that there was no way to rehabilitate them back to a long and productive life.

I especially enjoyed teaching the prenatal clinics, as this was uplifting and a stark contrast to the other world I saw. It was like light, joy, and life versus darkness, grief, and death.

Chapter 7
Our Adoption from the Adopt Indian Métis (AIM) Program

During this time, Wayne and I became friends with a couple our age. They had a young daughter and had just adopted a First Nations boy about five years old through the Adopt Indian Métis(AIM) program, which the Saskatchewan Government began in the sixties. This boy's name was Roger.

This couple had Roger for about six months, but we found out that they were not going to complete the adoption. They were having marital issues and soon moved from the beach.

Before Wayne and I got married, we talked about adopting a child, indicating that this would be something we'd do at some point. We would not have adopted at this time with all that was going on in our lives, but hearing about Roger being returned changed everything.

We notified Saskatchewan Social Services requesting to take Roger. He'd be an older brother for Lincoln.

Soon, a Child Adoption Social Worker, Mr. Tingley, drove out to our home to begin a home assessment. We were soon told we'd passed the assessment and that arrangements were being made for us to adopt Roger. We were so excited!

I was about to go into overdrive getting everything arranged when we got a call from Mr. Tingley stating there'd been a change in the circumstances of our being able to have Roger.

He explained that Roger had been in foster care since he was an infant with the same foster parents. When he was returned to the ministry, they returned him to these foster parents. They'd decided to stop fostering children and adopt Roger.

Our disappointment was replaced with a sense of what was the best outcome for Roger, and certainly, this seemed best. Mr. Tingley assured us that there were lots of children in need, like Roger, who needed to be adopted, and since we'd been approved to adopt a child, he asked us if we'd like to go ahead with their placing another child with us.

We told him we'd discuss it and get back to him.

Moving Forward to Adopt Again

It was sometime in November 1971 when we got back to Mr. Tingley, telling him we'd go ahead with adopting a child. He did a home visit one evening to get the process underway.

We sat at our dining room table, and he said that he had five children's portfolios to present to us, and we could choose from one of these children. This was unexpected.

He knew that we did not care what gender the child was, but we wanted the child to be closer to Lincoln's age for them to grow up together.

Mr. Tingley spread out the five presentations, and Wayne and I read through all five, trying to digest the information and looking at their photos.

Surprisingly, Wayne was managing this better than I was. I thought I was going to have a panic attack because I found this totally overwhelming.

When asked what child we'd like, I said that this was too hard for me, as I would likely say, let's take them all. With that, I asked Wayne to choose one of them while I made us coffee. Wayne must have looked them over again, as by the time I came back with the coffee, he said, "Arlene, what about this little girl?"

I looked at her photo, and she wasn't smiling and looked frail. I recall saying that she sure looked like she needed a home and love. So that was the child we both decided to adopt, our daughter.

Her name was Melinda. She was around 17 months old. Her mother had issues with alcohol, and we later learned that she had been murdered. Her dad was still living, but he also had issues with alcohol. We were told that there was no one in the family in a position to care for her, and she had been placed in foster care, and a sibling had also been taken into care.

Melinda was to be placed with us before Christmas. Once again, we were so excited.

Another Setback

One Friday evening at the beginning of December, we received a call from Mr. Tingley telling us there was a problem with our going ahead with the adoption of Melinda.

He explained that two social workers visited the foster home in preparation for the upcoming adoption, and they discovered that she was very much delayed in her growth and development.

They strongly advised that she be taken to Saskatoon, SK, to the Alvin Buckwold Clinic, where they do child development assessments.

The next question was, do you want to consider another child or wait to see what the results of the assessment are? Even though Wayne seemed to handle this adoption process much better than I did, he did find it stressful, too. We told him we'd discuss it and get back to him.

With minimal discussion, we told him that we'd wait and see what the assessment determined before we made our final decision. Mr. Tingley said the department would fast-track the assessment for us. Towards the end of December, we received their report.

The highlights that I recall were that Melinda had developmental lag. She was underweight, her IQ was 91 (a low average), and she was nonverbal and not walking.

The prognosis or conclusion was that with loving parents and a stable environment, she should progress and reach her developmental milestones. Furthermore, they recommended she be reassessed when she turns five years old.

I was 25 years of age at the time and knew little about how the alcoholism of the parents can affect their unborn child, particularly if Mom consumes alcohol in the first three months of pregnancy. Therefore, I never asked questions about whether she had Fetal Alcohol Syndrome (FAS), and it was not queried in this report.

So, with what we read, we were certain we could provide her with enough love and care to overcome her developmental lag and that Lincoln would be a role model for her.

We called Mr. Tingley back (hereby referred to as our Worker) to tell him we'd like to complete the adoption. He confirmed he would put everything in place and let us know the date we'd need to travel to Meadow Lake, SK, to receive her.

We became very excited and began sharing our news with close family and friends. The varied reactions were surprising. Some were excited, and others, like my mom, stated, "You'll be sorry for adopting an Indian!"

Wow! That was so shocking to hear my mom say this. On the other hand, not so much, with my knowing mom's 'critical spirit' and negativity about a lot of things. I knew Mom would be alright once she knew her. Dad was pleased for us but said little, as was often the case.

Two Cultures Collide

There were lots of First Nations families, and interracial marriages, and relationships around the beach.

Wayne grew up with Métis and First Nations friends all his life, as they lived close to the reservation land like Kinookimaw. For those two years of his life in Fort San, when he had tuberculosis, most of his friends there were Métis and First Nations.

I noted that he interacted with them with ease. Often, he'd joke with them, and they with him. Wayne said he loved how they'd laugh, as it was from 'the soles of their feet,' and he enjoyed that. He said they were not phony but genuine.

New Year's Eve, Wayne and I planned to bring in 1972 by attending the celebration and dance at the Regina Beach Community Hall.

Shirley, who was Métis, became one of my friends at the beach. Our sons were around the same age. She was at the dance with a friend of hers who was also First Nations.

I stopped by Shirley's table to say hello, and she introduced me to her friend Loretta. I could see Loretta was very drunk. She said to me, "I hear that you and Wayne are going to adopt one of our people!" I said we were and that we were very excited about it.

Well, she became enraged that we would adopt one of their own and was ramping up her disapproval wherever others heard her. I said to Shirley that she and Loretta could come to my place during the week for coffee, and we could talk about this then.

With that, I got up and began walking away, and then, without warning, she jumped up behind me, grabbed my hair, and flung me to the floor. I lay there semi-conscious, thinking that an ambulance was going to be here at any moment.

I am told that Loretta was reaching down to grab my hair again and, with a beer bottle in her hand, was about to hit me in the head. Fortunately, Jim's best friend Keith grabbed her and prevented her from delivering what may have been the deadly blow.

I was now fully conscious but in shock. I got up and turned towards her, yelling, "You're no Indian. You're a damn savage!" and with that, someone led me away to sit down while Loretta was kicked out of the hall.

Of course, I wanted to go home after that altercation, and I asked someone to get Wayne for me. I was told he was outside fighting with Dr. Lloyd Barber.

Fighting each other over what? I had no idea to this day. I only knew that Wayne and he weren't friends. Wayne got along with almost everyone, including the Barbers. Their family was prominent on the beach, as were the Dobsons. Likely, alcohol was involved there, too.

Well, the ambulance did not come, and Wayne and I went home. In the morning, I had a huge headache, with my neck feeling as if it were broken. I looked in the mirror to see a large bald spot on the top of my head where my hair had been yanked out.

A few months later, I was admitted to RGH hospital, and my neck was put in traction. It was Peyton Place, for sure, and we were residents immersed in it.

As a footnote, back then, First Nations' peoples were called Indians, just like in the title Adopt Indian and Métis (AIM) Program. So, my referring to Loretta as an Indian was in no way disrespectful at that time, but calling her a savage was how I saw it or experienced it!

At that time, I had no idea of the residential schools and the historical trauma suffered by the First Nations peoples. Perhaps I never paid enough attention in school, but I don't recall it being discussed at home or in school, other than hearing how the fur traders exchanged spirits with the Indians for their furs and land disputes that were going on.

The Adoption – *The Placement*

On January 3rd, 1972, we went back to our normal life of working. After work, I was busy buying diapers, girl clothes, and a brand-new snowsuit to put Melinda in.

When the placement occurred, she would be 18 months old, and Lincoln would be 26 months old. It would almost feel like having a set of twins.

On Sunday night, January 09th, 1972, Wayne and I drove to Meadow Lake to stay in a hotel so we could be on time for the placement the next morning. Lincoln was cared for at home.

That night in the hotel, I had a dream that I was pregnant with Melinda and that I was in labor, ready to deliver her. That was so real that when I woke up early in the morning, it felt like I was actually having contractions. Needless to say, I never got back to sleep.

Monday, January 10, 1972, at 10:00 a.m., we arrived at the Social Services office in Meadow Lake, SK to meet our Worker with another woman Worker, to finally meet Melinda. There was no Melinda.

Mr. Tingley and a female Social Worker arrived to tell us there had been a snowstorm during the night and that the country road to Melinda's foster mother's farm was snowed in.

The workers told us they had been trying to figure out how they could get into the foster mom's home, indicating they thought of getting a snow plow to clear the roads, but they wouldn't do anything until tomorrow. They had even considered using a small plane to go in to bring her out, but that plan could not happen that day either.

The workers wanted to get this placement over with that day if possible, because they had other things to attend to come Tuesday.

Wayne told them that if they could rent two skidoos, then he would guide them to the farm where Melinda was. He said he could bring her out on his skidoo, holding her while the other two workers would be on the second skidoo.

I panicked about that plan not because Wayne was not an experienced skidoo driver, but because he sold skidoos at the beach and was very adept with them, but it was these two workers who likely were not experienced.

Lastly, but most importantly, how was Wayne going to hold Melinda in front of him while driving a skidoo through heavy snow in winter? I had no idea how many miles they had to go.

This plan seemed doomed to fail, but as I was processing all of this, the two workers went to check if they could rent a couple of skidoos, and they came back to say they had them reserved. I didn't voice my concerns and went back to the hotel to wait while the two workers, along with Wayne, left to get the skidoos.

I took myself to the hotel's restaurant and waited and waited until I finally went back to the hotel room. Back in my hotel room, I began pacing and praying. I was very anxious.

Around 4:30 p.m., they arrived. Wayne came in first, and I was in the hallway in front of our hotel room when Mr. Tingley came walking down the hall holding her.

She had tears on her cheeks and a runny nose, and I began talking softly to her. I didn't want to reach up for her to take her right away as she'd just been through quite an ordeal.

I validated her 'big ride' to come to see me. As I looked into her sweet brown eyes, I asked her if it was alright for me to be her mommy. I said something like I would love to be your new mommy, and for you to be my little girl.

She stared right through me and then leaned over, still being held in our worker's arms, and bent herself over and kissed me on the cheek. That was such a touching moment, and the workers and Wayne thought so, too.

I then reached my hands towards her, and she reached back, and I took her in my arms to start our new life together. The workers left, and I changed Melinda and put all new clothes on her and her new snowsuit, and we headed home. Wayne told me that the workers flipped over their skidoo a couple of times, but he managed to get them going again.

He told me that when he came into the farmhouse, Melinda was sitting in her highchair, and she had just finished eating chicken with the bones lying on her tray. He noted that the foster mom was very nice and that she became emotional saying goodbye to her.

It was getting dark when we stopped at the Chinese restaurant in North Battleford to get some supper. We had milk for Melinda, but little food on hand.

We gave her a bowl of rice and a baby spoon. It was so comical to watch her eat that. She cupped her little fingers into the rice and just kept shoveling it in like I've seen Oriental people do in movies. She had to be starving because we gave her a second bowl, and she polished that off in no time. She slept the rest of the way home, and we arrived at the beach around midnight.

Once we got her out of her snowsuit and set her down on the floor, we watched her crawl, going straight to the cat's dish of milk. We could see she would have lapped that up if we'd let her, but of course, we didn't. We gave her a bottle, settled her down in her crib, and went off to bed ourselves.

The next morning, we were now a family of four, with Melinda getting to know all three of us and us three getting to know her.

Soon, we extracted 'lin' out of Melinda and began calling her Lin, as Lin and Lincoln sounded well together and was easier to say. We added a middle name for her, Helene, after Wayne's mom, Helen and mine, Arlene.

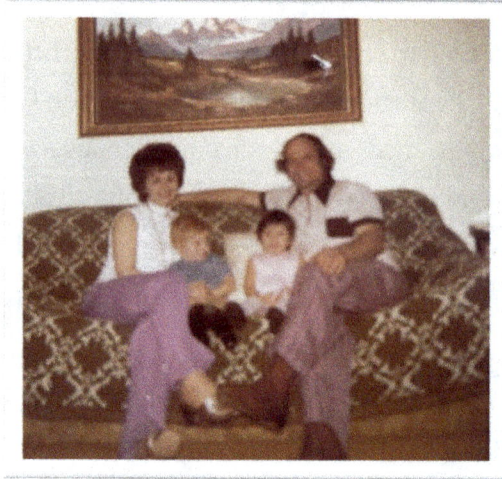

Lincoln and Lin with us. Photo is not too clear.

Meeting Some Milestones

Lin was very interested in her surroundings. She was not a fussy baby and soon put on some weight and began to walk. We noticed that if she got excited, her gait in walking was somewhat spastic, but as time went along, that lessened and was no longer visible.

Wayne's sister, Lydia, and her husband decided to get their daughter, their first child, baptized when visiting. Wayne and I decided to also have Lin baptized at the same time.

However, Lydia said to me that they'd prefer that Wayne and I didn't have Lin baptized at the same time as their daughter, as this was a very special occasion for them. Well, this was a very special occasion for us too, but I guess we weren't to share in this.

This was distressing and hurtful for me to hear this request. I thought this was unreasonable. Was this racism? I didn't answer her right away, but told her I'd pass it by Wayne.

Wayne felt as I did and said, "We are going to get her baptized."

I told her that we'd be going ahead with the baptism as we'd arranged for that.

Through the years of raising our kids, we had holidays with Wayne's sisters and their husbands and children, and for the most part, those times were enjoyable. The cousins got to know one another as children, as that was important, but as adults, they never stayed connected.

Chapter 8
Addictions—From the Pit

There's a Definite Problem

I was in my late twenties when I recognized that too much drinking was going on with Wayne and his buddies. Actually, there was too much drinking going on in the town of Regina Beach. Wayne's brother, Jim, was getting in trouble with it, and I was tired of all of it.

Therefore, I thought this whole beach needed to be enlightened as to what alcoholism is about, so I arranged for Dr Saul Cohen to come to the beach and give a talk on alcoholism. After all, life is not one Big Party!

Dr. Cohen was well-respected and very personable, so I reached out to him.

The following highlights his background, which is on Google:

"Dr. Saul Cohen moved to Regina in 1954. In 1959, he became a consultant to the Bureau on Alcoholism and continued his teaching and research in the field. Dr. Cohen was a founder of the Physicians at-risk Committee, the author of the Physician's Manual on Alcoholism, and a charter member of the teaching program on chemical dependencies at the College of Medicine, University of Saskatchewan."

As you can see, he was an excellent person to have come to the beach to speak. I arranged for the Regina Beach Community Hall to be available to host this event, and I began to advertise for it. There was no social media, so it was done by flyers and posters and, I believe, radio announcements.

On the day of the event, the hall was 'jam-packed,' and I was thrilled. Some never showed up, like Wayne, who needed to hear this, but a lot of others did, so I could only hope they would benefit from the talk.

Downs and Ups 1973 – 1975

In the fall, Dore decided to get into a farmer's field that was nearby and killed a few sheep.

Remember, he was part wolf. Cork was on his way to Regina to have him put down when Wayne 'got wind of it.' Wayne took off in his truck and told me he caught up to his dad, and when he wouldn't pull over, he almost ran him off the highway.

I am sure there were words between the two of them, but Dore came home with him. Dore was a significant link to his mom, and as you may recall, he was a hero in preventing her from being raped.

Months later, Wayne came home to say he found Dore lying in a ditch, dead. I knew he'd been crying and asked him where Dore was now. He said, "He's in my truck, and I am going to bury him with Mom."

It was dark already, but I knew he needed to be alone and do that right then. When he came home, he told me that he buried Dore next to her on the other side of the cemetery fence, as her grave bordered on the fence. Dore was like the one remaining link to his mom, and his grief had surfaced again.

Job # 3

In August, after having worked for just over a year in Public Health, I saw Nursing Instructor positions posted by the Saskatchewan Government.

They needed to fill these positions to teach their Cored Nursing Program to nursing students who were enrolled in this program to become either Nursing Assistants, Diploma Nurses or Psychiatric Nurses. As a cored program, they were all to receive basic nurses' training and skills, and then they'd complete the portions of the program they'd enrolled in to graduate.

The Wascana Institute of Applied Arts and Sciences (WIAST) was newly built, and this program would be delivered from there. I was sure it would be the perfect job for me, as in university, I majored in Teaching with a minor in Public Health.

I got the job and absolutely loved teaching the students. One time, when I went for my coffee break after having done my lecture, my coworkers laughingly said, "We always know when Dobson is lecturing with all that laughter." Well, I guess I still had a sense of humor.

The 'back and forth' traveling was really getting to me. Life was busy, and weekends were to be just family times, but that still became difficult as the same friends came by, and I was often entertaining them and taking care of the family.

Finally, I told Wayne that we'd need to rent a place in Regina as I couldn't continue commuting, and he agreed to move.

Moving to Regina

We found a two-bedroom bungalow to rent near the Regina General Hospital. Wayne was tied to his life at the beach, so he commuted for his business there.

Doing clinical instruction was much different from lecturing. Clinical instruction is when you take the student nurses in the nursing homes and in the hospital to do patient care.

My sense of humor was on hold. I thought I was becoming like my mom, and that was a bit scary, as she was over the top with her 'dos and don'ts' and so on, which had driven me a bit crazy.

I had two groups of students who were doing their clinical practice in nursing homes. I was rather a perfectionist in doing everything by the book because, after all, each patient deserved the very best care.

At the end of the clinical of that first year of teaching, I was questioning my effectiveness as an instructor when a knock came at our door at my home, and standing there were fifteen students, some from each group that I'd taught.

They presented me with a card and a silver goblet with all of their names engraved on it, listed under each group. That was so generous and so special. Even though I was strict with them, I believe they knew that I loved and cared about them and that I had their best interests at heart, as well as the nursing home residents.

That goblet has sat in my china cabinet for almost five decades. On occasion, when I feel down, I stop to take it out and smile, thinking about that day and those students.

That year also came with personal challenges. Yet, through one of those times, another miracle occurred that I need to tell you about.

Miracle # 5: – Heaven's Instructions – Again!

This would be in January 1974, when Lincoln got the croup, which is bronchitis. He was just over four years old. He had to be hospitalized and put in a croup tent.

A few days later, Lin came down with the same and spiked a fever. I had given her medication to bring the fever down, and gave her a tepid sponge bath to help. She began coughing and throwing up, and aspirated her vomit.

I was trying to clear her airway, and at the same time, I told Wayne to call an ambulance. He called the ambulance, and right then, Lin had a mild seizure, and she stopped breathing.

I was panicking as to what to do as I had already given her a few breaths to get her breathing, and she was not coming around. I didn't know if her little heart had stopped because she was an ashen blue color and limp.

Lin had improved a lot in her growth and development, but she still lagged behind and was not very strong. I knew from experience that this situation was a race against time.

Again, in my spirit, I cried out to God, "What shall I do now?" He told me to take her outside. It was 40-something below, and I was not going to question Him. I picked her up and went outside with her, carrying her facing upwards in my arms. I just stood on our front steps.

I hadn't a clue what I was doing and just stood there on our front steps when I heard His voice say, "Take her back in." I did that and laid her back down on the living room floor and saw her inhale a big breath.

Her color returned to normal, as did her breathing, but she was in a deep sleep. Right then, the ambulance arrived. When we arrived at the ER, we were immediately put in an examining room. I looked over at Wayne, who was outside the examining room, leaning into the wall and breaking down. He took himself outside to collect himself and then returned.

Lin was also admitted to the Children's Ward next to Lincoln. Wayne and I went home that evening without our children.

Once again, I give no credit to my intellect or nurses' training to take her outside, as that was entirely His doing.

Hazel – *My Blind Spot – My Shame*

I was working, and I needed to get the house cleaned before the children were discharged. I needed bedding washed and a thorough cleaning of the house before we brought the kids home. However, I didn't have time to do this as I was still teaching and needed to be with the kids as much as possible while they were in the hospital.

I had heard of the Regina Community Switchboard, where you can call for babysitters, house cleaners, house sitting, and the like. So I called there and told them my need for a housekeeper, and was told that they'd send someone there by 8:00 a.m. in the morning.

At 8:00 o'clock in the morning, the doorbell rang, and of course, I answered it. Standing in the doorway was the housekeeper. Her name was Hazel. She was an Indian woman, and I remember saying to myself, 'Damn, nothing is going to get done!'

Well, she was very pleasant, and I had the day off to help her. I had written down what I wanted accomplished, and she started to tackle the list.

She stripped all the beds, sorted the wash, and got it going; she cleaned the bathroom in a way that I'd never seen before, sanitizing everything. She washed all the floors, vacuumed even the mattresses, and flipped them. She did the dishes and wiped down all the areas I had asked her to clean. She did even more than I asked her to do. She dried bedding and clothes and helped me make the beds.

I was absolutely shocked at this woman, and later, I hung my head in shame for even thinking this. What a disconnect I had when I saw she was native.

This is racism. We assume things based on what others have told us. I had such a 'blind spot' that I didn't think it was even there until that day. It was a lesson I definitely needed to learn and did learn.

Hazel – *A Wonderful Friend*

After that day, Hazel became a staple in our home as I had her for several years as my housekeeper, but most of all as a friend.

She got to know my kids and Wayne very well, and we got to know her children, too.

She called Lin 'powerful,' and we'd laugh because Lin was so petite and certainly not powerful. We lost touch in the past few years, but writing about this, I must look her up.

Grafted-in x 2

Milestone Three
Lin is 'grafted-in' to the Dobson family, and I, to Lin's First Nation Family.

Lincoln and Lin at 3 years old

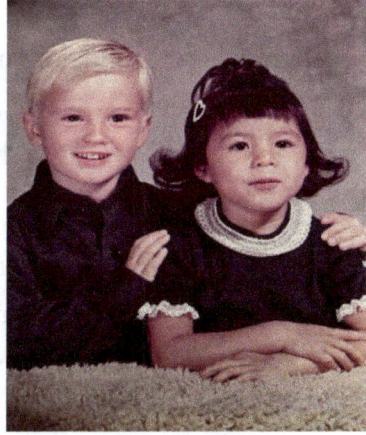

Lincoln and Lin at 5 years old

The Children – *Ready for School*

Before the children started Kindergarten, we wanted to purchase our own home. So we bought a three-bedroom home by Turtle Park in Regina. The children would start school at Athabasca School.

At that time, we took Lin for a follow-up appointment at Alvin Buckwold Clinic in Saskatoon. I cannot recall all the findings and do not know where I placed the report, but what I do recall was that she was now within the normal range for weight and height. In particular, I remember they said that her IQ had improved from a score of 91 to now a high average. We were told that the increase in her IQ was due to us providing her positive experiences for stimulation. I think Lincoln helped there, too.

They mentioned her gait in walking was still a bit spastic, but I told them how that had improved and that she didn't slap her foot down when walking anymore. I told them that I only noticed that when she became overly anxious or excited. The examiner's general impression was that she had made good progress, and we were all pleased with it.

I love children. They say and do the things that often surprise us as parents. Lin often surprised me with things she'd say and do. Some were nice surprises, and other times, they were questionable.

One day, she was out playing in the yard when she came into the house to present me with a dozen or more tulips, "Here, Mommy, I got these for you!"

I thanked her, and after placing them in water in a vase, I went outside to check on the elderly neighbor's flowerbed, who lived right next door. As I feared, she only had leaves left on her tulips, which she'd planted all around her home.

She was a cranky old woman, so I didn't tell her what happened to avoid her losing it on me. I tried to teach Lin a lesson that when people plant flowers, we can't pick them because they belong to them to make their yards look beautiful. I didn't want to take away her loving gesture; after all, she was only four years old.

Spoiling the Kids – *Wayne's Thing*

Wayne was always buying the kids high-end clothes. One afternoon, a small crane came to bring Lin the fanciest doll house I'd ever seen. He'd buy her anything she wanted. He loved and spoiled the kids, for sure. Lincoln was into sports, and we went to all his games.

Wayne and I took trips to Las Vegas, where Wayne would act like a 'high roller' playing Craps and Blackjack. He taught me how to play Blackjack. I enjoyed playing that, but hated losing, while Wayne said he always came out on top. I thought that this wasn't likely.

We also went to Vegas with friends, took in shows, swam in pools, and had food delivered to our rooms. It was a great getaway, but there was always too much alcohol.

Chapter 9
Mom, Hard to Figure Out! Thank you, Dad!

Mom used to call me a lot. She would talk about any and all things that were not very interesting, or she'd tell me news about her neighbors. All I had to say was 'Uhum, Uhum, O' Yeah' because 'you couldn't get a word in edgewise!'

Wayne would be reading the newspaper at the kitchen table, and he would take over for me, saying a series of 'Uhum, Uhum, O' Yeah' as I went about doing my work, like washing clothes. Mom never knew it wasn't me.

Finally, I began to set boundaries with Mom and interrupt her, telling her I had to go because I had something to do. Of course, she did not like that. So she called me on the phone one day and said, "Arlene, your dad and I would like to talk to you."

"What about?" I asked.

She said, "I will tell you when you come over."

I wasn't sure what to expect. When I got there, we went and sat in the living room; I sensed tension was in the air.

After I sat down, my dad stood up and said, "Arlene, it is actually your mom who wants to talk to you, and what she is about to say I don't agree with, so I am going downstairs to my office, but when she has finished just call me, and I will come upstairs and have a coffee with you before you go."

"Sure, Dad," I said.

I knew I was in for a load of 'dodo' from Mom. Then she started in, and I will summarize what I recall: 'Arlene, I have been so disappointed in you over the years. Your dad and I adopted you to give you a chance in life.

She went on to say, "I always tried to make you look nice, and I never could. You had flat feet, crossed eyes, and had to wear glasses. No matter how hard I tried, you never looked nice. I bought you nice dresses, but I'd find them in a heap on the floor in your closet because you never hung anything up. I could never have you look nice, and we worked hard to give you lessons in this and that, and you didn't make use of them."

Finally, I stopped her by saying something like, "Mom, I think you did a great job of raising me. You should be proud that I achieved great marks in grade 12, and because of my strong academic performance in nursing, I received a government bursary, which enabled me to pursue a degree in nursing. I have a great job. I am happily married (since I was at the time) and have two children that we love.

My life is good. Also, Mom, I am happy with how I look. You may have had a hard time making me look nice as a kid, but I am happy with how I look today."

I was determined to tell Mom that I was no longer 'The Ugly Duckling.' I had transformed into 'The Beautiful Swan.' She likely did not want to know that. I told Mom I needed to go, but reminded her that before I did, I was going to call Dad up for a coffee, and I did.

I was so proud of my dad that day because he didn't go along with Mom and stood up for me and himself by removing himself from what he knew she was about to say to me.

After Dad retired from the Post Office, he'd drop by my place to have coffee. He was never specific but said it was hard being around Mom all the time. I validated his feelings. Mom was a difficult perfectionist to live with, and she had Dad jumping through hoops, so to speak. Yet they did love one another and made it work; I did witness their commitment to each other.

Mom still made the odd 'off the cuff' toxic remark towards me after I confronted her, but I ignored or refuted them. She knew I would not tolerate an entire load of them ever again.

Personally, and as a therapist, I know only too well how parents' words to their children can either 'build them up' or 'break them down.' We need to help our children build healthy self-esteem and not tear them down, leaving them with 'poor self-esteem and self-image.'

I know I struggled with repairing mine, and I still struggle with it at times, but I work through it more easily now.

Did I do this to my children and grandchildren? Ask them, and they'll give you the odd example, and yes, I know I did. If I didn't catch myself, they'd catch me. I know I did more positive and healthy affirmations with them because I made an effort.

Positive affirmations and saying, "I love you," don't come easily when you have not received it, but you do it because you know it is important.

Of course, this was not easy to do at first, as it was not natural for me, but it became purposeful and soon became natural. I soon realized why we had not received their spontaneous love and affection because neither had received much, if any, themselves.

I told them that I loved them, and we exchanged hugs and reassurance. When, on occasion, I messed up, I'd say sorry, please forgive me.

I have always loved my mom and dad, and I am grateful to them. For the most part, I did honor them. I never talked back to them and did try to please them.

When they were getting up in years, I had them over every Sunday for supper. I always welcomed them with a hug and kiss, coming and going.

I noted that when they were leaving to go home, they'd line up like two young children who needed a hug, a kiss, and an affirmation from their daughter that she loved them. I did not receive that back, but they warmly smiled when they were told, and that was enough for me.

We had no liquor in our home, but Mom's addiction was perfection and her need to control, which is codependency. Perhaps she had some hidden liquor, as I recall the vodka she gave my bridesmaids and me.

Everyone has some demons to overcome. I am only able to address mine with God's direction and help. I decided to enjoy my journey of self-discovery, leading to personal growth and healing, because it really is liberating and a never-ending journey while here.

Today, it is my privilege as a therapist to assist others in pursuit of the same. I learn from them, too, as that's how it should be.

Expanding Our Family

Wayne and I were excited to be able to increase our family to one more. The pregnancy went very well. Here is a photo from December 1975 when we were expecting Caine.

The Birth of Our Son Caine
– *Don't Leave, Please!*

January 27th, 1976, came, and I had to be induced again. Wayne hung in there through my labor until the nurse said, "Mrs. Dobson, you are almost fully dilated, and we'll be taking you into the delivery room very soon."

The nurse left the room, and Wayne announced to me that he would be right back because he needed to go to the YMCA to have a massage. What???

That was shocking because the hospitals were now allowing fathers in the delivery room, and we were excited about this special experience, so I said rather frantically, "You can't go now, Wayne, because I am going to deliver real soon!"

He assured me that it wouldn't take long for his massage and that he'd be right back, and off he went. As the stretcher rolled me down to the delivery room, there was no Wayne. I felt alone and very sad. I couldn't believe he'd miss the birth of our baby.

Well, it was time to deliver, and just as I finished giving birth to our beautiful baby boy, the double doors of the delivery room crashed open with Daddy standing there in a mask, gown, and gloves. It was almost humorous, but it wasn't.

Months later, I heard Wayne talking to a friend on the phone whose wife was due to give birth any day. Wayne insisted that his friend be there to see his son being born, as it was such a great experience, and he wouldn't have missed it for anything. The problem is, he did miss it!

We named our son Caine Deon Wayne. There wasn't maternity leave like now. So, after a couple of weeks, I was back teaching.

Arlene, I'm Sending Caine and You to Hawaii.

Wayne's cousin, Nita, was about twenty years older than me, but we became very good friends when I lived in Regina Beach. Her husband, Sam, and Wayne got talking, and it was decided by them that their wives should go to Hawaii.

I wasn't keen on it, but Nita was, and she was taking her teenage son along and said she'd help me with Caine as he was only a few weeks old. So we got on the plane and went to Hawaii for a couple of weeks.

Likely, Wayne wanted a break as Caine was colicky like Lincoln was, and he'd have peace and quiet. Of course, I didn't really know why he was so keen to cart me off.

Becoming a Stay-at-home Mom

When Caine was about nine months old, I had another miscarriage. Again, there was no time to grieve, but we decided to stop at three children, so I got my tubes tied.

I was looking for my car keys frantically as I had to get to work in the hospital ward with about ten nursing students.

The sitter was already there. I don't know what made me think to check Lincoln's coat pocket. I didn't know how he got them in there because the hooks were too high for him to reach. When I asked him, he proudly showed me how he did it by putting the broom handle under his jacket, and you can figure out the rest. The message was clear, "No more sitters, Mom! I want you to stay home!"

Before Caine was born, we decided I needed to stay home with the kids. So, I took a break from teaching. Wayne thought he could manage our finances with his work.

During the day, I had more time with Caine. I took him to the Lawson Pool for water-baby lessons. Here, I had to drop him in the water and see him close his mouth off and swim to the surface. He actually did that along with the other babies. What a surprise! They have that natural instinct to do that.

It was nice being a homemaker. I grew a garden and canned and froze some food for the winter. I enjoyed baking, too. One day, Mom and Dad dropped in unannounced, and I had about 10 pies baked to freeze that were sitting on our kitchen table. Mom kept saying, "Arlene, you never baked those!" Dad finally said, "Mae, she did bake them!"

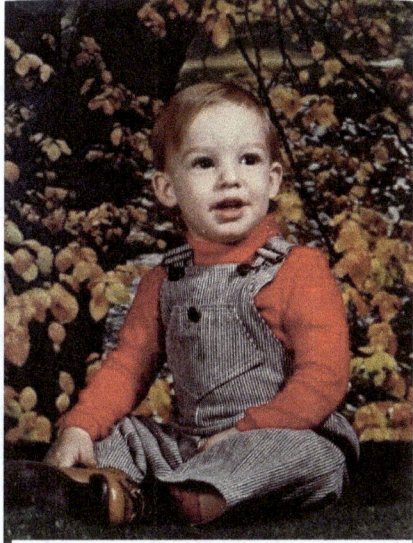

Caine at one year old

Her surprise was likely because she never let me bake anything, including pies. Yet, I watched how she did it and did what she did. It almost seemed to me that she did not ever want me to be able to bake as well as her.

That year, Wayne was diagnosed with high blood pressure, and he often had migraines. I figured he had anxiety, but it was never treated. I knew he had a problem with alcohol, but he always denied there was a problem and told me that it was my imagination. I wanted it to be my imagination, but deep down, I knew it wasn't. I was asking God to help me as I felt that things were not going to end well for us if we didn't get help.

Chapter 10: Grafted into The Vine –
I am Born Again

The Invitation – *The Beginning of a New Direction.*

In September 1976, I invited my friend Pat to come with me to Women's Aglow. This was a Christian Women's organization that was non-denominational. Veronica Klebuc, who I had met along with her husband, a prominent justice, at a Bible Study, had invited me to this gathering. She greeted us at the door and showed us where to hang our coats and sit.

At the beginning of the meeting, the women were singing praise and worship songs. Then the music stopped, and my attention was drawn to someone speaking out loud. I noted that who was talking out loud was a Catholic nun.

You Must Be Born Again! – *What?*

This nun was speaking in a language that I had never heard before, and I didn't know what that was, but I felt moved in my spirit by this and said to myself, "I want what she has!"

The host of the Women's Aglow meeting explained what had just occurred. She said that what the nun spoke was called 'speaking in tongues' according to Biblical scripture.

Then she told us that the other woman who spoke in English had interpreted what the nun said. I had paid no attention to what the interpretation was, but for some reason, I wanted what that nun had, as it witnessed to my spirit that I needed that.

The host indicated that after the main speaker had given her message, there'd be an invitation for anyone to come up front to accept Jesus Christ as their Lord and Savior and to also receive the gift of the Holy Spirit, which was 'speaking in tongues.' This 'gift of tongues' was news to me.

The woman who was the guest speaker told us that she was a former United Church minister. She was asked to leave that church because she began to preach about needing to be 'born again' and the baptism of the Holy Spirit, which was receiving 'the gift of speaking in tongues.'

She thought she was saved, but realized that she wasn't. She preached that speaking in tongues was a heavenly language and a gift of the Holy Spirit, and every Christian should desire it. This fell on deaf ears within the congregation she pastored, and she was let go or fired, to put it simply.

Her talk was that Jesus Christ said, "You must be born again." She read this passage:

6 That which is born of the flesh is flesh, and that which is born of the Spirit is spirit.[c] 7 Do not marvel that I said to you, 'You must be born again.' 8 The wind[e] blows where it wishes, and you hear its sound, but you do not know where it comes from or where it goes. So it is with everyone who is born of the Spirit."

John 3:6-8

So this was all news to me! I had never understood the concept of being 'born again.' She spoke about a second baptism in the Holy Spirit, with the evidence of one 'speaking in tongues,' which I had just witnessed. The scripture for speaking in tongues also caught my attention:

135

22"Tongues, then, are a sign, not for believers but for unbelievers; prophecy, however, is not for unbelievers but for believers."

1 Corinthians 14:22

If 'speaking in tongues' was a sign for nonbelievers, and this nun's 'speaking in tongues' was just witnessed by me, and I did not recall the interpretation, then I must be a non-believer.

So, I began reasoning. I've talked to God many times, and He has helped me many times, so how can this be? Perhaps I never saw myself as a sinner?

The 'old lady' told me about Jesus at four years of age, and my parents took me to Sunday School. I knew that Jesus was a wonderful man who healed people and did amazing things when He lived here. I even knew the Christmas and Easter stories, so what was missing? I am a believer, so this can't be right.

I Needed A Savior – *Wayne and I Needed a Savior!*

The speaker's message and the nun 'speaking in a heavenly language' convinced me that when the altar call was given to be born again and receive the Holy Spirit with the gift of speaking in tongues, I realized I needed both.

I had just finished deciding this when my friend Pat, who was sitting behind me, touched my shoulder and said, "Arlene, are you ready to go?"

I said, "Yes, I am!" and proceeded to walk to the front where the altar was.

Once there, I realized Pat was not with me. I looked back and saw her going into the coatroom. Obviously, we had a miscommunication, and she meant 'to go home.'

Afterwards, I realized that His Holy Spirit had been communicating with me all along. When we cry out to Him as I had, He answered me, but I never declared I was His or that I was 'born again.' Jesus wanted a relationship with me and wanted a commitment from me that I'd be His. As it says in the Bible, He listens to us and answers us:

"Surely the arm of the LORD is not too short to save, nor his ear too dull to hear."

Isaiah 59:1.

He'd never left me, yet what became apparent was that even though I had attended church and was confirmed and knew that my prayers were being answered, I had not recognized that I was a sinner in need of a Savior. I hadn't recognized the need to be 'born again.'

Yet my going forward for prayer was a heartfelt decision to follow Him as my Savior and become 'born again':

16"For God so loved the world that he gave his one and only Son, that whoever believes in him shall not perish but have eternal life."

John 3:16.

To be born again, I had to sincerely say sorry to my Creator's Son, Jesus Christ, for my sins and sincerely ask him to forgive me, which is called repentance. Then, I needed to do my best to not sin again, but of course, that was not 100% possible.

Why? Because I'm flesh, and it says that our flesh and the spirit are enemies of one another.

137

"For the flesh desires what is contrary to the Spirit, and the Spirit what is contrary to the flesh. They are in conflict with each other, so you are not to do whatever you want."
Galatians 5:17

For example, bad habits are hard to break. Such as when I'm driving, and someone cuts me off, I blurt out something not so nice, which has me realize I'm still a work in progress. So we ask for His forgiveness, and as the Bible says, 'we go from glory to glory' but remain saved.

"So our faces are not covered. They show the bright glory of the Lord, as the Lord's Spirit makes us more and more like our glorious Lord."
2 Corinthians 3:18. CEV

We Are Going to be Alright!

I was excited to tell Wayne about my being 'born again' and having 'the gift of tongues.' I knew if he got what I'd received, that we'd be alright.

Wayne didn't deny my experience, but he did not seem much interested in exploring this, so nothing much changed there. I began to take the children with me to a Pentecostal church, where I met some precious families and friends.

Wayne would come to church with us sometimes. When a new church was being built just off the highway, he'd make and deliver his fancy lunches to the workers, like stuffed peppers smothered with tomato sauce.

Wayne had many wonderful qualities, but he carried a lot of hurt within him. As a therapist, I came to recognize it as unresolved 'complex trauma,' and I was better able to understand him, as well as myself and others I have counseled.

Milestone Four
Grafted-in x 3
1976 – to Eternity

Miracle # 6: – I Am 'Born Again!'

The greatest miracle of all was my adoption into 'The Tree of Life.' I asked this question: How was I grafted-into the 'Family of God' once I was born again? I struggled with that until I came to this understanding. The Bible says that if you are not a Jew, then you need to be adopted into the Jewish lineage.

Jesus said that He grafts us into Himself, who is the 'root of the tree.' The branches on the tree that are natural branches are the Jewish people since God chose His only Son, Jesus Christ, the Savior of the world, to come through the Jewish nation for all nations.

So Jesus, born to Mary and Joseph, was born a Jew. Jesus came first for the Jew and then for the Gentile (a non-Jew). Gentiles receive the same promise as Jews when we are *grafted-in*. Yet, every Jew must also become 'born again!'

So, Why the Jewish Nation? – *Was Another Nation Not 'Good Enough?'*

It had to be the Jewish nation for the following reasons:

The Torah—called the Pentateuch, the first five books of the Old Testament—laid down the foundation for the Jewish faith.

The Jewish religious custom was to give a blood sacrifice to atone for their sins, which was to 'cancel out' their sins and be forgiven. No other nation or culture did this.

The blood sacrifice they gave was to kill a perfect lamb, whereby the shedding of that blood became the atonement to cancel their sins, so they could go to heaven. – Easter.

Jesus Christ became the perfect 'Lamb of God' who truly was without sin but was PERFECT! Now, it was only His blood that could cancel out the penalty of our sins.

God knew that their sacrifice of animals could never atone for their sins. So God came down and dwelt among us, and that is why one of His names is Emanuel, meaning God with us. – CHRISTMAS.

God is the first of the Triune (three-part) existence of God: God the Father (Our Creator), God the Son (Jesus), and God the Holy Spirit (Great Spirit).

The part of the Triune God (Creator) is the Holy (Great Spirit) who convicts us of the Truth of the Word of God and convicts us to say, I need you, Jesus, to be my Savior. When you and I say sorry for our sins and ask for His forgiveness, called repentance, then we are born again. Now we have our ticket to HEAVEN. We cannot earn salvation, and it is God's gift to us, His son Jesus.

Since Jesus paid the penalty for your and my sins, now when His Father looks at us, our sins are covered because you and I belong to His Son, who redeemed us from the curse of the law, the grave, and hell. We live in a spiritual world, and we are more spirit than flesh.

You may ask, "Do you need to be baptized by water and 'speak in tongues' to be born again?"

The answer is "No." We should seek water baptism as a confession of our faith as a follower of Jesus Christ, and also seek the 'gift of speaking in tongues' since the Great Spirit desires you to have it so the devil can't interpret this heavenly language, and you have a direct uninterrupted line of communication to God.

These two baptisms are not a prerequisite to get you into heaven, and the Biblical story of the two criminals on their crosses on either side of Jesus affirms this:

"39 One of the criminals who hung there hurled insults at him: 'Aren't you the Christ? Save yourself and us!' 40 But the other criminal rebuked him. 'Don't you fear God,' he said, 'since you are under the same sentence? 41 We are punished justly, for we are getting what our deeds deserve. But this man has done nothing wrong.' 42 Then he said, 'Jesus, remember me when you come into your kingdom.' 43Jesus answered him, 'I tell you the truth, today you will be with me in paradise."
Luke 23:39-43, NIV

God Declares that He has No Favorites

Peter's declaration that "God is no respecter of persons, "John 10:16 affirms that the gospel of Jesus Christ is available to all, irrespective of nationality or social status.

If you are a natural-born Jew, then you don't need to be *grafted-in,* but as a Jew, if you reject Jesus Christ as your Jewish Lord and Savior, you'll be cut off from the tree, which is the 'root of the tree.' If later you repent and believe in your Jewish Savior Jesus Christ, you can be grafted back in.

141

23And even they, if they do not continue in their unbelief, will be grafted in, for God has the power to graft them in again.
Romans 11:23

The Grafted-In Symbol – *How Cool Is This Symbol?*

The Grafted-In symbol consists of three iconic images aligned vertically:

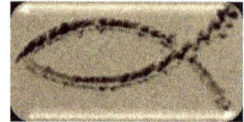

The Jewish Menorah: This seven-branched candelabra of the Tabernacle and Temple has long been a symbol of the enduring faith of the Jewish people.

The Star of David: It is identified with the Jewish nation. Universally, it represents the connection between God and humanity and heaven and earth. It has two triangles, with the gold triangle pointing downwards, reflecting earth and mankind, while the blue triangle points upwards, reflecting God and heaven.

Menorah #1 sits at the top of the 'Star of David' # 2, which reflects the lineage of David through which Jesus Christ was born.

The Ichthus (fish) Symbol: In the Messianic Seal, some see this fish also representing non-Jewish Believers, called Gentiles, whom Jesus came for. In Biblical times, when two people wanted to inquire if a person was a fellow 'fisher of men,' each casually drew an arc in the dirt, and the other person drew an opposite arc, turning it into a crude fish.

12"For I am not ashamed of the gospel of Christ: for it is the power of God unto salvation to everyone that believeth; to the Jew first, and also to the Greek (non-Jews).

Again, Jesus spoke to them, saying, I am the light of the world. Whoever follows me will not walk in darkness but will have the light of life."

John 8:12 (ESV)

Jesus, the Good Shepherd, asks us to follow Him and acquire deep peace and full confidence that we will spend eternity in heaven. It is His gift to man to accept or reject.

God's fatherly care is summed up in the following scripture:

"Are not two sparrows sold for a penny? And not one of them will fall to the ground apart from your Father. But even the hairs of your head are all numbered. Fear not, therefore; you are of more value than many sparrows."
Matt. 10:29 – 31.

Millions of people know the Easter story and that Jesus died on the cross and rose again from the grave. Before the Roman soldiers nailed Him to that cross, they whipped him with 39 lashes as they knew 40 would have killed Him.

They mocked and spat on Him and put a crown of thorns on His head. He went willingly to that cross to save us by shedding His blood for our sins so we could live out this life, knowing He faced abandonment, rejection, humiliation, and persecution for us by taking all of that to the cross. He has freed us. He loves us and wants us with Him.

If you have rejected God's Son, Jesus, and His gift to you of salvation for your sins to be forgiven, then when you die, you will travel to utter darkness known as hell. Satan, the Angel of Light, the Great Deceiver, the Devil, the 'Trickster' has 'demons' assigned to each family to do 'his dirty work,' and he also wants you and I and our families to spend eternity in hell but Jesus wants us even more, after all, He died for all of us.

If you find Jesus and accept Him, you will walk into the 'Light' where you will find Jesus, and you'll never regret it. Some who have denied Him have been given a second chance in having Near Death Experiences (NDE). He will show Himself to you as He has to me, in special and even profound ways, some of which I am about to describe here. I pray that each reader comes to accept Him, for He is Truth!

Chapter 11
1978 to 1982 –Goodbyes and Hellos

Wayne's Dad's Death – *1978.*

Wayne's dad, Cork, died in 1978. I talked to him about the Lord, and he said that in the summer, he used to sit on a hill when the Kettleston Bible Camp services were on.

I talked with him, and he told me he'd accepted Jesus Christ as his Savior and believed he'd meet Jesus and be reunited with Helen, his wife, and his parents, John and Lyla Dobson.

When he was very sick, he told me twice that he was outside of his body but came back into it. Each time he was hovering above the bed, he was watching the nurse working on him and heard the doctor and nurse talking.

I asked him, "Which one felt like you, the one in the bed or the one outside looking at you in bed?"

Without hesitation, he said, "It was me outside of myself, just looking at me in bed and seeing and hearing everything that was going on."

There is much documentation of people having this same experience. So, when you think that it is simply 'lights out' when you die, you are wrong! I have listened to YouTube testimonies where people who have died came back to life, and their experiences are very similar. Those who have had NDE tell about going to the Light and the peace and love they experience, and that they see Jesus and feel only love and no condemnation. Others describe descending into utter darkness and meeting Satan and his demons, and describe hell. Most fortunately, the latter came back to tell us that they were provided a second chance to accept Jesus.

1978 – *Time to Find My Birth Mom*

My parents had lifelong friends who also adopted their two children. We often visited them. Gordon and I called them our aunt and uncle, and their kids were like our cousins, James and Sandra.

I was going on 33 years old when I wanted to find my birth mother. I knew Sandra had found her birth mom, so I asked for her advice on finding mine. She was eager to help me.

I searched the adoption records and found out that I was born on February 03, 1946, in Moose Jaw, Saskatchewan, at the Union Hospital. My mother's name was Helen Gertrude Duncan, and my father's name was listed as Norris Lawson.

Helen gave me the name Katherine Frances Duncan. I was placed for adoption immediately, but could not be adopted until around seven months of age. Perhaps it was because of the surgeries I had to remove two large hemangiomas.

1979 – *What if She Doesn't Want to See Me?*

Sandra suggested I do an album of my life from a baby until now to give her when I meet her. I thought that was a great idea, so I started that and began tracking down the family photos.

Through some detective work, I found a brother of hers with the name Duncan living in Moose Jaw. His wife told me that

Helen was married to Emil Glass, and they farmed near Val Jean, Saskatchewan. I now knew where their farm was.

So Sandra and I planned a day in the summer of 1979 to go to her farm and hopefully meet her. We decided that I would park the car a little away from her house and that Sandra would take the album that I made for her, and if she didn't want to meet me, then she'd leave the album and my contact information with her if she changed her mind.

This was exciting, and I was so happy that Sandra was helping me. We did exactly as planned and parked the car at the side of her house, and Sandra walked around to her door. Apparently, she said to her, "My name is Sandra, and I am wondering if the name Katherine Frances Duncan means anything to you?"

She replied, "Yes, it does. Are you a Social Worker?"

"Today, She's Coming Off of my Top Shelf!"

Sandra told her that she was just a friend of Katherine and that Katherine was sitting in the car around the corner if she wanted to meet her. If not, Sandra could leave the album and my contact details with Helen.

She said, "No, I had her on my 'top shelf' all these years, but today, I am bringing her down, and I want to meet her."

With that, both Sandra and Helen came around the house, and I got out of my car to meet her.

We smiled and gave one another a hug, and she said that she had often looked down this road, wondering if I would ever come down it, and today was the day. She was very happy and invited us into her home.

Soon after, her husband and son came in as they'd been on the field farming, and we were introduced to them. They also had a daughter, but she wasn't there at the time. We didn't stay long and exchanged our phone numbers before leaving.

Time to Meet Her Family

Soon, Helen called to invite my family and me for dinner. Wayne and the kids were excited to meet Helen and the family.

We went and enjoyed the visit with all of the family and had a delicious home-cooked meal. When we got onto the highway to come home, Wayne said, "Well, Arlene, you know now you didn't come from royalty but from hillbillies." He was relating to the popular television series, The Beverly Hillbillies. We sure had a good laugh.

Shortly after I had come home from work and had just gotten out of the bathtub, Lincoln came to say someone was here to see me. It was Helen and her family. They came unannounced and said they were in Regina and thought they'd just stop by to say hello.

After this, I would go for visits, and Helen often came to stay with me on occasion. I was also introduced to her extended family.

My Birth Dad – *Where Does He Come into the Picture?*

As I got to know my birth mom, she told me how she came to be expecting me. She had gone to a country dance, and the gals were to make two bagged lunches with their names on them; one was for the guy who'd pick the other bag of lunch.

Well, Buster (Norris) Lawson picked her lunch. Buster was his nickname, and his family farmed around Parkbeg, Saskatchewan. He had a car and offered to drive her home, and she told me that's when it happened. She said that he was as quick as a cat, and then she found out she was pregnant. She must have made a very good lunch!

On my own, I found Buster's sister, who lived in Parkbeg. She lived there with her husband. Both were quite elderly. I told her who I was, and she said there was some talk at the time about you. Then she said she was going upstairs to get a photo of Buster. I definitely saw myself in him, particularly my eyes and smile.

Wayne called Buster, who lived out of province, and told him about me, but he denied that I was his. Wayne mentioned that he had declared he was with Social Services, and it was documented in the file that he left $100 for them to get me a layette for when I was born. He did not want to get into it further, and of course, Wayne didn't press it further.

When I was in the Seminary, taking a class on 'family systems,' the professor asked me to do two family trees for the class: a family tree of my adopted family and another one of my biological family.

So I had to do some digging and research, and I called what would be my cousin on my dad's side, whose mom was a sister of Buster's. She lived in Edmonton. She, too, acknowledged knowing about me, but the family never spoke much about it. She told me that I was related to someone very famous, Henry Clay.

He was known as the Great Orator and ran to be President of the United States and lost.

He was the Secretary of State and fought to abolish slavery. I bought a couple of books on him, and I think I saw in his photo a resemblance to my son Lincoln.

I have yet to do Ancestry.com to confirm that I am related to him, but I still plan to do this. It would be important for my children to know this for certain.

Squashed – *And Nowhere to Go!*

Helen told me that she did not want her sister or her parents to find out that she was pregnant. She was in grade 12 at the time. So she got a girdle and wore that, and as she got bigger with me, she had a second girdle that she cut in strips and would sew into the one girdle, one strip at a time, as she needed to.

When she was in her eighth month, her dad came to her and said, "Helen, are you in a family way?" Her secret was out.

She told me that when she was in grade 12, a boy in her class saw that she was expecting and began bullying her. When he was outside under the classroom window, she got a pail of water and dumped it over him. I found this humorous and interesting as it demonstrated her feistiness. Perhaps that's something I might have done, too.

Helen told me that her older sister Maggie had a boy out of wedlock a year earlier, and she brought the baby home for a short time. She told me that neither Maggie nor her mom would get up in the night to feed and change him, so Helen did that every night.

Then, one morning, her mom and Maggie took the baby to the dad's farm near Swift Current, SK, and "just dropped him off on their steps. The dad farmed with his parents.

She felt that, with how Maggie's situation was handled, she'd have no support to bring me home and had no choice but to give me up.

I thought that with my being squashed so tight inside her with that very tight girdle, it was no wonder that I had crossed eyes and hemangiomas and even flat feet. I don't think I really believe this, but I can't help but wonder what may have transpired in those cramped quarters.

If abortions were readily available as they are today, I likely would not have been here at all. God had another plan.

Miracle # 7: – God Doesn't Want You Yet.

This is Helen's miracle. After she was married, she had a tubal pregnancy, as she got an infection after I was born that was never treated. She said that it had scarred her fallopian tubes and resulted in her having a tubal pregnancy.

She had another tubal pregnancy and found that out while shopping in Moose Jaw when her fallopian tube ruptured, and she had to have emergency surgery. The doctor told her that if she'd been on the farm when this happened, she wouldn't have survived.

So Helen and Emil adopted their two children, Randy and Tammy. Randy seemed to have no problem with me, but it was a very different story with Tammy.

The children's affection towards their parents seemed somewhat divided, with Tammy being daddy's girl and Randy being mommy's boy.

My Parents Meet Helen

I had told my parents much earlier, before meeting Helen, that one day I would look her up, and they didn't seem opposed to it.

So I planned that when Helen came to stay with me for a couple of days, I would have my parents over for supper, and they could meet.

That day came, and after supper, Mom had a gift to present to her, which I thought was nice of Mom. It was a very lovely Wedgewood brooch.

While I watched the presentation, Mom said, "I want to give you this gift, Helen, as a thank you for you having my daughter Arlene. If it wasn't for you fallen girls, I wouldn't have had her."

I thought it was just fine until the last part, and thought surely Mom could have left out the part about her being a 'fallen girl.' It had to be there as, after all, that was Mom!

Chapter 12
1983 to 1987 – From age 36 to 41

Going Up In The World – *Before the Slide*

I was worried about our marriage, and I knew I needed God to come in and help us. I asked Wayne if we could go to church with the kids and me, and he agreed. I think he also realized that something was not right and that he also needed Him, but his denial of alcohol being an issue was still there.

We began attending church regularly and enrolled the children in Sunday School. We even started attending a Bible Study Class. Yet, nothing improved.

With addictions, many try to have others see they are doing well, but it is deception. So we moved to 24 Lynn Bay in Regina. The home was very nice and had an Olympic-sized pool in our backyard that was jointly owned. It was built by some of the families who lived on that Bay. I was the one maintaining the pool, such as shocking the pool, testing the chlorine levels, and doing yard work.

The home had a fancy bar, and Wayne had it stocked with fine wines, liqueurs, hard liquor, and beers. There was a sauna, too. We were living beyond our means. There were a lot of parties at the house. Voicing my concerns fell on deaf ears.

I was worried that we might get in trouble trying to keep it up. Wayne was away working, and besides taking care of our children, I was trying to work part-time, keep up with paying the bills, and maintaining our home and the pool.

We did have some fun times, going to hockey tournaments and spending holidays with family. We still went on our Las Vegas jaunts, and we still slept in the same bed, but we were becoming more distant.

Wayne suggested that I take a real estate course, as he thought I could make a lot of money fast. I hoped that was the case to help keep us afloat. So, I became a realtor and began working for Frances Olsen Real Estate. None of what I

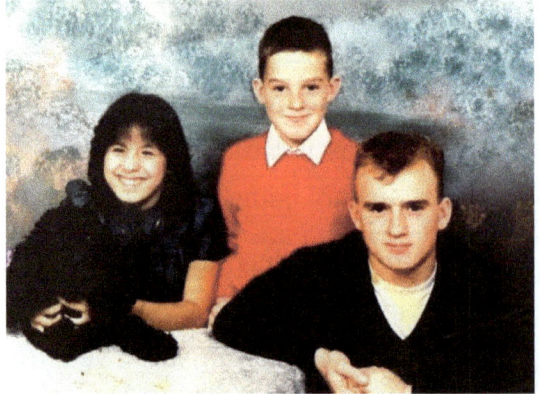

Lin holding our Cocker Spaniel Ode, Caine & Lincoln.

did could fix us, and we continued to drift apart.

Addictions – *Heading to the Abyss*

Our marriage was in trouble, and the children knew it too. Hope was fading.

Lincoln and Lin graduated from grade eight. Wayne never attended the ceremonies. They were dressed in their best, as shown below, but underneath, they were hurting because our family was falling apart. Once, we were connected, loving, and enjoying family life, but now it had come to a stop.

One summer day, Wayne and I went for a swim. We were the only ones in the pool. We were playing around when he decided to hold me down underwater. He wasn't letting me up. I became scared, as I knew he had been doing it for far too long and not for fun. I was just about to give up when he let me go. I exclaimed, "What were you trying to do, drown me?"

He just laughed. Then, there was the day the doctor's office called me to come in to hear my lab results. The doctor told me that I had a Sexually Transmitted Disease (STD), and I exclaimed, "How can that be?" The doctor said that I should go home and ask my husband.

That was such a shock, as I never thought he'd cheat on me, but it was obvious he had. I confronted him about my having an STD and told him he also had to go on antibiotics. I asked him whether he had hired someone, or was he-having an affair, or just sleeping around? He never answered and just walked away from me, having no defense, nothing!

He had become a shallow man, and I felt broken. I knew then that he was not the man I had fallen in love with, and for the first time, I was scared of him.

Soon after, he let me know that he was in trouble financially and blamed me. He screamed at me, saying, "You bitch! You always wanted to see me go under!"

This was the first time he'd called me a name in the 20 years we'd been together, and it remained the only time. Obviously, he had to blame someone.

Around that time, he'd taken Caine to a hockey game. When he came home, he became ballistic, going into his bedroom, yelling at him uncontrollably, telling him he hadn't skated hard enough, and began throwing his toys against his wall.

I ran upstairs to Caine's room and demanded that Wayne get out of his room immediately. He left without saying a word and went out of the house.

I was numb myself and had just started back on antidepressants. Caine was sobbing, saying, "Mommy, I can't live here anymore." I told him that Mommy was going to do something about this, and he wouldn't have to go and live anywhere else.

It took this incident for me to finally act. For the longest time, I never understood how a man who had values and would never have done these things earlier in his life could now be doing such shocking things. I was certain that the brain was affected, but back then, I was not fully aware of the moral decay that came with addictions.

The Jellinek Curve, known in lay terms as The Valley Chart, is an excellent tool for us to understand the abyss that addictions take a person to.

The path to recovery is on the other side of the valley. This link describes it: https://www.therecoveryvillage.com/drug-addiction/what-is-jelinek-curve/

Addictions are a 'Family Disease' – No, A Family Disaster!!

Addictions are a 'family disease' affecting you and every area of your family's life. I couldn't see that clearly at the time because I was right in the 'swamp of addictions' or better described as quicksand, as addictions 'suck the life out' of you, as well as your family.

The other day in counseling, as I explained to this couple who were facing addictions in their own marriage and family that addictions are a family disease, I had a 'light bulb' moment and said, "No, not so much a disease but a 'Family Disaster!'"

Disaster more fittingly describes what results from one's addictions as they impact every aspect of one's life physically, socially, emotionally, and spiritually. Marriages and families are left devastated. To think it does anything less than that is denial.

Shame and guilt hang over the family. One doesn't want others to know that you and your family are falling apart. So you ignore the 'red flags' of addiction, and you either outright deny there is a problem or you minimize what is occurring, hoping tomorrow will be better.

The two wheels that addictions run on are DENIAL and BLAME. BLAME is riddled with excuses for one's behavior. The addict will say over and over again, "If it wasn't for you, I wouldn't drink," just like Wayne said that if it wasn't for me, he wouldn't have his problems, financial troubles, and everything else that was going on in his life. The lie is this: "I would have succeeded – but for you!"

The addicted one is not only dependent on 'mood-altering substances' but also dependent on others around them. Everyone becomes a means to an end to keep them from sinking into their own quicksand. The addicted person is in survival mode and depends on others to survive.

The list of excuses goes on and on! They do not take responsibility for their actions. They do not say they are sorry. They are sinking 'like a ship at sea,' and they will do anything to make the pain go away. They don't care about you. That was so shocking to me.

Why was I so shocked? Well, it was because we loved one another. I knew that he respected me, and he certainly loved our children, and now this. The grief was so real, and yet I coped by continuing to put one foot in front of the other and staying protected by becoming numb.

After the incident with Wayne blowing up on Caine, he returned home the next day, and I told him that we needed to live apart, and he needed to get help for his drinking. He didn't argue. I told him I'd be gone for an hour, and I wanted him out of the house by the time I returned.

When I came home, he was gone. Caine said, "I saw Dad pack. I asked him, 'When are you coming back, Dad?' Mom, he said he's never coming back."

At that moment, I regretted not taking Caine with me, as he shouldn't have witnessed that. He was ten years old. I think Lincoln and Lin were home, too, but I was so stressed and thought I would only be gone for an hour.

I wasn't thinking clearly. I didn't protect our children emotionally by ensuring they weren't around when their dad was packing up.

Going to Addiction Rehab Centers – *'Grasping At Straws'*

After he left home, Wayne agreed to go to a rehabilitation counselor. Then, we were both to attend an 'addiction rehabilitation center' at Pine Lodge at Indian Head, SK.

Back then, both the husband and the wife were encouraged to attend the 28-day program. We were to get ourselves there

159

separately. That felt like the longest day of my life, watching for Wayne to come through the door and praying he would come, but he didn't come.

I stayed for four weeks on the advice of my counselor at Pine Lodge. The children visited, and I had them stay in a hotel. Lincoln said to me that he couldn't see the addiction, as it was like not seeing the forest for the trees. Exactly! The clarity and wisdom of children and youth, as when you're in it, you can't see it until you walk out of it.

Shortly after, Wayne agreed to go to a second 28-day inpatient addiction rehabilitation program in Regina, SK. He said he would come every day but not stay overnight, and they made an exception and allowed it.

He did come every day. During one of our group therapy sessions, the therapist, Dr. Rick Lebell, said, "Arlene, Wayne is not going to change because he is too far into his addiction!"

He broke through my 'thin veil of denial' that had still remained, and in that moment, it just evaporated. I knew now that our marriage was over and our family would never be a family again. Addictions had won!

With no more denial during the group therapy session, I broke down crying out to God and speaking in tongues, not being aware of others in the room, including Wayne. It was just God and me.

When I was finished talking to God, Dr. Lebell called a coffee break. Then he came over to me and asked, "Arlene, what just happened there?"

I am sure he was referring to my 'speaking in tongues.' I just said, "I was grieving," as I wasn't about to explain it.

I felt like 'Humpty Dumpty' who had just fallen off the wall, but it was I who had fallen off my wall. Now, all the King's horses and all the King's men couldn't put Arlene back together again. Hopefully, God could.

Our Children Suffer – *Never Fool Yourself – Not for a Minute!*

I was called to the school one day because Caine was not well. The Principal said he was crying and asked for me. He had an anxiety event or panic attack. Lincoln and Lin were older, but they were definitely also affected; however, they just didn't talk about it.

Lin was in Marion High School, and she was acting out. I was getting calls about her behavior. I had her switch to Miller High School, as they had programming that she might fit into. Things were not much better there, and she got pregnant.

In any crisis, I go into 'high gear' to stabilize the situation as soon as possible. I went and bought a crib, a high chair, and baby clothes. She wasn't even three months into her pregnancy. I was always preparing for the worst and trying to 'keep my ducks in a row' since I never knew what crisis would come next.

Lin miscarried at three months. She was very difficult to manage, and soon, she quit school to begin living with friends whom I knew very little about.

Caine had been sleeping with me because he had anxiety. A Christian addiction therapist I was seeing at the time told me to just let him sleep with me since his psychological health was more important than my concern about his sleeping in the same bed as me.

When he was 13 years old, I told him he needed to go to his own bed, and he did. He never once asked to come back into my bed again. You see, we were all coping in every way possible.

1985 – Helen Has Bowel Cancer – Stage 4 – *She Needs A Miracle!*

Helen was now 59 years old. I had met her in 1979, so I had known her for six years.

Dr. Wigmore and Dr. Young were the surgeons in Moose Jaw, SK, who did her surgery. While she was in surgery, they did five quick sections, which are biopsies of the lymph glands. What they found in all five of them were cancerous cells together with melanin cells. Melanin cells are pigment cells found only in the skin, but they can also be found in association with cancerous cells.

The cancer clinic gave her only months to live due to the spread to her lymph glands. The surgeon also said he had to scrape the wall of her abdomen since the tumor was attached. He could not have removed all of it, so she was definitely a stage 4.

The Regina Cancer Clinic decided not to give her chemotherapy and sent her home to get her affairs in order and die. Upon getting that news, her first reaction was that she'd go across to the States, book into a room, and shoot herself. I told her that this wasn't going to happen and that we'd pray and have faith in Jesus to heal her.

My first reaction was crying out to God, saying, "Lord, I just recently found her, and now this. Please, Lord, heal her!"

I was crying out to God in the living room, sprawled out face down. When I got up, I saw my Bible on the dining room table. I didn't know how it got there, as I didn't recall sitting at the dining-room table reading it.

I sat down and read where it was opened, and it was Psalm 34. What stood out to me was when it said:

"The righteous person may have many troubles, but
the Lord delivers him from them all."

Now, I am only righteous because of my accepting God and His son Jesus. Yet, I felt heard and that God was on this.

On a follow-up exam, her doctor thought he'd again palpated a hard mass in the wall of her abdomen. Helen insisted that the surgeons open her up again and remove it because now she was ready to fight and wanted to live!

Dr. Young called me on Helen's instruction because I was a nurse. She wanted the doctor to discuss this second surgery with me, as they did not want to open her up again.

I told him that Helen believed she'd have a miracle. I mentioned that Helen told me that he was a Christian and sang in the United Church choir, so she had faith in him. I said to him, "Please do whatever she asks!"

So, these doctors agreed to perform a second surgery on her, which was a miracle in itself.

Miracle # 8: – Helen is healed of Stage 4 cancer!

I knew Helen had a Bible, and I asked her to read from The Book of James, chapters 5:13-15. This passage is known as The Prayer of Faith:

13 Is anyone of you suffering? He should pray. Is anyone cheerful? He should sing praises. 14Is anyone of you sick? He should call the elders of the church to pray over him and anoint him with oil in the name of the Lord. 15And the prayer offered in faith will restore the one who is sick. The Lord will raise him up. If he has sinned, he will be forgiven."

James 5:13-15

Further, I told her that the Elders of my church would come to her in the hospital to anoint her and pray over her before the second surgery. After she read this scripture and thought about it or prayed about it, she could call to let me know if she'd like the Elders to come.

She soon called me to ask that the Elders of the church come to the hospital and pray over her. The day before the surgery, the Elders came up and prayed over her.

Before I left for Moose Jaw to be with Helen after her surgery, I called Rose Bell (Pelletier), who was a very dear friend and a prayer warrior. I knew she had a direct line to the Throne Room of God. I asked her to pray for Helen's surgery to go well.

At the time, we prayed Helen would be just going under the knife. As Rose was praying, she had a vision. She saw Jesus standing at the end of her surgical bed with His hand extended over her, as it was very large, covering her entire body. She declared, "Jesus has healed her!"

So, I headed out for Moose Jaw. The highway was not yet twinned. We had our first snowfall. Someone was mad at me as my car began to spin around, and I had no hands on the wheel. As the car went out of control, I called out, "Jesus, help me!"

When my car came to a stop, I was directly facing the oncoming traffic, perfectly perpendicular to the ditch, but on the highway's edge. I sat there for a few minutes, thanking God for sparing my life and likely that of someone else as well.

I definitely was expecting to hear 'a good news report' from Dr. Young when I called him. Before going to see Helen, I called his office from a pay phone in the hospital lobby.

It was an excellent report as he told me that they found only adhesions and released them, and did another five biopsies and quick sections of her lymph nodes as they'd done before. This time, they could not find any cancerous cells but only melanin cells.

Dr. Young said that they had no explanation for this. They were going to send the slides they'd made to the Saskatchewan Provincial Lab for review. The Saskatchewan Provincial Lab also found no cancer cells but only melanin cells. She was healed, and *she had a miracle!*

When I went to her room, she had a note pinned to her gown that she had written before going for surgery: "If you need to put the stomach tube in, you can go down the right side as the left is too narrow, but I don't think you'll need to because I have sent Jesus ahead on this one!"

We all had sent Jesus ahead on this one with 'child-like faith.' I thought Helen went from wanting to shoot herself to having faith in Jesus as her Healer and receiving His healing.

Helen had received an answer to her prayers and mine, as well as those of others, particularly from her persistence in asking the Elders of my church to visit her in the hospital before the second surgery.

Glory to God in the Highest! He heard our prayers and did exactly what He said He'd do according to His Word!

Her husband, Emil, was not a believer and yet wondered how this miracle was possible.

Struggling as a Single Mom

I'd already been a single mom for almost two years, but God made a way for me to support myself, and it became clear that I'd need to sell this house to survive.

My Dad is Dying

It was the summer of 1987, and my dad was dying of prostate cancer. Gordon and Sheila came out to see Dad, and they enjoyed playing the accordion together one more time.

As Dad became more ill, I took care of him at their home, even getting him in and out of the tub. It was difficult for him to see his daughter doing this. One of those days, he looked in the bathroom mirror and said, "How much longer?"

It wasn't much longer. Finally, it was near the end, and Dad was in the emergency room waiting to be admitted.

When I arrived in the emergency room, I heard my mom singing to him, "You are my sunshine, my only sunshine. You make me happy when skies are gray."

She sang it over and over again, and everyone could hear her, but I wasn't going to ask her to stop.

When I was alone with Dad, he said, "I need to tell you that Mom isn't right, and her mind is going. She might have dementia."

He asked me to look out for her. Dad had just turned 75 years old in June, and Mom would soon be 78. I think he'd been seeing her decline for a while, but covered up for her and carried on. He deeply loved Mom.

He also wanted to share with me an experience he had. He told me he had a preview of heaven, and when he was there, he was looking down a tunnel, wondering if Mom was going to make it. He said, "I kept watching for her to come, and she wasn't coming, and I was so concerned, but finally I saw her coming."

Of course, I was glad Dad saw that Mom made it to heaven, but I wanted to know what heaven was like. Dad told me that it's hard to put into words, but that it's stunning. The flowers were incredibly colorful and beautiful. The grass stood out to him because it was like stepping on a soft, thick cushion.

Dad had never spoken of ever having personal spiritual experiences until that day. I believe God reassured him where he was going by giving him a preview. What a loving and personal God He is!

Dad asked me, "Arlene, are you going to be alright?" I reassured him that I would be. Dad knew I'd likely remain a single mom raising our three children and the emotional and financial weight that would be on me, so while on his deathbed, he was worried about me.

My parents were sad that Wayne and I were separated because they loved him too, but they knew about the difficulties we had. They never 'bad-mouthed' him or interfered, which I was thankful for.

On July 25, 1987, my dad went to heaven, and this time, he wasn't coming back.

Dad's Funeral

I was focused on Mom, helping her through this heart-wrenching event. When one is extremely stressed, one only remembers snippets of events, and that was one of those days.

What I do remember is someone pointing out to me that they saw Wayne drive out to the cemetery, but he stayed in his truck. He was not at the funeral, but he did honor my dad and our family by doing that.

In helping Mom after the funeral, I began to see what Dad was talking about. She was, indeed, getting dementia. Soon, she was diagnosed with Alzheimer's disease, and I knew their home would need to be sold. She was mostly at home, so I figured she needed to move into an apartment first.

Keeping My Head Above Water – *Again!*

I was still hoping and praying that Wayne would be struck by a 'bolt of lightning' from heaven to bring him back to his senses. My denial crept back in momentarily, but it soon passed.

Wayne would tell me that he wanted what he saw that I had because he noticed that I had changed, relating to my faith, and it had brought me peace. I told him he could have what I had, but he wasn't open to discussing this any further.

In that same conversation, he brought up his girlfriend. "Arlene, you'd really like her. She's funny like you are!" he said.

I thought, 'Wow! That's the deluded thinking of an alcoholic who is very far gone.' I couldn't even get mad, and he left that afternoon after our visit

I gave up all hope that we could be back together again and filed for divorce. I wasn't sure what my long-term career would look like as I had to let my registered nurses' license lapse. I decided to take a nursing refresher course. It was challenging, but I accomplished it.

I then worked in nursing homes, taking shifts, but I still wanted to be home more. I founded a company called Coordinated Rehabilitation Services (CRS). I was contracted by insurance companies to provide services on their behalf. I also decided to start a Christian counseling business, and I discussed it with God.

The Lord gave me a vision. I was looking over a wheat field covered in sheaves. It was dusk. As I looked at this field, one sheaf stood up and walked towards me. As that person got close to me, they turned to the right.

Then, the next sheaf stood up and came towards me, turning to my left. As I watched this happening over and over again, I heard the Lord say to me, "Arlene, when I bring these people to you, you are to do five things: One, you are to love them. Secondly, you are to speak into their lives, My Truth. Thirdly, you are to encourage them. Fourthly, you are to admonish them in love, and lastly, you must pray for them."

I asked Him, "Do I lay hands on them? Do I anoint them with oil?"

He said, "No, but you are to pray with them (only if they are open to it), but always pray for them."

(Note: The Biblical reference for the 'laying on of hands' is Hebrews 6:1-3)

Therefore, let us move beyond the elementary teachings about Christ and be taken forward to maturity, not laying again the foundation of repentance from acts that lead to death,[a] and of faith in God, 2 instruction about cleansing rites,[b] the laying on of hands, the resurrection of the dead, and eternal judgment. 3 And God permitting, we will do so."

Since this vision was such a revelation for me, I registered my first counseling business, Revelation Christian Counselling.

I continued to go to church with the kids. Caine and Lin were water-baptized by immersion. Lincoln, however, was going through a lot of grief and anger over our marriage breakup, and likely confusion. So he decided he didn't want to do it. All the children were baptized as infants, but they had never dedicated their lives like this before.

I was distraught in my spirit for Lincoln, whom I felt had 'the weight of the world' on his shoulders. During a church service, as I worshipped, tears began to fall from my eyes. Then the music stopped because this woman, whom I knew to be a simple but sweet, gentle, and down-to-earth soul, began 'speaking in tongues,' and she also interpreted the message.

The interpretation was: "My daughter, I see your tears, and I hear your prayers; do not be troubled, for I will deal with your son in My time."

I'd heard this woman give a message before, and what was so interesting to me was that she was so unassuming, but when speaking in tongues and interpreting it, her voice was strong and emphatic. I would say that she had 'a direct line to God.' That is how God often works, taking the humble and lowly to work through:

"...God has chosen those whom the world considers to be puny and powerless — even laughable. These are the very ones God will use to confuse, frustrate, and baffle the political powers of the world!"
1 Corinthians 1:27

I took that message wholeheartedly to heart and thanked the Lord for His encouragement and comfort. Later, I asked the pastor about the message, as a message is usually intended to edify, which means to build up the church, not just one person.

He said that there may have been more than me who received this message, but he emphasized that it was directed personally, stressing that God can do whatever He wishes to do.

That man was a wonderful pastor, but for some reason, the Board of Directors dismissed him after he and his family had been there for a few years.

1989 to 1991 – *Surviving – Thanks be to God!*

I also had my home to sell and downsize, as well as selling Mom's home. I needed to get her into an apartment. By the grace of God, I was able to do both. I moved to 11 Hudson Drive, which was just off Lynn Bay, where we'd lived. The house was very adequate. The children could continue at the same school and still be close to their friends.

During this time, I got hired as a Rehabilitation Counselor with The Cooperators. I stayed there for two years. For me, it was a very toxic environment. My work was successful, and I was informed that my statistics showed I was saving them money, as confirmed by their Actuarial Department. However, it was an environment I could not survive in.

One day, being fed up, I wrote on the white message board just outside my office, "This place makes me sick, and I am off indefinitely!" Then I returned the next day, which was a weekend, and packed up.

Perhaps that was not so professional, but there was no easy way to do this, and there was more to that story. I hired a lawyer and asked him to write a letter on my behalf, which I had drafted, and I requested close to twenty thousand dollars. He did write it for me and sent it off, but also told me that I'd never get it, as I'd only worked there for two years.

Shortly after, the lawyer called me and said, "I have a check for you, and it is for the exact amount you asked for." Again, God was taking care of me.

I was not receiving financial help from Wayne, and there was no hope for reconciliation, so I began divorce proceedings with the hope of getting some financial support. After all, we still had two children to raise. Lincoln was ready to go out on his own.

Summer of 1991 –*Surgery and a Divorce*

In the summer of 1991, I ended up in the hospital. I had to have a bowel resection because I had a diverticuli rupture, leading to an abdominal infection. Since my surgery was an emergency, I had the doctor and the porter wait for me while I wrote my Last Will and Testament. I had my doctor witness it, and then I put it in the bedside drawer and asked the doctor to let my family know about it if I didn't make it. He agreed, and off I went.

When I was recovering, Mom called the hospital, saying she needed to talk to her mom, which was me. Her dementia had progressed. I knew I'd need to move her from her apartment.

Surprisingly, when I was in the hospital, Wayne sent me a beautiful flowering plant. He also filled in the swimming pool in the back of 11 Hudson Drive. The pool was beyond repair, just like our marriage.

I applied for a contract with Great West Life Insurance as a Rehabilitation Counselor with my business, Coordinated Rehabilitation Services. The woman who hired me was from Nova Scotia, Canada, and she came to interview me for the job while I was still in the hospital. Fortunately, I got that job. Again, God was looking after me.

Maintenance Enforcement was going after Wayne for support. He and his siblings were trying to settle their dad's estate, and the Canada Revenue Agency (CRA) was after Wayne for unpaid taxes. Wayne's sister, Lydia, paid me a visit with her husband, Jerry, and requested that I ask Maintenance Enforcement to close my case against him.

I told her that wasn't going to happen. She followed up that visit by sending me a handmade wooden pull toy. I guess it was her way of telling me I was childish. At the time, she and Wayne's other siblings didn't seem to care how I or our children were doing.

Yes, God hates divorce, but I sought Him diligently on this matter and got the 'green light' to proceed. I thank God that I was divorcing Wayne at the time of settling his dad's estate, since CRA could only take Wayne's half. Wayne had inherited 25% of the land, and CRA and I split it, each taking 12.5%.

Wayne and I were to visit the lawyer's office to sign our divorce papers. I was surprised that he showed up. We were about to sign them when he said, "Arlene, I have somewhere to be right now, so I will come back in the morning to sign them."

I'm not sure why he didn't want to sign the papers then, but I knew he wouldn't be back in the morning, and they needed to be signed. So I said firmly, "Wayne, it will take a few minutes to sign these, and I need you to sign them now!"

With that, the divorce papers were signed.

Chapter 13
1992 – 1993 – Finalizing the Divorce

Dating After 21 Years

In 1992, a few months after my divorce went through, a friend of mine suggested that this man call me to ask me out. So I began dating Jock, who was also divorced. He was a Christian. I only wanted to date a Christian, if at all, as it says in the Bible that we should be 'equally yoked,' which in lay terms means you should only be hitched as a team, believing and serving the Lord.

Lin's Layers of Trauma

Lin and her boyfriend Donny were expecting a baby. I knew Lin had Fetal Alcohol Syndrome (FAS). She'd suffered neglect and abuse before we got her, and she also had challenges and traumas during the time we raised her. I became increasingly worried about her mental health.

When we adopted Lin, I found cigarette burns on her body, like the babies I saw when I interned as a nurse in the children's ward at the Royal University Hospital. In making rounds with the pediatrician, he told me that every fall, there's an influx of Indigenous babies admitted from the northern reserves.

He explained that parents would put a drop of coal oil in their milk bottle, just enough to make them violently sick. They'd get high fevers and become dehydrated from vomiting and diarrhea, and then would need intravenous fluids. He added that the parents did this so they could go hunting.

175

He pointed out cigarette burns on some babies. He explained that some parents do that to condition the baby not to cry. They did not want them to cry to have to feed and change them when they were drinking. The baby soon associated the pain of the burn with their crying, so they knew not to cry or they'd get burned.

After noticing the cigarette burns on her body, I was horrified. I knew that Lin and her siblings were left in their home in freezing weather. Their parents were out drinking and left them all night. The door of the home had blown open, and it was so cold the older children did not want to get up to close the door. Lin was the youngest of six children and an infant when this happened.

Fortunately, she'd been wrapped tightly and only suffered frostbite to her cheeks. Tim, who was next to Lin in age, froze his fingers, leaving some disfigured.

Many times, I was alarmed and concerned about Lin's behavior. In her preteens, she, at times, would talk with different voices. When I asked her why she was talking differently, she'd say, "Oh, that was Molly," or another time, saying, "That's Lily." She'd assign names to the different voices and behaviors she displayed. This was very troubling, and I never knew who would show up.

Certainly, this was abnormal, so I had her seen by a Child Psychiatrist who said he didn't deal with this apparent condition of Multiple Personality Disorder (MPD), now known as Dissociative Identity Disorder (DID)

I found Dr. P. Bastian, a woman psychologist who worked with patients to integrate their various personalities. She confirmed her diagnosis and suggested I have her seen by a Child Psychiatrist, Dr Colin Ross, who focused his practice on dissociative disorders and trauma. So, I made a trip to Winnipeg, Manitoba, and he confirmed her diagnosis of DID.

In my clinical counseling practice and in my reading and speaking with scholars on DID, the child has to be intelligent to be able to do this and maintain their hierarchical personalities that have split off from the host personality.

The personalities that 'split off' from the host, which is Lin, are called Alters. Each alter serves a purpose for the individual to cope with their life. Lin's IQ was a low normal at 91 when we adopted her, and she had FAS and had experienced abuse, but when she was reassessed at Alvin Buckwold Clinic at five years of age, her IQ was now a high average. So, obviously, she was and is intelligent.

We were told that this dramatic increase was a very good indicator of our love and care as parents and our exposing her to stimulating and learning experiences.

How Could Lin Acquire DID? – *She Had To Have Experienced Severe Traumas:*

It should be noted that all children and adults will dissociate. We do it every day, like when we momentarily daydream or have a minor blank spell, when carrying on a conversation with someone, or when we are tired or under sustained stress. Most never do it to cope with life and acquire DID.

Besides the very early childhood traumas mentioned prior to our adopting her, she disclosed to Wayne and me about bad boys

177

taking her to their house and then letting her go and telling her to get home. What she described was sexual abuse. This was devastating to hear, and we contacted the police. Nothing came out of their investigation.

The nightmare was not over, as a month later, in the evening, a teen came to our door asking for Lin. It was almost dark.

"Who are you?" I asked. With that, he took off running.

Evil came stalking again, and the nightmare continued. Lin told me that those two boys were coming to the playground at recess, calling to her through the fence.

We had notified Connaught School about the situation. We told her to go to the teacher, who would call the police and call us. So, a 'safety plan' was put in place.

Again, the police looked into these occurrences, but nothing came of it. They thought they knew who these boys were and told us they spoke to them, and finally, their appearances stopped.

I had a couple of young girls babysit Lincoln and Lin. Wayne and I knew the parents and thought these girls needed some spending money, so that turned out to be a disaster when Lincoln told me they were having them undress and run around.

After that, I realized you can never be too careful with babysitters, and you need to vet them. I am putting this in here because it may seem like you can trust a babysitter, but be sure you know if they are responsible and have babysat others, and not just take the parents' word.

The breakup of our marriage was tragic for all of us. Lin didn't show that she was very affected by it. She would say,

"Well, we're down to four now." Yet knowing that she was 'daddy's girl,' I am certain this negatively impacted her.

Lin did not engage consistently with her counseling with Dr. Bastian, so I don't know if she was ever fully integrated.

More Trauma – *She was Going to Have a Baby*:

Now that Lin had to give birth, this event could serve as another trauma for her, and I was worried she'd resort to her usual 'coping strategies,' which were addictions and dissociating.

Both Lin and her brother Tim became part of the Sixties Scoop. Now Lin was expecting a baby with Donny, who, along with his sister Victoria, was also part of The Sixties Scoop.

I thought Donny was more responsible than Lin, but I had learned that before he was a teen, he started a fire under his parents' car, blowing it up. He might have suffered FAS also.

Lin stopped using alcohol as soon as she found out she was pregnant, which I was very thankful for. During her pregnancy, she was admitted to Martha House, a Catholic Home for unwed, 'at-risk' mothers that was operated by nuns.

This was a wonderful facility. Sister Margaret was also wonderful, and she helped Lin and me as I visited and supported Lin throughout her pregnancy.

Can She Parent? – *"God, I Will Need Your Help – Again!"*

On January 25, 1993, Lin was in labor, and I was stressed. When I got to the labor room, I picked up a paper cup of apple

179

juice from her bedside table, asking her if I could drink her apple juice as I was parched.

I was about to drink it, thinking she'd be fine with my request, when she blurted out, "Mom, that's my pee!" We sure laughed. I was glad I'd asked.

Donny and I and, of course, the obstetrician were in the delivery room with Lin. The obstetrician was going to use forceps to pull her baby out, but I pleaded, "Please let her have two more pushes," as I stood between her legs, holding her feet in place of stirrups and preventing him from gaining access to her.

He laughed and said, "Okay, two more pushes!" and he started to

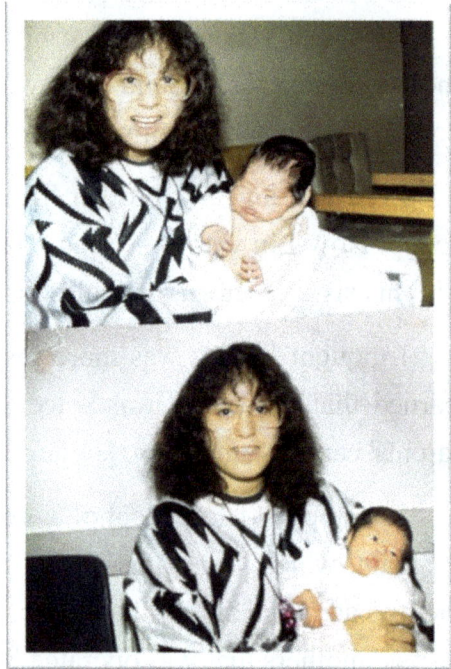

Lin holding Charlene

clang the forceps in the air. I started coaching her with those two pushes, and after the second push, I quickly got out of the way so he could deliver Lin's beautiful, healthy, sweet baby girl without forceps.

Donny was supposed to name their baby if they had a girl, and Lin was to name the baby if they had a boy. Well, Donny didn't get a chance to name his girl because as soon as the nurse asked what her name would be, Lin blurted out Charlene Marie. Later, Lin told me she named her Charlene because she wanted my name to be included in her name.

Once Lin was released from the hospital, she went back to Martha House. It wasn't long after that Sister Margaret called me to meet with her as she had concerns about Lin. She told me that she'd find her spaced out, not caring for her baby or interested in breastfeeding her.

My worst fear for Lin surfaced again, and I said, "God, I will need your help again!"

My Meeting With Sister Margaret – *Plans for Lin and Her Baby*

I was all in to help Lin if possible. Sister Margaret had conveyed her concerns to Child Protection Services. I contacted an addictions' counselor who had seen Lin before she delivered, and he agreed to be involved in a meeting that was arranged with the Department of Social Services.

In attendance were Sister Margaret, the Child Protection Worker, the Addictions Counselor, and I.

It was decided that Lin would attend a 28-day addiction program up in northern Saskatchewan at Sandy Bay, which was an Indigenous Addiction Healing Lodge.

Further, I would look after Charlene while she was in treatment. There was no follow-up plan, and this concerned me. She was told that she had to complete this program if she wanted to have her baby back.

I was concerned she'd run from there, and then what? So, I planned to be away by visiting my friend Angela in Sarnia, Ontario. I was so glad I did this, as I found out later that Lin thumbed a ride to Regina every weekend that she was in treatment to be with Donny. That was quite a distance to go to Regina and back to Sandy Bay, but she did it.

If I'd been at home with Charlene, she might have taken off with their baby to Donny's sooner. She apparently put in four weeks in Sandy Bay, minus the weekends. I learned later that the 'healing center' wanted her to repeat the four weeks, but of course, she had no intention of repeating it.

At the end of the fourth week, I was back home, and Lin showed up and took Charlene with her. As she took her in the stroller, I recalled what Sister Margaret said, "Arlene, you will need to be the one to look out for the well-being of her baby." I had a sinking feeling that things may not go well. In the meantime, I'd need to become 'a helicopter grandma.'

Initially, Lin lived with Donny and his sister, Victoria. Both of them had a 'big influence' over her, and it was not a good one. Victoria had three sweet little girls.

Lin and Donny went on their own, renting a two-bedroom home in a low-income neighborhood. I was always checking in on them. I came there one Saturday morning to find only Lin at home, bathing Charlene.

I noticed some of the living room furniture I'd given her had blood on it, and the floor lamp with a glass shade on it was smashed. Beer bottles were all over. Obviously, there'd been a brawl there. I told Lin that this was no environment for her and her baby. I asked her to pack her things and come home with me.

After settling her down for a few weeks, I got her into a nice two-bedroom apartment in North Regina with security. Donny was still coming around even though she had a new boyfriend. Again, I was always popping over to check on Charlene to be sure Lin was taking care of her.

The Engagement–*Short But Not So Sweet!*

All the time that this was going on with Lin, I was still dating Jock. I wanted a life of my own, and after dating for two years and going to Holland with him to get his mom's approval of me, we got engaged. That lasted for one week.

At the time, we'd been attending a 'far right' evangelical church. One week after we got engaged, Jock told me that he'd setup a meeting with this Pastor. I figured he was getting 'cold feet.' So before I met him there, I talked to God, and He told me that it was not going to happen; that is, our marriage. So, I was prepared for this meeting.

In case you are wondering how I hear from God, I will try to explain. It isn't that I have a constant download from Him, which is His Holy Spirit, but when I pray and get quiet before Him, I often get a picture or a vision of what is lying ahead, sometimes right away and sometimes in three days or even weeks later.

Sometimes, He shows me things that will happen in my future, but waiting for His timing can be difficult. Many times throughout my life, I have had dreams, and often, they are to show me what is lying ahead for me or to give me a warning to not do something, to do something, or to pray.

Around age forty, a dear friend of mine who had a close walk with the Lord told me that I am a Seer. I had no teaching on this, but I looked it up to know what that meant. A Seer is 'one who sees' into the spiritual realm with their senses. This is how I came to understand how this operates in me, which is described in this two-minute link:

https://www.youtube.com/watch?v=aTkGJ_c3tCo.

So when I arrived at the Pastor's office to meet with Jock, God had already prepared me for this meeting, although I had no idea just how it would play out.

Jock got there ahead of me, and he appeared on edge. The Pastor told him to help himself to any refreshments in his bar fridge, saying there was pop or beer, and to take whatever he wanted. I passed on any refreshments.

Jock soon began to communicate his concerns to the Pastor. He brought up my daughter Lin, who had problems, and he wasn't sure what was going to happen there; he told the Pastor how he'd hired my son Caine, who was in his late teens, to do some work at his business, complaining how he'd doused a red ant hill with gasoline and lit it on fire instead of working. Later, I checked with Caine, and he said it was on his break when he did this.

Jock went on that he was concerned that because I was divorced, he'd not be in God's will to marry me. He must have forgotten that he was also divorced. Both of our spouses had been unfaithful, so although this is not God's perfect will, it is his permissive will.

He was throwing everything at the wall, so to speak, including my mom having Alzheimer's disease. He went on to tell the Pastor that when he came over, he found my vacuum in the middle of the living room. He liked things to be tidy at all times, saying it would only take a minute for me to put things away.

After hearing all of this, the Pastor tried to alleviate his fears by saying, "Don't worry about any of this, Jock, because after Arlene has been under my leadership for one year, your concerns will be over. I'll have her just how you want her!"

'WHAT???!!!' I thought. I had not seen this side of Jock or this Pastor before that meeting, but God saw it all and went ahead of me. I was already familiar with a few of these controlling and toxic behaviors with certain Pastors, but sadly, he was just another one.

So, while trying to take off his beautiful carat diamond ring, I stood up and said, "With all due respect to you two gentlemen, this engagement is over!" and I headed downstairs to my car.

Jock hurried out and drove up beside me before I could get in my car. He said, "Don't take it off!" I had just managed to get the ring over my knuckle and had it clasped in my fist, and as I held onto it, I pretended to throw it. He gasped, "Oh my God, that's just what my ex did! She threw it too, and I had to crawl in the grass to find it."

Wow! I assured him that I'd spared him from crawling through the grass and handed him his ring, got in my car, and left. When I got home, I broke down and cried, grieving deeply, like I did the day I was in the rehab center with Wayne when I realized our marriage was over. Yet, I knew this time I would be alright because the Lord went ahead of me again.

To bring closure to all that went down, I asked Jock to attend one counseling session with me, which I initiated and paid for. He came. I now had closure and peace that it was over with.

Chapter 14
Churches – And Wolves in Sheep's Clothing

I am going to take the opportunity to give you my insights on churches from my experiences. Now, more churches are doing a wonderful job of 'guiding the sheep.' No person, leader, or church is perfect.

Yet, certain leaders and churches are toxic. Toxic refers to having the capacity to make you ill (spiritually) if you hang with them for too long. Some Pastors hope you will blindly follow this scripture:

*"Obey your spiritual leaders, and do what they say. Their work is to watch over your souls, and they are accountable to God ...
"*

Hebrews 13:17.

If I had obeyed all of my spiritual leaders, I would not have been in God's will. There are times we need to pass things by the Lord, the Shepherd of us all, to receive His guidance.

Jesus tells believers to be wise as a serpent and as gentle as a dove, and that even goes for our interactions with church leaders.

187

Favoring the Sheep – *The 'Well-To-Do' Sheep*

The 'well-to-do' sheep in certain churches often get much more pastoral attention and services rendered to them because 'money talks' even with Pastors.

Jock likely got this Pastor's sympathies because he knew that he was worth a million or two. It is all a farce, but Jesus sees it. Was I going to stay under this man's leadership? The answer was 'No!'

A couple of years after Jock and I met with this Pastor, he was written up in the Regina Leader Post and on the news in various outlets. The gist of the story was how he'd swindled the sheep in his fold, taking their money, left the church, and headed down to Arizona, USA, to start another church.

Wolves in Sheep's Clothing – *Ravenous Wolves*

The Bible warns us about them:

"What sorrow awaits the leaders of my people—the shepherds of my sheep—for they have destroyed and scattered the very ones they were expected to care for, says the LORD."
Jeremiah 23:1

"Beware of false prophets, who come to you in sheep's clothing but inwardly are ravenous wolves."
Matthew 7:15 ESV

I have had too many encounters with these 'ravenous wolves,' yet just one was one too many.

One such encounter occurred after my divorce. The evangelical Pastor of the church I was attending at the time asked to come and visit me to see how I was managing. I thought that was kind of him.

He was married and had a lovely wife and family. After a cordial visit, and while standing at the front door to leave, he made a move on me, telling me how attractive I was.

I turned away from him, opened the front door, and thanked him for his visit. I soon left that church and later learned that he had an extramarital affair with some gullible woman who did follow her leader.

There was one other pastor who tried the same thing.

The Last Days – *The Kind Who Worm Their Way into Households*

2 Timothy 3:4b-7 tells us what will happen in the last and evil days on this planet:

"Rather than lovers of God, 5 (they) having a form of godliness but denying its power. Turn away from such as these! 6They are the kind who worm their way into households and captivate vulnerable women who are weighed down with sins and led astray by various passions, 7 who are always learning but never able to come to a knowledge of the truth."

Churches can have cultish leadership, particularly the 'far-right evangelical churches.'

These charismatic evangelical churches can attract Pastors who are not so much interested in letting the Holy Spirit work in the lives of the sheep that God entrusted to them. Instead, they 'get high' on controlling their flock and wanting to be the Holy Spirit for them. This is an addiction, too.

Leaders and their flock can be very religious and self-righteous to exert control over the flock, leading to submission.

They believe it is their 'god-ordained duty' to do so, which is not guiding the flock but ensuring they do this and that.

This stifles the love and work of the Holy Spirit. I had had enough of 'do this and do that' from my mom and Ms. Hitzman, my grade six teacher, but I can never have enough of His Holy Spirit working in me and through me and guiding me.

Jesus loves His Church! As believers, we are His Church. He tells us that He's coming back for His Church, which is us! He is not interested in denominations but in your heart, my heart. He asks us to seek Him, that is, find Him and believe He is who He claimed to be. Then He becomes our Savior, and we stand on the 'Truth of His Word' and have faith.

The Christmas Story is so beautiful, how God came down from heaven to us as Emanuel, and Jesus Christ was born of the Virgin Mary in a lowly stable with Joseph at her side. The angels rejoiced on the first Christmas, and we felt His love come down.

The Easter Story tells us of two stark realities: How this precious child of LOVE, Jesus, became the sacrificial Lamb of God. On Good Friday, we celebrate that He died for our sins.

It was not a Good Friday for God to have His Son crucified on the cross, but He did that for you and me. Yet, we insist it is 'Good' because if it were not for Jesus Christ shedding His blood on the cross to save us from our sins to be 'born again,' we'd have eternal separation from God and utter darkness, which is 'hell. 'Christ went through hell to give us His gift.

No one should coerce, bully, or guilt you into accepting Jesus Christ as Your Lord and Savior since you have free will. The gift you give to God is accepting His Son's gift to you, which is waiting for you with open arms, a gift you can never earn as it is free.

I Felt like Jesus in a Local Church – *Rejected!*

I love God's people, but I often felt like the leadership was non-accepting of me. I sensed it and knew it. They appeared to tolerate me until the Lord led me out.

A Seer is a prophet, and in my senior years, I came to recognize that I do have the anointing of a Seer. I do see what God shows me. Do I see everything or get it right all of the time? Of course not!

Jesus was rejected in His hometown of Nazareth:

4 Then Jesus told them, "A prophet is honored everywhere except in his own hometown and among his relatives and his own family." 5 And because of their unbelief, he couldn't do any miracles among them except to place his hands on a few sick people and heal them. 6 And he was amazed at their unbelief."
Mark 6:4 (NLT)

Jesus disdained or hated religion in His day, and He does so today. Religion stifles a relationship with Him. He asks us to have a relationship with Him, to follow Him and learn from Him, and He'll be our Shepherd.

The church is God's doing, and so we should gather together to share His Word, worship Him, and do the will of God in helping others, particularly the orphans and the widows:

27 "Religion that God our Father accepts as pure and faultless is this: to look after orphans and widows in their distress and to keep oneself from being polluted by the world."
James 1:27

Church is wherever two or three are gathered together anywhere, in His name, because He will be present there as much as when thousands gather together. Love and unity need to reign, or His Holy Spirit will depart from there.

My mom walked around the house singing, "He walks with me, and He talks with me, and He tells me I am His own," and that ministered to me as a child.

Today, I know that He does walk with me and talks with me. He'll do the same for you.

The Learning Curve Never Ends... *Churches and Cults...*

After I received my nursing degree, I began taking university classes at the University of Regina and at the Canadian Biblical Seminary in Regina, SK. The classes I took were geared toward counseling. I just wanted to learn more. Some crucial insights I want to share with you.

I learned that getting high on 'mood-altering substances' was destructive, but so was getting high on mood-altering behaviors, such as sex, religion, overeating, hoarding, shopping excessively, making money, and the list goes on.

Substance abuse is always coupled with destructive behaviors. Instead of each of us going to His 'Living Water,' the Word of God, we go to addictions. This leads to our destruction and the destruction of our families.

"For My people have committed two evils: They have forsaken Me, the fountain of living waters, and hewn them out cisterns—broken cisterns that can hold no water ..."
Jeremiah 2:13

All addictions are broken cisterns, and all are destructive. Some addicts, including some pastors, have put the bottle away, but they get high on other behaviors, which now get them high. Pastors and denominations can become super controlling, ensuring the sheep see the world through their lenses rather than loving and guiding them, and encouraging each person to have an intimate relationship with Jesus.

Codependency 'underpins' all addictions, and in fact, it is an addiction. Narcissism accompanies addictions, being on a spectrum from mild to extreme. It is like being a little bit pregnant. You may not see the pregnancy early on, but in time, you will.

Narcissism is about being self-absorbed, where that person's needs override anyone else's needs. We all need to examine ourselves and, with God's help, do better, but accept the journey and count it 'all joy' as He perfects us from 'glory to glory' until we are with Him.

There are many types of narcissism. There is 'covert,' which is hard to spot, or 'overt,' like grandiose narcissism, which is on display for all to see.

The covert may be the one who flatters, like 'love bombing' and putting you on a pedestal, until they switch, whereby he or she becomes abusive, controlling, spiteful, and angry. Then, your life becomes a living hell.

The narcissist will objectify you, where your existence becomes 'a means to an end' for them. That person uses you to get what they need, with no regard for you. If you no longer serve their purpose or you don't do what they want you to do, they'll 'chew you up and spit you out.'

There is nothing worse than the betrayal and trauma that a supposed loved one can inflict on their victims. They are always right, righteous, and unrepentant.

I experienced this through the school of 'hard knocks' like many of you. Those who go into caring professions, such as nursing and counseling, are often called 'wounded healers.'

I wanted to learn more, and I wanted to first heal more for myself and then be more effective for my counselees. We are always learning, and that journey is exciting and humbling.

A renowned doctor in psychology, a professor, told his students to study Trump to learn how a narcissist and sociopath operates. Trump's own niece, Mary Trump, who has her Doctorate in Psychology, knows him all too well.

Trump is a classic example of grandiose overt narcissism who capitalizes on being a narcissistic leader of 'communal narcissism.' His MAGA Movement has led too many of the sheep down a path of allegiance where they operate like a cult. The devil is laughing! *But God is not!*

Too many evangelicals have fallen into this trap because they're vulnerable and gullible. Trump took one cause and magnified it, like abortion, hiding behind the 'anti-abortion movement 'to appear like he's God's chosen one to save the unborn and bring justice. All the sins of the nation that are plaguing the USA, he'll fix. They begin to believe the braggart.

Yes, abortion is wrong in God's eyes, yet some abortions are necessary to save a mom's life. God, the person who is pregnant, and the father of the child, along with their doctor, need to decide what to do in every situation. Hopefully, they seek God to guide them.

The army of narcissists backing government leaders to get into power and dictate how we should live is trying to take over for God and the Holy Spirit. These are the Pharisees whom Jesus encountered when He was here in person.

Instead of following the real Shepherd, Jesus Christ, and The Word of God, which is the TRUTH, they get what Jesus calls 'itching ears' and, in the example above, follow an overt narcissist as their leader, who loves 'power and control and allegiance' and believe the 'lie.'

Trump launched his media platform called Truth Social, which is a far cry from the truth and is a farce. It indoctrinates gullible Christian people who have wandered away from His Truth.

The sheep don't even realize that they've been 'communally brainwashed.' The Deceiver, the Devil, is very much at work doing what he does best, deceiving.

Yet, there is hope for anyone to make changes in their life and 'get right' with God, as 'we have all sinned and come short of the glory of God.'

Our pride is hard to swallow, to become undone before God, which is called repentance. Positive change begins by saying "I'm sorry" and doing it with humility and sincerity.

I know that when you have been emotionally wounded as I have been, it is at times hard to trust another, trust yourself, and at times even to trust God. I have come to recognize that healing is a lifetime journey.

Addictions stop that positive process until you face them and overcome them. My journey will be ongoing until I meet my Healer, Jesus. I am alright with this.

Chapter 15
1994 to 1996 – Two More Years of Challenges and Decisions

My concerns over Lin continued. She had a new boyfriend, Calvin. It was exhausting to keep tabs on her and Charlene, monitoring to see if she was caring for Charlene adequately.

The kids still connected with their Dad. Below is a photograph from 1994 of Caine (18 years old) and Lincoln (24 years old) with their dad:

I finally realized that I was not responsible for my loved ones' addictions, but that I was responsible for my choices, and I couldn't fix Lin! I was not able to fix Wayne, and in hindsight, I saw that Jock had his own addictions. What were my addictions?

When I first began taking counseling classes, the professor had us visualize ourselves counseling someone. Then, we were to share what we came up with. I pictured myself in a very large rocking chair with counselees on either side of me. We were all rocking endlessly 'back and forth' with no one saying a word.

Yes, I was in the middle of that rocking chair, but we were 'all in the same state' with trauma, needing comfort and healing. When counselors, or people in general, have not healed enough from their own trauma, they will attract those who also have trauma.

Unfortunately, most do not have the tools to heal themselves or help others. Unresolved trauma leads to addictions.

At least I wasn't trying to fix them, but I was one of them. Yet, I needed that realization so I could address my own traumas and heal more so I could be an effective therapist.

As time went on, I became an effective therapist, but this process goes on and on as it should. I now visualize Jesus behind my counseling chair to help me be more effective.

Alcoholics Anonymous (AA) describes the 3 Cs for those living with someone who is suffering from addiction. You need to know that you never *caused* their addiction; you couldn't *control* it, nor can you *cure* it or fix it.

I was not responsible for fixing people but for providing them with knowledge, tools, and a means to overcome their fears, grief, and addictions.

We all have addictions to a lesser or greater degree because that's our flesh, with its desires and demands, but we need to be aware of them and deal with them.

Lonely One Evening – *What is this Man All About?*

A year had passed since Jock was out of my life. It was the spring of 1994, and I was on my own at home on a Saturday evening, reading The Regina Leader Post, when I came across a page about meeting others, like a dating site.

This page was a forerunner to what are now dating sites on the internet. I wasn't looking for anyone, so I thought, but I wanted to be entertained by reading these.

Participants gave their first names and a description of what they were looking for in someone. I came across this particular write-up where this guy's description of what he wanted in a woman was oddly put, but interesting.

What really caught my attention was his stating that he wanted a woman "who truly loved the Lord." I thought, 'Who would write that?' and I became curious.

So you were able to call the phone number and leave a message without your phone number being revealed. You could listen to the recording, and if you liked it, you could leave your name, at least your first name, and phone number for him to call you back. This seemed not too risky, so I was tempted to call his number, which I did.

The message was very straightforward, in which he introduced himself. After listening to it, I hung up and did not leave a message. I called back a few more times, and it was not the message that caught my attention but his voice.

His voice was kind and effective. Finally, I decided there was no harm in my leaving my first name and phone number.

He called back and told me that he was taking classes at the Canadian Theological Seminary in Regina, like I was, that he had an undergraduate degree like I had, and that we were both working on our Master of Arts degree in Counseling. We both had gone through a divorce.

He lived on his own in an apartment less than ten blocks from me. He worked as a freelance writer and a disc jockey, having worked at various radio and television stations. He had an excellent voice for that.

The Date – *Not My Type!*

He asked me out for coffee and said he'd pick me up. Now, I would never have someone pick me up before meeting them in a public place first, but I never thought about that over thirty years ago.

He did not have a very good car, and it smelled of stale cigarettes. He told me that he'd recently quit smoking. He wasn't a classy dresser at all, but clean and pleasant. As we walked into the restaurant, I noted he had a tail comb sticking out of his back pocket, and that was rather odd, like back in the '60s or '70s.

He talked a lot, and I could see he would make a great radio announcer as he had 'the gift of the gab,' so to speak. He told me about his life and how he was raised in Montreal, Quebec. He was an only child and had one daughter who lived in Toronto. We shared about our careers, goals, and our faith.

Then he took me home. I thought to myself, 'You are not my type.' I was not attracted to him in a physical way, or not so much in any other way, except he was a Christian. I was actually glad to be home again.

Well, the phone rang within the hour of being home, and he asked me, "Well, what do you think?" I told him I thought he was very nice and I enjoyed our visit. I was not about to tell him my first impression of him, nor was I going to say You are not my type.

I know, in hindsight, I was dealing with Post-traumatic Stress symptoms and anxiety from what I'd been going through in the past few years, and I was definitely lonely. I know he was also. So I decided we could at least be friends.

When he asked me out for lunch the next time, I said I'd meet him there. That went somewhat better. He was definitely intelligent and kind and not too bad looking, but too serious. He lacked a sense of humor, which was always a plus for me. Humor would occasionally bring relief to the difficulties in life.

Prior to meeting Chuck, my mom had broken her hip, and I brought her home, nursing her in a hospital bed in my living room. Soon afterward, I was able to get her into a nursing home. I then began to have Mom over for supper every Sunday, as the Easter Seal bus could bring her. I also invited Chuck for supper since he had very few home-cooked meals.

The Proposal – *Did I Say 'Yes'?*

One evening, Chuck took me out for supper. I now knew him for about four months.

During the meal, he asked me to marry him, and I paused and could hardly believe what he'd asked me, but I couldn't believe myself because I said, "Yes!"

Perhaps it was the glass of wine I had with my meal, or perhaps the biggest factor in hindsight was what I saw in my spirit, a future chapter of my life, which I wasn't sure how I'd deal with concerning Lin and her children.

A part of my future flashed before me. It was going to be extremely difficult, and I didn't want to navigate it alone. Lastly, I knew this man loved me and would not abandon me. I knew after the last two, he'd be around for the long haul, which was very important.

Perhaps God was arranging this, but I felt somewhat selfish thinking of my own needs.

I definitely had two out of the three love connections with him. Filial, friendship, and love were there, and Agape was definitely there, which was our spiritual connection, but the Erotica, I was still not feeling it.

As soon as we got engaged, his dad passed away, and his mom was on death's doorstep in a hospital. He rushed out to Montreal. He got there just before his mom died, which was only three days after his dad passed. He had no funeral but buried them together in a Veteran's plot, putting one casket upon the other.

He hurried back to Regina after that and started taking Seminary classes and working some. I kept working. I began to learn more about him, and it was concerning for me. He had been married twice.

His first wife ran off with his supposed best friend. When he was in Saskatchewan, he met a woman in a small town where he was a disc jockey. They got married, and that lasted only three years. He said she was always complaining about him, and the marriage was toxic. They decided to go their separate ways. This last situation was not good, and I was still getting to know him, and here I was engaged to him.

We had not decided when we'd get married, as so much was happening that summer. I was still keeping tabs on Lin and Charlene and also working.

Seeking Mom's Approval to Marry Chuck

I recalled when Caine drove my mom out to Jock's place a few miles north of the city. I was out there already. Mom became upset and very agitated in his company.

One afternoon, Chuck and I were having a visit with my mom in the common area of the nursing home. I thought it may have been the ride out to Jock's that she became upset, but with dementia, your spiritual connection can be sharpened. Of course, there's no empirical research on that, but it is what I sensed.

Mom was comfortable in Chuck's presence. She was now in the latter stages of Alzheimer's disease, but I thought I would see what she'd say if I asked her this question: "Mom, this man asked me to marry him. So, Mom, do you think I should marry him?" She actually took in what I was saying to her and turned away

203

from me and stared at Chuck. I am sure she stared right through him, which seemed forever, and then turned back to me, smiled, and shook her head yes.

So, getting my mom's blessing, who is in this condition, is not ideal, yet somehow it felt like she had a connection to Him, and her approval was important to me, a blessing.

A Motor Vehicle Accident – *Becoming His Private Nurse.*

It was near the end of September, around suppertime, when I received a telephone call from Chuck, saying, "Darling. I am alright, don't worry, but 'the jaws of life' are cutting me out of my car as I was going to the Seminary, and I swerved to avoid a car and hit a telephone pole. I will be going to the Pasqua Hospital emergency." The car was a total mess, and he'd broken all of his ribs on one side and had some other cuts and bruises.

He was in a very bad state, and they had to stabilize him as his breathing was very much affected. He finally stabilized and was put on a medical ward.

About a week later, while I was visiting him, his doctor came in and said he could go home if he had anyone to care for him because he could not look after himself.

Immediately, Chuck said, "My fiancée is a nurse, and she can look after me, can't you, honey?" I thought, 'I can, but I don't want to.'

The doctor asked if we lived together, and I told him that we had our own places. He said that I would let him go home with you if you could take care of him for a couple of weeks. Again, I said yes when I felt like saying, "No, please keep him here until he is well enough to be on his own."

So, I resigned myself to reconciling my decision to take him to my home as just another life event or crisis that needed to be met. He came home with me, and I became his private nurse, bathing him, preparing his meals, and dealing with all of his needs.

Just before his accident, I was having my own 'cold feet' that he never heard about. Now, he was compromised and vulnerable, so it was still 'full speed ahead' to get married.

Getting to Know You – *Yes, All About You!*

During this time, I got to know Chuck even better. There were some positive revelations, and yet a couple of them were very troubling.

205

Chapter 16
The Tragedy of Sexual Abuse—When a Parent is the Perpetrator

As I mentioned earlier, he was an only child. He was a surprise for his parents, having him in their early forties. He told me that growing up, he'd been sexually abused by his mom.

I asked Chuck, "What did she do to you?" He told me how she flaunted herself, exposed herself, and tried to get him sexually aroused. He said the worst thing she did was to dress him up as a girl and call him Dorothy.

She started this when he was a toddler, and I am unsure just how long it went on. He told me that the reason she did this was because she always wanted a girl and a boy, and since she knew she would never have another baby, a girl, she told him that she needed to do this.

Alarm Bells Went Off – *My God, He's a Cross-Dresser!*

Hearing that she dressed him up as a girl and called him Dorothy, alarm bells went off, and I said, "What!? She was nuts!"

So, guess what this led to? As an adult, he became a closeted 'cross-dresser.' What! Again, more alarm bells went off! I was shocked that a parent would do this.

He said he left home after grade 12 and sought counseling. He told me his mom doing this messed him up really bad. It was messing me up just hearing about this, but I agreed with him that it must have done that. I needed to know how his mental health was now.

He said he was diagnosed with Generalized Anxiety Disorder (GAD), Post-Traumatic Stress Disorder, and Bipolar Disorder. He was no longer on medication for anything. He said his sexual orientation was messed up, so he sought therapy and considerable counseling.

He said, "Of course, I know I am a man, but being dressed up as a female for so long at such a young age caused me a lot of turmoil as an adult." So he'd cross-dress in private to calm his emotional turmoil by wearing women's clothes, makeup, and wigs.

'Oh my God!' I thought. I was able to comprehend this as a professional therapist, but to be in a marriage with someone with this history was another thing. I had come across situations like this in my own practice, with adults dealing with this, as well as a parent doing just what his mom did, for the same reason, but I didn't want a husband as a client or as a patient.

Today, children in kindergarten are coloring the Pride Rainbow flags, allowing them to join in mock Gay Pride celebrations, and parents questioning their child's sexual orientation if their daughter likes wearing boy clothes or playing with boy toys, or if a boy enjoys playing with dolls or Barbie dolls. The world feels upside down. My world was feeling upside down.

There is nothing wrong with boys enjoying playing with dolls rather than trucks or girls playing with guy toys, as this is perfectly normal. We all are 'two-spirited' with unique likes and dislikes, but we are born male or female, and God does not make mistakes.

Have You Healed Enough? – *Weighing it All Out.*

I asked him how his therapist helped him overcome cross-dressing. He told me that he had to sit holding a football while talking with the therapist.

I thought that all he needed to do was check out his privates while bathing or showering, and it would confirm just how God had made him, and he'd find out that he was 100% male.

Of course, I felt angry, even having to think about how messed up this was. I knew what this therapist was attempting to do, using visualization and Cognitive Behavioral Therapy (CBT) and so on, but I thought you just needed to keep it simple.

I told him that this is the therapy that I would have him do: at least once a day, he was to take a bath or a shower, and while washing his privates, he would reassure himself by stating, "See, you're a boy! And I love you!"

This is called 're-parenting of the inner child,' coupled with CBT, and he'd do this over and over again until he was convinced that he was a man.

You see, there's no conversion therapy required in letting him know how God created him and that he doesn't make mistakes. He made us male and female. God was never confused.

Although Mommy tried to convert him into Dorothy whenever she wanted her girl and put dresses on him, he was a boy all along and was now a man.

I'd give Arlene's therapy a new name: 'Fake It 'til You Make It!' This therapy is TRUTH because too many believe the 'LIE.'

The TRUTH is that he was 100% male. I guess it would be like 'putting lipstick on a pig' and pretending that it's a woman when it really is a pig!

A Flashback! – *The Day I Put Lipstick on a Pig!*

That imagery came to me when I recalled an incident when Wayne and I were still married. I came home one afternoon with my girlfriend Angela to find a frozen pig in our bathtub. I didn't know that Wayne was going to be having 'a big pool party' for all of his friends and roast 'that boy' or 'girl' on the spit on the huge barbeque by the pool, but I realized that's what he'd planned.

So Angela and I had a good laugh finding this frozen pig in our tub, and I am not positive, but I think it was me who decided to dress that pig up in a negligee, put a wig on it, add clip-on earrings on those lovely ears and complete the transformation by putting lots of makeup on it. I smothered those luscious lips with bright red lipstick, the kind of lips that women are dying for these days. Fortunately, I had all of these props.

We had to hurry before Wayne got home. Angela helped me with all of this, and we placed 'this cross-dresser' on my side of the bed and waited for Wayne to come home.

Yes, I remember now. It was I who came up with this great idea! When Wayne came home and walked into our bedroom, we heard him say very loudly, "Oh, Arlene! You're looking so beautiful!" My girlfriend and I had tears running down our legs—well, almost.

As I am describing this scene, I burst out laughing, thinking of it again, but I was soon reminded by the Holy Spirit that it was Satan who got the last laugh here. That day, I was no longer the 'ugly duckling' but a 'beautiful pig'—but definitely not yet a swan. There were layers of tragic irony summed up in this scene.

At that time, I did not know that Wayne was engaging in adultery, nor did I know that I had contracted a 'sexually transmitted disease' from him, nor was our marriage in total shambles yet. Now, I was about to marry a hopefully rehabilitated 'cross-dresser,' and there was nothing funny about any of this. I knew who wanted to get the 'last laugh,' and of course, it was Satan.

We discussed all of this, and I was thinking I should end our engagement, but I concluded that Chuck and I had the Lord, and so we'd be okay. As you will see, 'our future life together did throw some curve balls' that had to be dealt with, but you will also see that God was in it.

Fear began to plague me. I knew that this fear is not of the Lord and that the only fear we are told to have is reverend fear, which is love and 'high regard' and reverence for the Lord.

Yet, I am human. In the Bible, it says that the flesh and the Spirit are at war with one another. This scripture describes the battle between the flesh and the Spirit, and it described mine!

For the desires of the flesh are against the Spirit, and the desires of the Spirit are against the flesh, for these are opposed to each other, to keep you from doing the things you want to do.
Galatians 5:17 ESV

Decision Time – *To Marry or Not To Marry – What Would Jesus Say?*

What would Jesus say about this situation? Again, I read John 8 in the Bible. I encourage my readers to also read it. Here, Jesus comes upon a group of people about to throw stones at a woman who was caught in the sexual sin of adultery. The Pharisees, the religious leaders of the day, were there to watch it all.

When Jesus came upon this scene, He challenged the crowd to examine themselves by saying, "Whoever is without sin, cast the first stone," and with that, they all turned and walked away.

Then Jesus approached the woman to minister to her, saying, "Neither do I condemn you. Now go and sin no more."

Then Jesus spoke sternly to the Pharisees, saying,

211

[43] Why do you not understand what I say? It is because you cannot bear to hear my word.[44] You are of your father, the devil, and your will is to do your father's desires. He (Satan) was a murderer from the beginning and has nothing to do with the truth because there is no truth in him. When he lies, he speaks according to his own nature, for he is a liar and the father of lies."

John 8

Don't you just *have to* love Jesus? He was and is so full of grace and mercy towards this woman and us. Jesus called out these religious leaders who were acting like hypocrites. He confronted these pompous religious leaders, the Pharisees, to condemn them, stating they were from their father, the devil.

Jesus does not condemn those who desire to change, but when He sees 'the hardness of the hearts' like these Pharisees, He doesn't hold back His righteous anger. After all, they should have known better as scholars of the Old Testament, where its prophecies were being fulfilled in their own time. Yet, they did not recognize Him but were blinded by Satan.

Those who refuse to believe in Him and deny Him are rejected by Him because they believe the Liar, like the Pharisees.

As I was trying to reason and rationalize my dilemma to marry or not to marry Chuck, it was not because I thought I was more spiritual than he was. It was because I knew the 'death grip' that addictions can have on someone, and this addiction was one of those, considering the emotional damage that his mom had created for him.

I knew he was kind and generous with what he had, which was nothing in terms of material assets. He loved the Lord and wanted a woman who truly loved the Lord, which I did. Plus, I never questioned his love for me, but was this enough?

I prayed the Lord's Prayer, "Thy will be done," and then asked, "So what is Your will?"

Jesus had to 'die to self' and do His Father's will. He knew that meant taking the sin of the whole world in being sacrificed for us. He had to carry on His bleeding and whip back His own cross. He was humiliated, scorned, spit on, and mocked by the crowd, and the Roman soldiers pushed a crown of thorns on His head, finally nailing Him to that rugged cross.

He took the penalty for our sins so we can be redeemed and spend eternity with Him. That should excite all of us who believe!

The Roman soldiers didn't even break His legs, as was the custom and prophesied in the Old Testament. In breaking the legs of the one being crucified, that person will die more quickly. By not breaking His legs, they wanted Him to suffer even longer.

Have you ever felt like God had abandoned you? Well, Jesus, who had the sins of the entire world nailed to that cross, felt utterly abandoned by His Father. Before taking His last breath, He cried out, "My God, My God, why have you forsaken Me?"

In my decision to marry Chuck, I knew that God wouldn't go against my 'free will' nor if I decided to not marry Chuck would I lose my salvation, but what was at stake for me was completing the purpose for which I came for, which was my destiny, but the question remained, were Chuck's and my destinies to be intertwined?

He Gets the Last Word

"Keep a cool head. Stay alert. The Devil is poised to pounce and would like nothing better than to catch you napping. Keep your guard up. You're not the only ones plunged into these hard times. It's the same with Christians all over the world. So, keep a firm grip on the faith. The suffering won't last forever. It won't be long before this generous God, who has great plans for us in Christ—eternal and glorious plans they are!—will have you put together and on your feet for good. He gets the last word; yes, he does."
1 Peter 5:8-11 – The Message

What stood out for me was this: 'He gets the last word.' So now I need to pass all of this past Him. The answer came to me that He was in this, and I was to go ahead with the marriage, and Jesus would be with me, well, with us. With that confidence, I received His Shalom (Peace).

As I mentioned, Chuck's parents died three days apart. His dad's death was expected, but not his mom's. He arrived at the hospital just hours before her death, and as he was going to enter her room, he heard a Pastor leading his mom in the sinner's prayer.

Chuck knew his dad had accepted the Lord, but he wasn't sure about his mom. Now, he was sure. After burying both his parents, he came back to Regina, but he still had to continue paying the rent on their apartment until he settled their affairs and cleared out their apartment. Knowing that, we decided that we'd take our honeymoon by going to Montreal, Quebec, after getting married on December 17th, 1994.

The Wedding – *"Run Arlene Run"*

I insisted we have a prenuptial agreement in place, considering he had hardly two cents to rub together, and I had a home that was paid off and some savings. It was nothing to really brag about, yet it was my only financial security.

I could not have made this wedding scenario up because it was so humiliating and embarrassing. There's always a lot of stress in planning and getting through any wedding, no matter how small or big, but this was 'over the top.'

The wedding was at Chuck's church, Westminster Baptist Church. I had been attending a small house church, and my pastor was to officiate our vows. His wife would play the piano. My son Caine was to be giving me away, my friend Joy was my Maid of Honor, and Chuck's friend was to be his best man.

Decorations were up, the guests were all seated, and the piano was playing. What could possibly go wrong? The wedding was to begin at 3:00 p.m.

It was now 3:15 p.m., and there was no sign of Chuck or his best man. I needed a cell phone, but it was 1994, so there were none.

Time kept moving, and it was soon 3:30 p.m. The fingers were about to fall off the poor pianist's hands, and the guests were all wondering what was going on, with some looking at one another. I said to the Pastor, "I don't know if they had an accident," thinking of Chuck's last accident or what had happened.

215

I tried to calm my fears, but I heard a voice in my mind screaming, "Run, Arlene! Run." I then said to the Pastor, "I will go up front and tell the guests that I am not sure what happened, but to please come back to my home, and I will have the caterers bring the food there." Then I heard the Lord say, "Stay put, Arlene, I am in this!" Remember, He gets the last word!

It was 40 minutes past the hour, and Chuck showed up with his best man. The wedding ceremony was finally starting. Caine walked me down the aisle as Chuck and his best man stood there, having no explanation for the long delay.

Charlene was now 23 months old, and she kept herself busy running back and forth on the empty wooden bench behind us.

She had a sweet red velvet dress on with white lace, white leotards, and black patent shoes, courtesy of Grandma. She looked like a sweet doll because she was! She kept coming up to me, saying 'my grandma' and tugging on my dress.

In the photo below, you can see her running on the bench behind us, and her parents sitting behind her.

When Pastor said, "You may kiss the bride," I wanted to slap him more than kiss him. I just wanted it all over with! I was so humiliated and angry, and I needed answers. But I'd have to wait for that when we were alone.

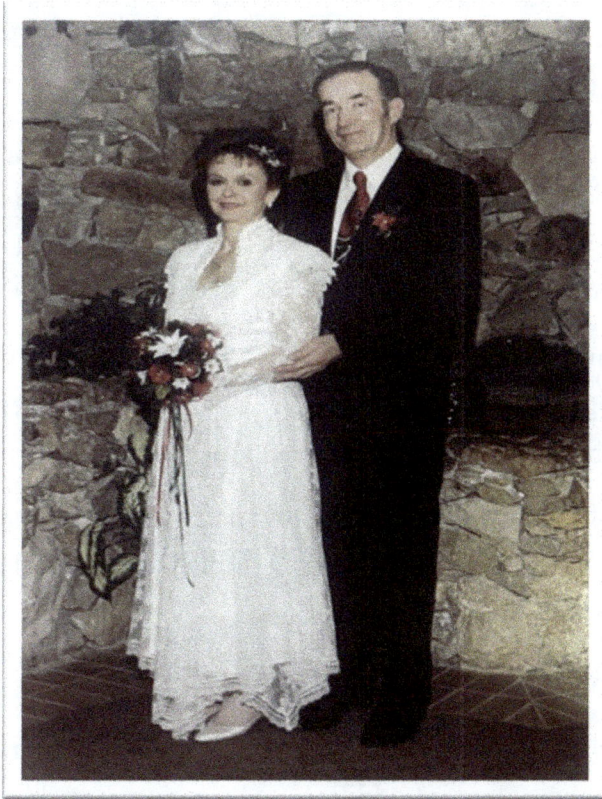

After we had our wedding photo taken at the Canadian Bible Seminary (photo above), we came back to the church basement for the reception and supper.

Charlene hung around me the entire reception. Lin and I sang a duet: Thy Word is a Lamp Unto My Feet. I think we sounded really good, and that was a special moment for both of us.

I learned why there was a huge delay in getting this wedding underway. Chuck told me that his best man had a problem getting his suit from the dry cleaners as they were trying to find it. To me, it was a very lame excuse, but I had to put it behind me and make the best of the rest of our wedding.

At the reception, I apologized to everyone on behalf of Chuck and his best man for the delay in getting the wedding started. It should have been Chuck apologizing, but I saw that was not going to happen.

During the almost 25 years that Chuck and I were married, I would bug him about our wedding day. He would get tired of hearing about it and say, "You need to get over it, Arlene."

Well, I have gotten over it now since I can now clearly see that God was in our marriage, even though, as you will later see, Satan was messing with it.

The Honeymoon

The honeymoon was fine, going to Montreal and seeing some of the sites in addition to clearing out his parents' apartment. We got everything packed up or thrown out and went to a New Year's Eve church function to bring in the New Year.

The next day, we were on our way home. There were some weird behaviors that I saw with Chuck, which were questionable and even troubling, but there was no fighting or name-calling. I have to admit that at one point, I thought this marriage might be over before it got started.

Once home, things settled down, and he gave up his apartment and moved into my home. Caine still lived with us for a short time. Chuck had two cats, and I had a Cocker Spaniel, Ode.

We attended church and Bible study and were very busy with our lives. Yet, there were some bumps along the way, some of which were normal in making an adjustment to marriage, and some were not expected.

As I mentioned earlier, I found Lin a very nice apartment in North Regina. She soon found a new boyfriend, Chris. This young man had a little girl, a few months older than Charlene, and he was also the sole parent. I was hoping that this relationship might work out, but I was not too hopeful.

Donny still kept coming over to see Charlene, and I never knew when another crisis could arise.

Come the fall of 1995, Chuck and I wanted to go full-time to the Seminary at Briercrest in Caronport, Saskatchewan. It would mean commuting daily, and it would mean that I would be paying tuition and books and living expenses for both of us, as Chuck had no money.

I had around $80,000 in cash in the bank, and my home and car were paid off, but going to the Seminary full-time for both of us would take a heavy hit on the cash.

I told Chuck that we should pray and ask for God's leading on it, and so we did. I had prayed to the Lord separately, telling

Him that although Chuck was kind and loved me, there were still times that I felt I couldn't trust him and was unsure if we'd make it.

I did not want to spend that money on our education if it was not His will for us to go to the Seminary and if our marriage would not work out. I asked Him for confirmation.

Miracle # 9: – The Fragrance of the Lord – An Answer to Prayer

A few days after praying this, I woke up one night, and the room was filled with a beautiful fragrance, an aroma that was something I had never smelled before. It was a smell of spices, yet a floral and fruity smell. I thought this was an odd experience and fell back to sleep.

The next morning, I told Chuck about it because he'd slept through it and had not experienced it. The next night, I awoke again, and there it was again, the same beautiful fragrance. I wondered if this was what mirth and frankincense smelled like. It was so gorgeous, and it was definitely 'out of this world.' I felt that this was a spiritual experience of some sort, but I could not understand it.

I had heard about the fragrance of the Lord, and I thought I would research that in the Bible to learn about it. I thought the Lord was trying to tell me something. I read these scriptures:

And walk in the way of love, just as Christ loved us and gave himself up for us as a fragrant offering and sacrifice to God.
Ephesians 5:2NIV

15 Our lives are a Christ-like fragrance rising up to God. But this fragrance is perceived differently by those who are being saved and by those who are perishing. 16 To those who are

perishing, we are a dreadful smell of death and doom. But to those who are being saved, we are a life-giving perfume. And who is adequate for such a task as this?
2 Corinthians 2:15,16 NLT

Author Prem Rawat describes the 'fragrance of the Lord' this way: "Peace is the perfume of God. When God is close to you, you smell His perfume. And this perfume is exquisite. It is beautiful. The senses dance, and life in that moment becomes complete."

Directly after the second night, there was a third night, and I was awakened once again. This beautiful fragrance filled the room again. This time, I woke up Chuck. I said, "Chuck, you have to wake up and smell what I smell!" He began to complain about me waking him up, and being half asleep, he said, "I don't smell anything." Then, a minute or so later, now lying there wide awake, he said, "Yes, I do smell it!"

Chuck fell back to sleep, and I lay there saying The Lord's Prayer that Jesus taught us to say, "Thy will be done, Thy kingdom come," knowing now that it was His will that we both go to the Seminary that fall.

Often, the Lord works in a sequence of three: three days in the tomb before He was resurrected The Holy Trinity—Father, Son, and Holy Spirit—is the most common example, and there are many examples of this threefold pattern in the Bible. Three signifies divine perfection and completeness.

I was reminded that I'd be spending His money anyway, not mine, as, after all, it was His provision. Finally, I had His perfect peace, His Shalom, because I was in His perfect will.

221

Chapter 17
December 1995 – A Month to Remember for a Lifetime!

Chuck and I had put in three months at the Seminary. We were commuting an hour each way, Monday to Friday. Chuck was up first, and then he'd get me up. He made breakfast and coffee for us, and I'd eat what he made and drink my coffee as he chauffeured me to class. He did spoil me in ways like this.

By the time we got there, I'd be fully awake. We were very much enjoying this experience of learning and meeting new people.

My Friend Sandra Was Dying – *The Dream*

Sandra, as I mentioned earlier, was the woman who helped me locate Helen, my birth mother, and went with me to find her. She was a very special lady, very sweet and pretty. She had many friends and was more of an extrovert than I was.

She was happily married with a now adult daughter. We went for lunch, not too long before I heard that she had breast cancer.

The cancer was very aggressive. When she was in the hospital, her family, understandably, did not want her to have a lot of visitors. So I never visited her.

I really wanted to go because I knew Helen had a miracle of being healed of cancer. So, I began to pray for the same outcome for Sandra. I couldn't ask if she wanted prayer like I did with Helen because her family was taking care of those needs.

The Dream – *What Does It Mean?*

It was sometime at the beginning of December when I had one of my 'spiritual dreams.' I always know the difference between a regular dream and one from Him. It is sometimes not clear right away as to why the Holy Spirit determines that a dream is necessary for me to have. Yet, I can be certain that it was absolutely necessary for Him to give it to me and that it would become clear. At the time of this dream, Sandra was still in the hospital.

The Dream

The setting for this dream was right after the funeral service that had been held for Sandra. I was at the luncheon or reception that was taking place after her funeral.

The table that I was sitting at was round, and several people were seated around it. I did not notice who the people were at the table because I was focused on this adorable boy who was sitting in the chair to the right of me. His chair was backed up from the table and angled towards me, and he was trying to get my attention, and he did manage to get it!

He was a bit fidgety, like young children can be, and he had his knees under his chin.

He'd be around five years old and nicely dressed. He noticed me, and it seemed he wanted me to notice him. He had a mischievous grin.

I was about to talk to him, and at that moment, he turned into a demon. He was still the size of the boy but had no color; he was a dull charcoal black, and he was grotesque. Now he had an evil grin and was hissing and laughing, relaying to me that 'he, they won!'

At that point, I woke up and lay there, knowing that this was not just a nightmare, though it could be categorized as such.

I thought, 'Lord, what are you trying to show me? Did you just want me to know that Sandra was not going to make it? Or was I to pray a certain way that Satan would not take her even though I knew she was gravely ill?' Nothing was clear about why He showed me this. Of course, I did pray for Sandra and for her healing before I fell back to sleep.

This dream occurred a few days before I heard of her death. Her death notice is still on Google search: Sandra Cheyne died December 09, 1995.

The Storm and the Viewing

Sandra's death notice was in The Regina Leader-Post. I read that her viewing was to be held at Helmsing Bremner Funeral Home on December 13, 1995, between 7:00 and 9:00 p.m.

I told Chuck that I really wanted to attend, and he agreed that we'd go after we got home from the Seminary that day. I can't be certain what time we got away from Briercrest to come home, but it would be no later than 6:00 p.m. The drive takes about an hour to get home.

Upon leaving, we heard that an early winter storm was coming in. As we were leaving, the wind picked up very quickly, and the snow began falling heavily and blowing. We soon became aware that this had quickly morphed into a blizzard.

The weather was so bad by the time we reached Moose Jaw that we'd considered going into Moose Jaw, SK, and getting a hotel room for the night. Yet Chuck said we'd keep going even if it was at a snail's pace. Chuck knew I really wanted to get to the viewing of Sandra, so I knew he hadn't given it another thought.

It was now dark out, and cars and trucks were sliding into the ditches in front of us. We hardly had any traction to stay on the road ourselves. The visibility was fast diminishing. We were now crawling at 20 to 30 km or less. Many commuters ahead of us were going into the ditch, including a semi-truck. Below is a Saskatchewan newspaper article on the storm:

It was 8:40 p.m., and we were now in Regina, and I'd just finished silently praying and saying, "It doesn't look like we will be going for the viewing, Lord, but whatever Chuck decides, that's what we'll do."

I had no sooner finished praying when Chuck said, "Arlene, it is going to be too late to go now because, by the time we get there, it will be after 9:00 p.m."

I said, "Well, I did want to see her, but that will be alright. I'll remember her the way she was."

We drove another dozen or so blocks to our turnoff onto Hudson Drive, where we lived. It was as if Chuck couldn't turn the wheel to go onto Hudson Drive as he came to a complete stop, saying, "Arlene, I'm not sure why, but we are to go there!" (implying even if we're late). Chuck's response amazed me, and I silently said to God, "I guess we're going!"

In the past, I had witnessed the Lord giving Chuck insights, but never such a clear direction like this. I felt somehow this was the Lord. It was now almost 9:00 p.m., and Chuck was heading to Helmsing Bremner Funeral Home.

We arrived at the door of the funeral home at about 9:15 p.m. We knocked and rang their bell, and a woman answered. I explained to her that we'd come from out of town through that blizzard and apologized for being late. I said that we were wondering if it would still be possible to have a viewing of Sandra Cheyne for just a few minutes.

She was very obliging and led us to the room where Sandra was, telling us to not feel rushed.

Raising Sandra from the Dead – *This Wasn't Planned!*

Miracle # 10: – Raising Sandra from the Dead!

The room was small and softly lit, and you could smell the beautiful flowers that lined the entire room.

I didn't notice where Chuck was as I slowly walked ahead of him up to the side of her casket and looked at Sandra lying there, looking as beautiful as any corpse I'd ever seen.

She was in a lovely black suit. On her lapel was the pink ribbon pin, the symbol for breast cancer. Her hands were lovely, and her left hand, with her wedding rings on, was resting over her right hand. Sandra was a very attractive woman with a beautiful smile and disposition.

As I took all of this in, I thought, "Sandra, you just started into your fifties, and until this cancer hit you, you were healthy. You should never have had to leave your husband, your only daughter, and your family."

I then had a flash of that dream where the cute little boy morphed into a demon and was hissing and laughing, saying, "I won. We won!"

At that moment, a sudden wave of 'righteous indignation' came over me, and with no reservation, I called out in a commanding voice, "Sandra, in the name of Jesus, arise!"

With that, I saw color come into her face and hands; I noticed her eyes moving as in REM sleep before you are about to open them; I saw her beautiful, warm smile come across her face, and

I saw her breathe. Her chest rose at least once, and likely twice, and I thought, "Oh my God, she's coming alive!" I was so excited and yet so afraid, and then it was all over, and she lay still again, as I first saw her.

The most troubling part for me was that it stopped, and she returned to her corpse state. Satan immediately taunted and gilded me, saying, "What little faith you had! Ha ha, you blew it!"

I realized that what I just witnessed was a 'sacred moment,' so I just stood there in awe by the casket until I heard Chuck say, "Arlene, I think we better go now because we haven't had supper yet." I agreed and turned around to leave. Chuck said he had to go to the washroom, but to wait for him in the lobby.

I never once thought of turning around to say to Chuck, "Did you see what I saw?" Right then, I was not looking for validation as to what just happened because I knew what just happened. I was perplexed as to why it stopped.

Processing this Miraculous Event – *Processing What Just Happened*

As I continued to process my reaction to what just happened, I realized that I, too, had 'great fear' like the shepherds had when the angel of the Lord appeared to them in the night sky, announcing the birth of Jesus: The Shepherds and the Angels:

8 And in the same region, there were shepherds out in the field, keeping watch over their flock by night. 9And an angel of the Lord appeared to them, and the glory of the Lord shone around them, and they were filled with great fear.
10And the angel said to them, "Fear not, for behold, I bring you good news of great joy that will be for all the people.

Chuck came to the lobby, and we left. As he was driving out of the parking lot, he said to me, "Arlene, what I witnessed tonight I will never forget for as long as I live!"

I exclaimed, "Chuck, please pull the car over, I need to talk with you!" He pulled over, and I said, "Chuck, I need to know exactly what you saw!"

He said, "Well, Arlene, when you called her forth, she came alive."

I said, "I know she did! But what did you see?"

"I saw her breathe, and her chest rise and color come into her face, and then I saw her smile. I was sure she was going to open her eyes as her eyelids were moving, and then it was over." Chuck had witnessed exactly what I had.

I had never attempted to or thought of ever calling forth anyone back to life, not before then or since. So I had to ask myself, "Why did God orchestrate our coming through a blizzard, my being alright without seeing her and then God intervening to press upon Chuck not to turn onto Hudson Drive, but to say, "I don't know why, but we're to go there," and then this happened.

Why did he give me that dream a few days before she died? I am convinced of one thing: God arranged for that private showing for Chuck and me. He honored my submitting to Chuck's leadership as my husband, not to go, but His Holy Spirit arranged for this all to come about, but why did he? Would I ever know?

I recognized that Jesus Christ had everything to do with Sandra coming alive. There have been many instances of a person being raised from the dead in His name in third-world countries, as they believed and had faith.

There are several Biblical accounts of Jesus raising the dead and healing the sick. His disciples also did these miracles in His name. Here are three such recordings of this:

Peter, Jesus' disciple, raises Tabitha from the dead:

"Now, in Joppa, there was a disciple whose name was Tabitha, which in Greek is Dorcas. She was devoted to good works and acts of charity. At that time, she became ill and died. Peter put all of them outside, and then he knelt down and prayed.
He turned to the body and said, 'Tabitha, get up.' Then she opened her eyes, and seeing Peter, she sat up."

Acts 9:36-37a, 40

Jesus Raises a Widow's Son

[11]Soon afterwards,[a] he went to a town called Nain, and his disciples and a great crowd went with him. [12]As he drew near to the gate of the town, behold, a man who had died was being carried out, the only son of his mother, and she was a widow, and a considerable crowd from the town was with her. [13]And when the Lord saw her, he had compassion on her and said to her, "Do not weep." [14] Then he came up and touched the bier (the stand that the coffin was being carried on), and the bearers stood still. And he said, "Young man, I say to you, arise." [15] And the dead man sat up and began to speak, and Jesus[b] gave him to his mother. [16] Fear seized them all, and they glorified God, saying, "A great prophet has arisen among us!" and "God has visited his people!"

Luke 7: 11-16

Jesus Raises Lazarus from the Dead – A Brother to Martha

When Jesus arrived, He found everyone there, including His dear friend Martha, grieving and crying. Jesus showed compassion and love, as the scripture records:

38 Jesus, once more deeply moved, came to the tomb. It was a cave with a stone laid across the entrance. 39 "Take away the stone," he said. "But, Lord," said Martha, the sister of the dead man, "by this time, there is a bad odor, for he has been there four days."40 Then Jesus said, "Did I not tell you that if you believe, you will see the glory of God?"41 So they took away the stone. Then Jesus looked up and said, "Father, I thank you that you have heard me. 42 I knew that you always hear me, but I said this for the benefit of the people standing here, that they may believe that you sent me."43 When he had said this, Jesus called in a loud voice, "Lazarus, come out!" 44 The dead man came out, his hands and feet wrapped with strips of linen and a cloth around his face. Jesus said to them, "Take off the grave clothes and let him go."

John 11:35-44

Some theologians claim Jesus did not just weep because He was moved by the grief of Martha and others, but for having to call Lazarus back from having been in the presence of the Lord for four days.

What amazes me is what Jesus said to whoever follows Him:

"Truly, truly, I say to you, whoever believes in me will also do the works that I do; and greater works than these will he do, because I am going to the Father.

John 14:12 ESV

I never had a sister. It is only now, as I am writing this, that I realize that I felt as close to Sandra as anyone would be to an older sister.

As children, our parents visited them in Rosetown, SK, and later in Lang, SK. Her parents were older, like my parents, and lovely people.

My brother and I called her parents Aunt and Uncle. She and her brother referred to my parents in the same way. So we thought of them as our cousins, but they really weren't. Yet, genetics didn't factor in because all four of us were adopted. That's how love should work anyway, and it certainly did here.

Sandra was so beautiful, kind, and pleasant. She had a smile that would 'light up a room.' She was a role model for me, a 'beautiful swan' like I always wanted to become.

As adults, we spoke on the phone on occasion or shared a lunch. In 1978, when we had lunch, she was excited for me, like a sister would be, to find my birth mother, and she was eager to help me plan and find Helen, which I described earlier.

Jesus Has All Authority, and He Has Given it to You And Me.

I don't think that I would have experienced this if it had not been for that dream God gave me, where that cute little boy sitting towards me at the funeral luncheon morphed into a demon, hissing and laughing to let me know that Satan won.

As I looked at Sandra lying in that casket, 'righteous indignation' rose up within me coupled with grief and compassion, and I determined that Satan would not win –and he didn't!

Getting the Answer – *It Now Made Sense*

I often wondered why Sandra only came back momentarily and questioned why she did not stay longer. Was it because I became afraid? Or my lack of faith? Or did I have nothing to do with her not staying longer?

Six months had passed, and I still had no answer or no peace. When I learned that a missionary was to be speaking at a Pentecostal Church, sharing the miracles he'd witnessed in third-world countries, including raising the dead, I was eager to attend.

As I listened to his accounts of these miracles, he explained that we hardly experience them in affluent countries because we do not just simply exercise the authority that we have in Jesus' name, nor do we have a 'childlike faith' as they have.

After the service, he was selling his book about this. I stopped to speak with him about what happened with Sandra and why it was only for seconds that she came alive, and then nothing.

He smiled and said, "My dear, when you exercised your authority in Christ as you did, she had to come back, but she had already been in the presence of the Lord for too long, and she did not want to stay."

Well, that made perfect sense. I had thought perhaps that would be the reason, but this was confirmation. Yes, she'd love to have been back with her husband and her daughter and family to alleviate their grief, but she saw the 'bigger picture' of God's plan in their lives and knew that one day they'd understand and join her. This scripture explains why we do not see the 'big picture.'

12"We don't yet see things clearly. We're squinting in a fog, peering through a mist.
But it won't be long before the weather clears and the sun shines bright! We'll see it all then, see it all as clearly as God sees us, knowing him directly just as he knows us."

1 Corinthians 13:12 MSG

Chapter 18
What Would 1996 Have in Store? –
Well, It was a Lot!

Another Baby is on the Way! – *This Could Be Another Crisis!*

That spring, Lin told me that she was pregnant and the father of her child was Chris, her new boyfriend. I knew she was cheating on Chris with Donny. Chris realized she was, so he left when he heard she was pregnant. Lin always said that Chris was the father.

I moved Lin closer to me before baby number two arrived. I found her an apartment in a two-bedroom four-plex, about ten blocks from our home. I furnished it and got another crib and all that's needed for the arrival of a new baby.

Lin found out she was having a boy this time. She told me about a dream she had two nights in a row. She described her dream: "I just finished delivering my baby, and the nurse asked me, "What are you going to call your baby?"

I told her, "I don't know." Then I heard a voice say, "His name shall be Jonathan Peter!"

The next night, she had the same dream, and Lin determined that it was God who gave her this dream. Lin did obey God and named her son Jonathan Peter.

For me, this was reassurance that God was with us and he was watching over this little boy, yet to arrive. I knew we'd need Him.

Something is Off! – *The Arrest!*

In the spring of 1996, Chuck began acting weird, leaving notes around for me. For example, I found one of them in a pot I was about to cook in, and when I approached him about this behavior being 'unacceptable' and asked for an explanation as to why he was doing that, he had no reasonable answer. Telling him it had to stop only resulted in him getting angry.

One of those times, I decided to take a time-out from what was becoming an argument, and as the front door closed behind me, I heard his coffee cup smash against it.

I was going to be sure that would never happen again, as I had zero tolerance for that. I called the police and gave them a report. It was a long weekend in May, and they picked him up and charged him, and he spent three nights there before court.

I decided that God wouldn't want me to stay in this marriage, which up to that point was around 6.5 out of 10, but had just taken a nose dive to a 1 out of 10.

I had previously told him that we would be done if I ever saw him cross-dress, as he knew that I had zero tolerance for this disgusting behavior. After Chuck was gone during this time, Caine told me that one time, he did catch him, which disgusted me.

So I am on my own again. Chuck got an apartment, and we both had lawyers. He had a No Contact Order against him, so that was good for me. His charge was stayed, so he had no record, which was 'which was a relief for him.

Jonathan Peter is Born – *God, Please Always Watch Over Him!*

August 14, 1996, Caine had Charlene with him at the hospital, and they were in the waiting room while I was in the delivery room with Lin. The doctor and the nurse had just finished delivering this beautiful baby boy, who was lying on the delivery table between her legs, not yet breathing, while they were chatting, I yelled out, "Get that baby breathing!" which they then did. What the heck were they doing? I had no idea!

They had to put Jonathan in the Neonatal Intensive Care Unit (NICU), which I thought if they'd gotten him breathing right away, he wouldn't have needed to be observed there.

After all, he was over seven pounds, and Lin was not using alcohol or drugs at that time, as she was around me most of the time. At that time, Lin still had enough sense to realize that using them could harm her developing baby.

Jonathan was a very alert and beautiful baby boy, so there was nothing wrong with him, thank God! I will never forget visiting Lin with Charlene in the NICU. Charlene was staring at her mom as she held Jonathan, and then Charlene put her three-year-old hands on her hips and, looking sternly at her mom, said with a 'voice of authority, "'Put him back!"

Charlene was not going to be four years old for another five months, and she already knew that her mother would not be able to care for him and that he'd be in danger.

237

I was not yet that aware until a few months later how dangerous that would be, but she knew! As I found out later, Charlene was already privy to things that no child should ever see or experience, some of which I will share with you later.

Bringing Jonathan Home – *A Helicopter Grandma for Sure*

I was taught by my parents to hope for the best and prepare for the worst. Will faith, hope, and love be enough for this scenario to be successful?

Jonathan was such a beautiful baby and so easy to manage. Charlene loved him and was looking out for him. If he needed changing or she thought he needed a bottle, she'd say, "Grandma, Jonathan needs this or that." On the other hand, Lin seemed totally disengaged in his care. I would encourage or outright tell Lin to do this or that for Jonathan.

On a usual Sunday supper at my home, Lin and the children were over. Jonathan was a few weeks old. I had placed his infant seat in the Captain's chair near our dining room table while we were having supper. Soon, Jonathan began to cry as he needed changing or a bottle, so I decided not to go to him and waited to see what Lin would do.

Lin did not make a move, nor did I. Finally, Charlene got up and walked over to him and, standing in front of Jonathan again with her little hands on her three-year-old hips, said in a very firm voice, "Jonathan, I am not your mother!" This was a very telling moment, and my heart sank.

I was still on my own, but fortunately, I had started a counseling business on the side and was managing well enough financially. I still had time to monitor Lin's situation, but not totally.

Heading for a Divorce – *It Will Soon be Behind Me!*

There was still a No Contact Order in place, but Chuck must have heard that Lin had her baby, so he sent her flowers and a card to welcome her new daughter. He forgot she just had a boy.

Towards the end of August, I received a call from the Pastor at the church we were attending. He told me that Chuck was receiving counseling from him.

I knew his wife as a co-worker when I was a nursing instructor. They were Jamaican and catered to the Jamaican community. They ministered to Chuck and seemed to have a direct line to the Creator.

A part of me was glad Chuck was being helped, but I did not entertain going back to him.

Chuck's friend came to my home to retrieve his two cats to take to him. I just wanted the divorce over with and to pretend that this marriage never happened.

The divorce papers were prepared, and it would be simple. I had a prenuptial agreement in place, and Chuck had nothing, so it was simply a matter of signing the papers, and it was all over with. I'd just 'chalk it up' to my having made a very bad decision, and God would forgive me, and life would go on.

239

On a Saturday morning at the end of August 1996, as I sat with my coffee, I thought I needed to be busy today. I was going to the lawyer's office after the long weekend to sign the divorce papers. Usually, when I am stressed or facing a crisis, I get very busy. That is often when the house gets an extra good cleaning, but I didn't have the energy for that.

So I got The Leader-Post newspaper to find the list of Garage Sales that were on and decided I'd go to as many as possible. I'd have a day to myself. I checked on Lin and the children, and off I went.

It was around 9:00 p.m. on that Saturday evening when I was again sitting at the kitchen table and being tired out from my running around to garage sales when I heard in my spirit the Holy Spirit speaking to me gently but firmly, "Arlene, my daughter, I allowed you to divorce Wayne but this time it is different. You are NOT to divorce Chuck."

I did not want to hear this, but I had come far enough along in my walk with the Lord that I knew that it was Him, and so I went to bed feeling disheartened. That night, I had one of those 'God dreams' that I get from time to time.

The Dream and the Interpretation

Miracle # 11: – "The Deliverance."

In the dream, I was walking along a mountainside, leading a group of young children down it. I was taking them on an outdoor excursion like one sees when a Daycare leader is taking a group of children outside for a walk.

The path had reddish sandy soil on it and wasn't very wide. It was a generous path, but you had to be careful walking on it because if not, you could easily slip off of it.

I looked downward to my left to see a beautiful, rather shallow body of water that looked like a very large pond. It was as clear as glass and turquoise blue in color.

In this beautiful body of water, there appeared a very large snake with three smaller snakes swimming alongside it. I became very alarmed.

I recognized that this was evil and the children should not see what I was about to do, so I asked the children to line up and face the mountainside while I dealt with this situation, telling them that it was not going to take long.

The children were not to turn around or witness what was about to take place. They were not told that it was evil or what it was!

Then it was like I had a very large 'spiritual gaff' in my hand, and with it, I firmly grasped the back of this large snake's head so it could not get away. Then I carefully guided it towards the three smaller snakes and watched as, one by one, they were consumed by this large snake.

With that being accomplished, I told the children that they could now turn around, and we continued on our walk.' I woke up.

The Interpretation

As is the case when I have these dreams, the Lord will give me the meaning of it or the interpretation of it. Usually, the interpretation comes right away, and such was the case here.

God always tells a story to the recipient because He wants us to get it. He wants to direct our path, and He will do that when we ask Him to.

There is always symbolism in these dreams, and so it was throughout the Bible. Whenever you are given one of these dreams, it will have a reference in scripture. A dream from God is a gift from Him. It may not always seem like that since it can be a warning, or it can show you something that'll occur in the future that you'll need to wait for it to come to pass.

No one enjoys waiting, particularly if it is a blessing that's coming. I knew right away that the large snake was Satan, the Great Deceiver, and the three smaller snakes were demons who had been assigned to Chuck. These demons were getting their orders from their 'Father of Lies,' the large snake.

The children in the dream were there to demonstrate that these 'evil spirits' are after our children. They'd attacked Chuck as an innocent child, and they didn't want to let go of him.

There is more to Chuck's story that I learned from him later on in our lives together, but what I knew at that point was that the abuse done to him by his mother, dressing him up as a girl and giving him the name Dorothy, had warped and damaged his psyche as a child. Confusion is one of Satan's greatest tools that he uses to deceive innocent children.

Now, as an adult, Chuck continued to 'role-play' this nonsense. Chuck's innocence had been stolen. Certainly, some warped sexual pleasure was attached to this, too.

Demons will torment their victim because that is their mandate. They attack your sexuality through sexual abuse and other perversions, which alter their victim's persona. Persona is how that person presents himself or herself to the general public.

They attack one's soul because our sexuality is tied to our soul. Only the love of God can set them free and give them an abundant life. This can only happen when you submit your will to God's will for your life.

Jesus said that He has given us authority over demons, and in this dream, I exercised His authority. I was ensuring that Satan was not going to steal these children's innocence and that these three snakes, which were demons, were going back to their daddy, the Father of Lies.

The three snakes attached to Chuck were:

1.   Perversion, having been sexually abused

2.   Addictions

3.   Death (Hell). They have attached themselves to millions of people, and they do not even realize it, because they're kept in the dark. They need to be free. Jesus came to set the captives free, and He announced in the synagogue the fulfillment of this prophecy:

"The Spirit of the Lord is on me, because he has anointed me to proclaim good news to the poor. He has sent me to proclaim freedom for the prisoners and recovery of sight for the blind, to set the oppressed free, to proclaim the year of the Lord's favor."
Luke 4:18-21 New International Version (NIV)

Jesus also said:

"I assure you and most solemnly say to you, anyone who believes in Me [as Savior] will also do the things that I do, and he will do even greater things than these [in extent and outreach] because I am going to the Father."
John 14:2 Amplified Bible

Yet, the Lord showed me that these demons are subject to Him just like death is. Through this dream, they were now dealt with, and Chuck was free.

Of course, I knew that this did not mean that he was totally healed, but free. I realized that Chuck's healing would be ongoing for a lifetime, at least in some capacity, as it is with me and all of us. There would be temptations or struggles at times because we are flesh and not all spirit, and it is the flesh that is weak, but His Spirit is there to help us.

Jesus Christ is the Light of the world, and His light will never be extinguished. He is our Healer, Bondage-breaker, Deliverer, and Savior, and He is our peace, our Shalom.

My Personal War – *My Spirit versus My Flesh –* *Abba Father Knows Best!*

As I lay awake after having this dream, I had to be honest; I still wanted to get this divorce. I didn't want to deal with the struggle that could lie ahead. I thought God would not hold it against me if I got this divorce.

There'd been enough burdens and struggles in my life already, and now Lin was a continuing challenge for me to deal with. There were times that I wished He'd quit giving me these dreams.

I thought again about getting the divorce and signing the papers, and I recalled the question that the disciples of Jesus asked Him about divorce, "Why was it that Moses gave petitions of divorce in his day?"

Jesus simply answered that it was because of the hardness of their hearts. I didn't want a hardened heart. I knew I needed to be in His will, and I knew what it was I needed to do.

I lay there and prayed as Jesus taught us to pray, and then I fell back to sleep.

The Lord's Prayer

9Our Father in heaven, hallowed be your name.[a]10Your kingdom come, your will be done,[b]on earth as it is in heaven 11Give us this day our daily bread,[c]12and forgive us our debts, as we also have forgiven our debtors. 13And lead us not into temptation, but deliver us from evil.[d]

Matthew 6: 9-13 ESV

Chapter 19
Our Truth and Reconciliation – His Way is Always Best

The Pastor called me the next day, Sunday, to tell me that Chuck was repentant and that he loved me very much and wanted to get back with me. He asked me if I would pray about it and consider that. He emphasized that God can heal a 'wounded heart' and bless our marriage.

From how the Lord spoke to me the evening before and then this dream, I knew what God's will was in this matter, so I said, "Yes, I will think about it and pray and get back to you."

I soon called back and agreed to the marital counseling he'd suggested. So we began that process and went to their church with Lin, Charlene, and Jonathan.

Back Together – *Starting All Over Again.*

Chuck was back at my home and gave up his apartment. In the fall, Chuck and I continued at the Seminary at Briercrest, SK. I had shared with one of our professors about the incident of the No Contact Order and what had happened with Chuck and me. I asked for prayer.

Now that we were back together and again attending classes, he and his assistant weren't supportive of Chuck in his recovery, and they wanted to see him expelled. The Dean was supportive of us, so we continued and graduated, even though a cloud hung over us.

After Chuck died, this professor let me know that he never understood that we were just married when we went to the Seminary. I had forgiven him, as we all need His forgiveness.

To my knowledge, no one was ever privy to the issues of his 'cross-dressing,' but if he reads my book, he will know now.

We'd Be A Team Effort!

Chuck loved me very much, and I knew it when he proposed to me. I know I saw in my spirit what was going to unfold with Lin, and likely Jock had an inkling of that; hence his getting 'cold feet.'

I positively knew that in the future, Chuck would be with me. Now, I had renewed confidence that Chuck would help me. God knew that all along. God is love, and He gives us the capacity to love ourselves and others.

"Anyone who does not love does not know God because God is love."
1 John 4:8

Our Healing Journeys

Chuck and I were now doing well in our healing journeys. I never did witness any further bizarre behaviors, and he was certainly healing more and more from a chaotic and highly abusive childhood that was never exposed until all of this happened. His secrets were now in the Light.

As he progressed through the Seminary, he began having flashbacks of more of his abuse that had been pushed down. One horrific flashback was when he was remembering his dad sodomizing him as a minor. He doesn't know what age he was exactly, so I didn't pry further.

He shared that his parents did not let him socialize and kept him at home as much as possible. He said he had a lot of fear. Both parents threatened him from an early age not to tell what went on in their home, and that if he wasn't good, they'd have nuns come to take him away to the convent. They'd look out the window, saying they were coming for him, and he'd feel terrorized.

As mentioned before, Chuck had buried his parents three years earlier, and he'd forgiven them and believed that he'd see them in heaven. The damage they did was no longer a 'dirty secret' and no longer had 'a hold' on him as he was now free.

At times, I'd see him dissociate when he was triggered by his abuse, but it was only momentarily, thank God! Addictions are used to cover up our traumas, but in the end, they cause more traumas for ourselves and for those around us. Untreated, they lead to addictions, divorces, family breakdown, mental illnesses, crimes, suicides, and a new generation of 'wounded children' who carry the traumas and pain of their parents and families.

We all need to heal! We all need the Healer—Jesus. If you think you can do it all on your own, of course, you can do it that way, but for me, 'He is the Way.'

Chapter 20
Troubled Waters Ahead – LORD, We Need You!

Chuck and I continued commuting to the Seminary and enjoying that very much. Our greatest strength as a couple was that we both loved the Lord, and also our family and friends.

We had little time to do much other than study, do papers, and keep our home up.

On weekends, I kept tabs on how Lin was doing and, of course, how Charlene and Jonathan were.

Lin is Unraveling – *What's Coming Next?*

It was always a worry as to what was happening with Lin, Charlene, and Jonathan. Donny, Charlene's dad, was in Lin's life again, and she was going over to Donny's and his sister Victoria's place. I was very worried.

I had reason to believe that they were doing drugs and using alcohol, and the children would be 'at-risk,' but I had nothing concrete to go by.

It was late November or early December of 1996, on a weekend, when Lin was not at home with the children, and I could not shake this heavy feeling that something was not okay. So I called Regina Mobile Crisis and explained my concerns about the children and asked them to please go over to Victoria's home and check on Charlene and Jonathan.

I soon got a call from a Social Worker that they had checked on the children and found Jonathan was only in a diaper and had no more clothes, diapers, or formula. They were dropping Lin off at her apartment because she was under the influence and bringing the children to Chuck and me.

I quickly made a list for Chuck to run out to get formula, bottles, diapers, and a few clothes. Lin was informed that I would be in touch with her the next day, but due to this incident, Child Protection Services would be in contact with her to determine how they'd proceed.

Lin made promises to Child Protection Services and to us that she was not going to be using alcohol and drugs around the children, and she'd take really good care of the children. She was also to let Chuck and me know if she needed anything, as we were there to help her.

A Year That Changed Our Lives – *1996-1997*

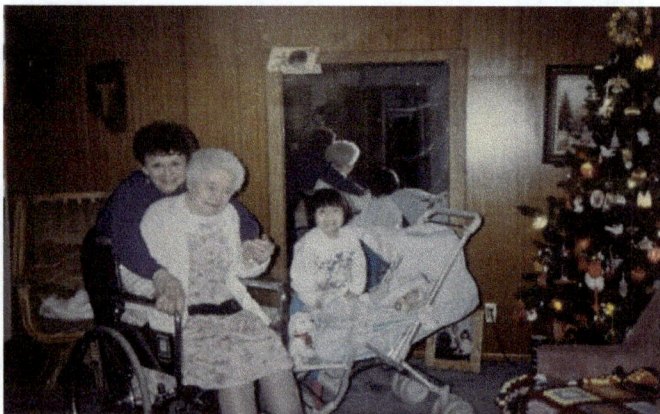

Christmas, 1996, Mom, me, Charlene, and Jonathan.

I had hoped that Lin would do better, but my hope was very thin. Chuck and I carried on our daily and weekly routine, checking in on Lin and the children daily.

Sundays were the same routine of Lin and the children coming over, along with my mom from the nursing home. They'd spend part of the afternoon with us, and after supper, Mom went back, and Chuck and I would drop Lin and the children off at her apartment.

What's Going On?

It was January 25, 1997. Charlene had now turned four years old. She was a very bright child, meeting her growth and development milestones very early. She had begun talking early, and I was amazed at how fluent and expressive she was.

In February 1997, Charlene began acting out, like taking Jonathan's formula, dumping the powder on the floor, and drawing on the walls with her crayons.

I knew she was troubled, and she was acting out, but she wouldn't say a thing when I asked her if something was bothering her.

Near the end of February, on a cold Sunday evening, I sat in the car while Chuck carried Jonathan in his infant seat into the apartment. As Lin was opening the door to her apartment, Charlene turned around and walked all the way back to the car.

I opened the car door and asked her if she was alright, and she said, "Grandma, I love you!"

Of course, I told her, "I love you too, sweetheart." I then told her it was very cold out and encouraged her to go inside with Mommy and Jonathan. She then turned around and went into the apartment.

When Chuck came to the car, I said my heart was heavy, and I could feel something was not good there.

The following Sunday, Lin asked me if she could go out with some of her friends. She said she had been unable to do so all week. I said, "Alright, as long as you're back for supper."

Charlene wanted me to go to the bathroom with her, so of course I did. When she was urinating, she began grimacing. I asked her if her potty hurt, and she started crying.

"I can't tell you, Grandma, don't make me tell," she said. She was crying uncontrollably. I held her until she settled and fell asleep.

Charlene was still asleep when Lin came back. I told her what happened when Charlene was going to the bathroom and what Charlene's reaction was. Lin said that she knew she was not wiping herself very well, and she'd been giving her heck about it, so it's likely that's why she reacted that way. Lin said she'd give her a warm bath to help when she got home.

On March 02, 1997, as I was putting on her boots and getting her ready to go back home, I noted some bruising around her ankles. I asked her, "Charlene, how did you get these marks around your ankles?"

Lin heard me ask her this and called out as she hurried into the kitchen, "Oh, I can tell you what happened there. She was playing with her cousins, and Blue-jean (this boy's nickname) was over. They were playing, tying each other up with a skipping rope, and he started dragging her around. When I untied her, she had these marks on her."

I didn't want to get Charlene upset by asking her if that was true, but I told Lin that she'd better ensure that this sort of thing was not going on, as she knew I didn't think much about her hanging around Victoria's home.

Victoria was Charlene's Auntie, and her three girls were her cousins. I'd mentioned them earlier when Donny brought the girls over for supper without Victoria.

I told Lin that I wanted an outing with Charlene this coming Saturday to take her for a haircut and that we'd go to McDonald's afterwards. I said I'd pick her up at 10:30 a.m. on Saturday, March 08th.

'I Have An Evil Mommy!' *Did I Hear That Correctly?*

I called Lin Saturday morning around 10:00 a.m. to let her know I was coming. Lin told me she had already given her a haircut.

I asked, "How's that?" Lin told me that she got hold of a pair of scissors and started cutting her hair. I insisted that it may need to be tidied up a bit. I asked her to get Charlene in her snowsuit, and I was on my way.

When I pulled up in front of the apartment, I found Charlene close to the street, sitting on top of a large snow bank left there from the streets being cleared of snow.

253

As soon as she saw my car pull up, she jumped off of it and came running to me.

"Where is Mommy?" I asked.

"She's in there with Daddy," replied Charlene.

I decided to just take Charlene to the car. As I was buckling her into her seat, she said to me, "Grandma, I love you!"

"I love you, too, sweetheart!" I replied.

Then she said, "Grandma, I need to come and live with you! Can I come and live with you?"

I said to her, "Why would you need to come and live with me, sweetheart?"

She responded, "Because I have an evil mommy!"

'Oh my Lord,' I thought, 'What is going on?' I didn't want to believe what I just heard. Alarm bells went off. I will never forget that exchange with Charlene—never!

I responded to her by telling her that after we had our haircuts, we'd go for lunch, and we would talk about her coming to live with Grandma. I reassured her that if she needed to come and live with Grandma, she would for sure.

Charlene was very clear about what she needed and why she needed to come and live with me. At lunch, she shared enough of her abuse, which was so troubling that I called Chuck. He met me where I was, and we agreed it was necessary to go to Mobile Crisis, and Charlene would not be returning home.

Once at Mobile Crisis, a childcare worker interacted with Charlene. They concluded that we needed to keep Charlene for now, and they'd let Lin know that there'd be an investigation. Chuck and I were instructed to take Charlene to the Regina General Hospital to be examined by a pediatrician, since they were concerned that she had been sexually abused.

That pediatrician came late in the evening, and from my medical background, I knew that his examination of her was very cursory. He did note that she was talking normally, but as soon as he began asking her questions as to what happened, she would resort to gibberish. That was concerning enough for him to say we needed to have her in our care.

Chuck and I knew that nothing would be done until at least Monday, when Child Protection Services could be briefed, and the next steps would then be decided for both Charlene and Jonathan. Jonathan was almost seven months old. The fact that he was still in the care of their 'evil mommy' was very concerning.

I reflected on what the Pastor's wife said to me one Sunday at church. I was changing Jonathan's diaper in the infant change room when she shared with me her concern about him.

She said that Jonathan was more than 'a good baby' because she observed him when we were at church, that he didn't fuss or cry at all, and that wasn't normal. This woman was a co-worker of mine and taught nursing students obstetrics. She was very astute.

As I thought of what she'd told me, I recalled what the pediatrician told me about the Indigenous babies I saw at the Royal University Hospital in Saskatoon, SK, whose parents had burned them with cigarettes to condition them not to cry.

I was very worried for Jonathan, too, but there was nothing I could do over the weekend. I did feel that Mobile Crisis should have taken extra precautions and brought Jonathan to me as well. In hindsight, I wish I'd been more insistent, as it may have made a difference.

Over the weekend, Charlene was very concerned for Jonathan.

"Grandma, he needs to come to you," she kept repeating. She was sick with worry. She knew a whole lot more than I did, as you will learn.

'The Thing I Feared The Most' – *The Rest of My Life Passed Before Me*

I did my best to keep Charlene entertained and keep her mind off her brother. On Monday, I took her for lunch at Burger King so she could play on their play structure.

When we got home, there were two cars parked in our driveway. As we went through the front door, standing in the foyer was a Child Protection Worker and a Constable.

Chuck was standing there holding Jonathan, who was still in his snowsuit. Chuck had the biggest smile on his face, as if he had just been handed not his grandson but his own son.

For me, I saw the rest of my life pass before me, even though God had prepared me for what was to come. I felt what can only be described as 'profound sadness and grief' for what this all meant for Lin and her children.

There was no time to focus on that, as there were two precious children in need. We didn't have a crib for Jonathan, but we put him on our closet floor, which we padded very well, as a makeshift crib, until we came up with something better.

Chapter 21
You Have Planted a Good Seed –
Now Walk Away…

That night, as I lay in bed with my thoughts with the children and Chuck already asleep, I heard the Lord speak to me, "My daughter, you have planted a 'good seed'. Now take your hands off the plow and devote yourself to these children that I have now put into your care." (*that is Chuck's and my care*).

When the Lord speaks to me, He will use words and phrases that I do not use, such as plow, planted a 'good seed', and the like. In this way, I know in my spirit that it is His Great and Holy Spirit directing me, comforting me, or saying whatever is needed in that moment. Lin had her addictions and serious mental health issues that would take a long time to overcome, if ever, and the children would be grown u*p by then.*

Regina Children's Justice – *The Injuries Found On Their Bodies*

I took Charlene down to the police station to have photos taken of her injuries. Charlene had to be examined by the Children's Justice doctors.

When one doctor asked Charlene how she got the marks on her body, she said, "Mommy burned me with a knife, and it was a very hot knife!" She had also burned Jonathan, but the burns were not deep enough to cause scarring. Charlene's burns were deep enough to leave scarring.

The doctor asked her how she got these marks around her ankles, and she told them, as she'd told me, that Mommy tied Jonathan and her up. The constable assigned to our case told me that in the days ahead, Charlene would tell me more and more as she felt safe to do so. She was absolutely correct because she did, and it was appalling.

The constable also told me that they (police officers) see these situations all the time, and nothing good comes out of them. The children are returned to their parents. She then added, "Some people live their lives differently than you and me."

My thought was, 'What?? Oh my God! No!!! Is this how the Child Protection and Children's Justice reconcile these awful situations?'

Children's Justice Had Their Own Agenda

It soon became apparent that those we were connected with to help Charlene and Jonathan had no intention of actually keeping her children safe from her.

It was so bad that I had to go to court to fight them and keep the children safe. I finally launched a lawsuit in July 2005 that was still alive until 2012. It went on for seven years.

Those seven years are certainly an integral part of my Memoir, but for this book, I will not go over the details of it as it is very triggering for me and could also be for my readers.

That part of my Memoir is, of course, very important considering the seriousness of it.

I have a website that has been professionally revised under my business name, Anchor Inn Rehabilitation and Counselling Center, at this link: www.anchorinn-hope.com.

Instead of having two additional websites, I have added details of what transpired at these two tabs: The Demands of Justice and Voices of the Bruised-Reeds.

Grief and More Grief

One day, the reality of the situation hit me very hard. I thought, here is our little girl that Wayne and I adopted and loved like our own, who was suffering from her own addictions and serious mental health issues, and had now lost her children. To comprehend what she and others had done to her children was another huge layer of grief, but that day, I cried not for her children but for Lin, as a mother who could not parent them, and they would likely not be together.

I had to protect them from their mother, and my focus had to now be on her children as I'd exhausted all my efforts to help Lin, and God knew it.

Then I had to witness Charlene's grief and her post-traumatic flashbacks, her overwhelming anxiety, her screaming, and my needing to settle her, and the times I had to find her in the house because she was hiding. When I found her, she would be in a fetal position in what is known as catatonic stupor. Then I'd sit beside her and gently rub her arm to ground her and tell her that she was safe and Jonathan was safe and no one could hurt you or Jonathan now.

I never saw a child as traumatized as Charlene was, and she wasn't a patient or a client, but she was my granddaughter. To keep 'my head above water' and my sanity intact, I decided to get proactive and see if there was any government funding that I could get to start up a rehabilitation program for 'at-risk' Indigenous young adults and their families.

I could not help Lin because she was with people who were in gang activity and ritually abusing children, as is detailed on the tabs on my website. I was at odds with Children's Justice and Child Protection Services, who had their own agenda by setting the children up to have visits with their mother. Afterwards, I had to deal with the aftermath of Charlene regressing.

This was painful for her, and very painful for me to help her. Her grief and ours were continually being reactivated. She had no opportunity to consistently heal from the hell she had been put through.

It is even hard for me to write about this, but the story needs to be told because of the situations that children are left in and the overwhelmed justice and social services systems that cannot address these dire situations.

That is why they say and do things that they should never consider doing, nor should they ever turn a blind eye to these situations. What they did to Chuck and me, which is on my website, should never happen to grandparents, as we need their support. Instead, they maligned us and conspired to ruin us emotionally and financially. Thank God we had our faith and Jesus.

Chapter 22
Busy is Good – We Can Do This!

Chuck and I had to take a break from attending the Seminary full-time, but we were both determined to finish our Master's degrees at some point, as we had the children to focus on.

Mom was still coming over on Sundays from the nursing home, or we'd visit her at the nursing home for a meal like this photo below of Charlene, Jonathan, and me:

Dealing with Child Protection Services was a huge ongoing crisis. I felt that if I sat at home, I would sink into such a deep depression that one of my family members would also need to look for me somewhere in the house, only to find me in a catatonic stupor that I may never come out of. I was sure that I might not even want to come out of it to face all of this.

Now, that may sound rather extreme, but you need to understand that even with my training as a nurse and my education and experience in childcare and psychology, this situation was so over the top.

I never could have imagined what went on with Lin and her group and the children, but I kept finding out as Charlene kept sharing with me, just as the Constable told me she would.

A Wise Judge – *A No Contact Order is in Place.*

I filed a request with the Court of Queen's Bench for Charlene's parents to have No Contact with her, and a very wise judge granted it. This was quite rare.

This was the beginning of my struggles with Children's Justice's doctors and psychologists, who were aligned with the government's mandate. Things got uglier as time went on.

1998 – *Making Lemonade out of Lemons*

So I had already started a business called The Anchorage Counseling and Rehabilitation Center, but I went ahead and incorporated it as a non-profit to receive funding for operating rehabilitation programs for 'at-risk' youth and young adults and their families.

Then I wrote a ten-month program that was 'holistic' and geared to help a target group of 'at-risk' young adults and their children who represented my daughter Lin. I was unable to help her as I had tried and tried, but perhaps others like her were ready for help.

She certainly could take this rehabilitation program when and if she felt ready to. I named that program A Focus On The

263

Future – Guiding the Young. Now, I had to find funding. I found funding through Human Resources Development Canada (HRDC) to operate this program on a very low budget.

Since the participants were those who had had children and weren't coping well, like my daughter Lin, they'd be on welfare or social assistance. They were also at higher risk. If they were accepted into the program, then they had to get permission from their Social Workers to participate. If allowed to come into it, they were provided the financial means to participate.

We rented a wonderful facility on 11th Avenue and Smith Street, Regina, SK. I went to auctions on Saturday mornings to buy computers for all of the participants to have, bought a photocopy machine, chairs, tables, and more to be ready for when the program started.

The Lord was providing for all of this. Those who were instructors and counselors did this for a minimal amount of money as a wage since they believed in the value of this program.

Evil Intentions – *Catch Them If You Can – Or Her!*

Everything was going well until Regina Social Services realized I was the Director of The Anchorage, and it was I who developed the program and retained funding. Then the participants' Social Workers were told to tell their clients, who'd already been in the program for a few weeks, to get out, or they'd cut them off from their financial assistance.

I encouraged the participants to push back and say how it was helping them and tell their workers to back off, and they did back off because it was about to become newsworthy.

Once they realized that, they made it their goal to undermine me, the organization, and the program. They should have realized that they were going to be denying these First Nations' participants this healing program, who had already suffered enough historical traumas at the hands of both governments. They didn't care!

I knew that there would not be ongoing funding because once the 10 months were up, the program would be done. I was shocked that this was happening.

During that time, an HRDC person who was assigned to oversee the program did an attendance check one morning. She asked me to have one participant at a time come to the phone to identify themselves because she decided to do a 'roll call.'

This was highly unusual and was intended to intimidate the participants and undermine the program, should there be high absenteeism. They knew with this 'high risk' group that some may be using alcohol and drugs and not show up particularly early in the morning.

There were around 18 participants, and it so happened that morning, all of them were there. I looked up and said, "Thank you, Lord!" Now, that, too, was a miracle!

I was also notified that there'd be an onsite audit by the Canada Revenue Agency (CRA) during the program, which, again, was highly unusual. This was orchestrated by HRDC in cahoots with Regina Social Services. Everything was found to be in order.

They were finding it very hard to come up with a reason to shut the program down, and The Anchorage. Again, there are more details on my website, Anchor Inn: www.anchorinn-hope.com

Wayne is Dying – *Yet He'll Live Forever!*

By September 1998, the program had just gotten underway when I heard that Wayne was dying of prostate cancer. I felt no bitterness towards him. I had remarried and understood more about trauma and addictions, and why our marriage fell apart.

I had forgiven him. Still, he had been my husband, and we had brought two children into the world and adopted Lin as our own, and we dearly loved all three of them.

Visiting Wayne – *Saying Goodbye*

My first visit was when I walked into his room, and he had a lot of visitors, including his brother Jim. He looked surprised to see me. Then he said to everyone in the room, "I appreciate everyone coming, and please come back shortly, but Arlene is here, and I want to visit with her."

Wow! I felt very special that he cleared the room just for me, as something like that had never happened before. His asking others to leave so he could be with me was huge for him. I sat down beside him, and he asked me how I was doing and asked about our children and Lin's children because he knew they were in my care.

Then he closed his eyes and said to me, "Arlene, I am so sorry that I gave you such a hard life."

I wasn't going to say, "Oh, that's okay," because none of this was ever okay, so I sat there in silence, trying to formulate a genuine response.

I finally said something like, "Wayne, all that has passed is in the past. I have forgiven you. We will remember the 'good times' we had together and will always be thankful for our three children.

With that, he opened his eyes and agreed and smiled. We had a little more small talk, and I told him I would check in with him again, to which he said that'd be nice. I knew he had a girlfriend. I came to know that she was there a lot, but that did not stop me from visiting him.

My second visit was when I went there to find our sons visiting. We interacted and laughed, and it was like all the past 'pain and suffering' was gone. Lincoln called me that night and said, "Mom, us visiting Dad today was the best day ever!"

I was astonished at how he summed up our times together as a family as being the best day ever. His dad was critically ill and dying, and just because we felt like family again and had a few laughs, he thought that this was the best day ever.

Then, I realized that even though I was remarried, we were connected as a family again for a moment 'in time,' and it was that which Lincoln's spirit witnessed. Family is precious, a God-given gift to us. Addictions and the grief that ensues when divorce happens leave our children with deep wounds that never really heal. That realization that this day was Lincoln's best day ever was definitely bittersweet.

On my third visit, I popped up there and took Jonathan with me, who was now two years old. Charlene was likely in Daycare. During our visit, Jonathan was all smiles, and Wayne enjoyed seeing him. It was a short visit, and I soon left.

My fourth visit occurred when I dropped in to find Lin visiting him. He smiled that I'd come, and he asked me to come to his bedside, which was on the opposite side of where Lin was standing. He said to me, "Arlene, promise me that you will help our girl. She'll need your help." I promised him that I would help her and left before Lin did.

My fifth visit would be the last time that I was able to communicate with him. As I sat by his bed, a nurse came into the room and said, "Wayne, who is this lovely lady?"

He didn't know how to respond, and I said in a low voice, "I'm your ex-wife," and he said right away, "She's my ex-wife." The nurse said that it was so nice that I came to visit.

As I was about to leave the hospital, I bumped into our Pastor, and told him that Wayne was there. He asked where he was since he'd go and visit him.

That evening, the Pastor phoned me to say that he had visited Wayne and asked him if he wanted to accept Jesus as his Lord and Savior, and he answered as expected, "Why would I do that?"

Pastor told him why, and when he finished explaining this, Wayne said, "That sounds good to me. Let's do it!" It had to be sincere since Wayne never agreed to anything if he wasn't sure.

I told Lincoln and Caine about their dad accepting Jesus as His Lord and Savior, as they were familiar with John 3:16 and knew that Jesus saves people and heals people even today.

Shortly after the Pastor's visit, Lincoln said, "What's with Dad? He's up in his chair, joking around, and is like himself. Do you think he's healed?"

I said it's certainly possible, as God can do anything.

Visit number six was a Celestial Visit, a dream that was a preview of what was about to take place. In the dream, I felt myself going out of my bedroom window and traveling in space through the dark of the night, traveling on an upward, gentle incline. Then I saw in front of me, in the distance, three figures. One figure on the left disappeared, and there were only two.

As I got closer, I was able to see that those two figures were Jesus and Wayne. I was traveling and coming closer to them, but positioned behind them.

I saw that Wayne had his head on Jesus' left shoulder as Jesus had His arm around him. I became so excited trying to catch up to them when, all of a sudden, it felt like a roll-blind was pulled down, and I woke up.

As I lay on my bed, now fully awake, I knew Wayne was going home, and He'd be with Jesus. He had fears and anxieties in his life that were only treated with his addiction, and seeing him with his head on Jesus' shoulder, I was struck that even in death, as we are transported to heaven, Jesus is our Comforter, and He was comforting him.

He was now free of his sick and broken body and mind. His 'pain and suffering' and grief were left behind. I thought of these two scriptures, which are such a great comfort and promise for me, and I pray for you also:

*⁴He will wipe away every tear from their eyes, and death shall
be no more, neither shall there be mourning, nor crying, nor
pain anymore, for the former things have passed away."
Revelation 21:4 English Standard Version*

⁸He will swallow up death forever, and the Lord God will wipe away tears from all faces, and the reproach of his people he will take away from all the earth, for the Lord has spoken.
Isaiah 25:8 English Standard Version

I knew that the Lord was even comforting him as he had anxiety about dying, perhaps seeing so much death while in Fort San, from those who had tuberculosis, as he had. Only God knows, but I was so thankful to know that Wayne was being comforted on his journey home.

It was sometime later when I heard a sermon by Billy Graham where he said that when we die, an angel, likely our guardian angel, takes us into the presence of the Lord. I had always wondered who that third person was that I briefly saw before it disappeared, and then I knew and was convinced that the third figure was Wayne's angel.

My Seventh Visit

Before Wayne died, the Lord had shown me in a dream that Wayne was saved and would be going home with Jesus.

I decided to go and see him once again. I heard he had no intravenous and was in his last hours of life. I went up to his room, and no one else was there. Wayne was unresponsive and unable to speak.

I knew that our hearing is the last sense to leave our body, so I talked to him. I told him it was me. I said it will be alright because Jesus will be there to take you home where your mom and other loved ones are. I told him that one day I would be there too, and that our troubles and sadness would be over with.

I told him that I loved him and I had always loved him, and with that, he began to move and make an effort to say something, but he couldn't.

I said, "Just rest, Wayne. Everything will be alright." I said a short prayer with my hand on him. He seemed to relax, and I left—*until we meet again.*

Wayne was escorted by his angel into the presence of the Lord Jesus on October 08th, 1998.

The Funeral was a 'Wake'

There was a 'wake' instead of a funeral at Regina Beach. The hall was packed. I attended with my friend Pat. Jesus never had a funeral or a wake, but it is simply a gathering of remembrance and a time to communally grieve.

Wayne's brother-in-law, Jerry, was the only one on Wayne's side of the family who made an effort to speak to me. At one point, I went over to Wayne's siblings and spoke briefly to them.

As I was leaving, Jerry came to me and thanked me for all the Christmases and visits his family had at our home and the lovely meals I'd made. I told him that it was my pleasure because it was.

Jerry was a very fine man and a vice-principal of a high school in Calgary, AB. I never spoke to him again after that. I heard that he had died of malignant melanoma. He also died too early. Wayne would be sure to be there to greet him.

As I was leaving the hall from 'the wake,' I noticed on the table by the entrance a beautiful wooden box. Lincoln was sitting there. I opened the box and was taken aback to find inside it a plastic bag of Wayne's ashes.

I soon realized that Lincoln had made this lovely box to hold his dad's ashes in, so I slowly closed the lid and said to Lincoln that he'd made such a beautiful box.

Keeping the Promise! *Promise You'll Help Our Daughter!*

My first promise to help my daughter was to God, and the second one was to Wayne.

God told me to take my hands off the plow and walk away from Lin and focus on raising her children. Certainly, raising her children would be helping her.

Wayne knew that I had been helping Lin through her teens, helping her with her pregnancies, and being with her after she brought Charlene and Jonathan home. He knew she was unable to care for her children, and of course, he'd ideally want her to have her children, as I did, too.

I'd set her up several times so she could have a stable environment for the children. I found apartments for her, furnished them, and helped her financially. I had found counseling for her, but that didn't work out.

I kept Charlene when she had to go to the Indigenous rehabilitation center at Sandy Bay, Saskatchewan. This was a prerequisite for Child Protection Services to allow her to have Charlene. Now Lin had Jonathan, also.

Now I knew that Lin and others had abused her children and that she remained in her active addiction. I knew in my heart that

I could only promise Wayne to keep Lin's children secure, safe, and loved.

Nothing could change unless Lin became rehabilitated, clean, and sober. But I could still help 'at-risk' young adults like Lin who were ready to get help.

God Knew Best – *He Always Does!*

"A person's steps are ordered by the Lord. How, then, can anyone understand their own way?"
Proverbs 20:24

I could have never ordered these steps for myself, as I am certain most of us could not have ordered theirs. We have questions in our minds about how life will work out. It always has twists and turns; some we authored and others we didn't.

Yet, God saw it all beforehand:

"I knew you before I formed you in your mother's womb."
Jeremiah 1:5 NLT

This means that God knew you, and you are loved. He did not make a mistake. He gave us all 'free will' to choose our own path and to choose 'good over evil' or the opposite. Through every trial in life, He desires to guide us, but we must ask.

Yet, the 'good news' is that we can change our minds and go towards God at any time because He is right there and will always work with us. He did that with David in the Bible and so many others, and He continues to do that with me.

If I had kept going my own way and had gone through with divorcing Chuck, I would not have had the best 'helpmate' that a woman could have asked for. I know he felt I was that for him also.

273

Chuck was completely involved with me in raising the children. He was there to hold me when I was grieving, and he never grumbled if I needed him to go for diapers, make a bottle, or change a diaper.

When we had to go to court to resist Donny's filing of the 'Variation of the No Contact Order' to have contact with Charlene, Chuck acted as the kids' lawyer. The Saskatchewan Minister of Social Services, Child Protection, was backing Donny through Legal Aid to have access to Charlene.

The judge decided that the Saskatchewan Minister of Social Services was to submit the name of a psychologist to the court, and we, in turn, were to submit the same. From these two submissions, the judge would choose one to do an assessment on Charlene.

The reason this had to be done was because Chuck and I were maligned by Children's Justice and their doctors and psychologists. The Child Protection Services under the Saskatchewan Minister of Social Services refused to believe Charlene when she described what Mommy and Daddy did to her, but we know she was sexually abused, that Mommy burnt her with a really hot knife, that she was tied up with her baby brother Jonathan, and left alone. She vividly described how she jumped into the kitchen and pulled a knife out of the drawer, then sat on the floor, sawing her way through the ropes around her ankles, and then went to Jonathan to cut the ropes off of him. Charlene proceeded to comfort him, change his diaper, mix formula in his bottle, and feed him, all the while being three and four years of age.

Just picture this in your mind for a moment. Then realize why I had to go on the offensive.

The government didn't believe all of this, or that Charlene witnessed Aunty Victoria bury Jonathan alive by putting him in a garbage bag and burying him by placing him into a hole dug in one of their back yards. Then she told how Aunty Victoria pulled him out of the hole to save him just in time. This created for Charlene and the other children a 'trauma bond' with her auntie being a hero.

They said Chuck and I were influencing them and that Charlene had likely seen a bad movie. More details are on my website: www.anchorinn-hope.com.

Thankfully, this wise judge chose the psychologist that Chuck and I chose, Dr. Gerald Farthing, who is a seasoned registered clinical psychologist with a practice in Saskatoon, SK.

The judge also said that the psychologist could take as long as he needed before submitting his report.

We made a few trips to see Dr. Farthing, who even came to Regina to do a home visit. He was very professional and very thorough. He suggested doing psychological assessments on Chuck and me. He implied that it would be in our best interest to have this done, so we agreed to this.

When Dr. Farthing had completed his assessments, we met with him in his office. He said that you and I know what happened here, but if I provide the court with my report, they will fight it, and in the end, you will lose. So my report will never be submitted to the court until the children are all grown up. After all, the judge had told him to take as long as he liked to complete his report.

I asked him how his assessments of Chuck and me turned out, and he said they were just fine and said, "I never had a concern that they wouldn't be." Thank you, Dr. Farthing, for your professionalism and wisdom, and for protecting our grandchildren, Lin's children.

Chuck was very involved in helping me with these legal issues when they had to be done. When it came to disciplining the kids, we had some tension there, but we got through it.

We also had the program to complete by the end of June, 1999. Chuck was totally involved there also. The participants in the program mentioned he was patient and kind. I was the one who, at times, was the disciplinarian in the program, but many still called me Mom!

Chuck cared for the participants as he did his clients, and they often told him so. We were so busy with all that was 'on our plate' that we didn't have much time to ourselves. We learned to work together as a team because we had to! We loved our grandchildren and were family.

I couldn't have understood the journey that God had me on, but in retrospect, I now can. This scripture was so appropriate,

"How then can anyone understand their own way?"
Proverbs 20:24b.

The Participants Graduated

By the end of June 1999, the funding was pulled. Each participant got to take their computer home. They'd enjoyed

Home Economics like making fry bread, sewing jingle and ribbon skirts, and the like. There were traditional teachings and individual counseling, as well as group therapy.

They had recreational times of movies and popcorn, and they bonded well as a group. Some needed longer than 10 months, but we all celebrated their collective and individual successes in a graduation ceremony.

The funding agencies were all invited, but only one from HRDC came. She'd always been condescending and miserable, but she showed up, gave a couple of words, and left early.

Others were also sent invitations, like social workers, but not one attended. Perhaps they were told not to come or decided not to.

Towards the end of the program, I asked another HRDC government official that I had to deal with, the only pleasant one by the way, if she knew why the funding was pulled. She said, "Arlene, the only thing I can think of is that the program was too good!"

She was right, it was too good, no, it was excellent! Of course, I knew why the funding was pulled, which is detailed on my website: www.anchorinn-hope.com.

Chapter 23
The Children Grow up – Another on the Way!

Charlene had to be reassessed by a Saskatchewan Government psychologist at Child and Youth Services, who said Charlene could now have supervised visits with her mom at the Salvation Army.

There was not as much concern for us about Jonathan having these visits, although he had trauma too, but he was under a year of age. We were still concerned that Charlene would be triggered.

Charlene and Jonathan at 5 and 2 years old

Charlene and Jonathan at 6 and 3 years old

After these visits, Charlene began to regress, and we had to deal with the aftermath. Her trauma being reactivated was extremely concerning for us.

It is professionally unethical to force any child who has suffered trauma like Charlene to engage with their parent—when Charlene had identified her mom as one of those who had abused and traumatized her—to just see how things go. They should know and do know that it will not go well when they minimize or deny the effects of the child's abuse and take the word of their parent over what the child has told them. In addition, Children's Justice and Child Protection Services had the physical evidence to corroborate Charlene's story. Instead, they tried to frame Chuck and me.

They should have known better and pulled their 'professional heads' out of the political sand.

Baby # 3 – *December 21, 1999 – Keep Her Safe!*

Lin had now given birth to a sweet little girl, whom she named Kayla Christine. I learned of this just before Kayla was born, and there was no way that Child Protection Services was going to approach Chuck and me to take her.

One thing I was pleased about was that they knew not to give Kayla to her mom because if they did and something happened, they'd have me to answer to, and that would not be pleasant.

Fortunately, Kayla was put in a foster home at birth. We later learned the foster woman's name was Judy, and we called her Mama Judy. Lin started to have supervised visits with Kayla at the Salvation Army, and Chuck brought Jonathan there also.

What Would 2000 Bring? – *A New Start but the 'Same Old'*

Chuck and I managed to complete our Master of Arts degrees, and my sons came to the exercises. We were glad to have this behind us as we were over the top busy.

I had heard that Canadian Heritage, along with the Aboriginal Healing Foundation, was joining their resources to implement youth centers across Canada to meet the needs of 'at-risk' Aboriginal youth and young adults. These centers were to be called Urban Multipurpose Aboriginal Youth Centers (UMAYC).

One of these centers was to be established in Regina, SK. There was an advertisement calling for proposals to be submitted to an Aboriginal youth panel that had been selected in Saskatoon to review all of the submitted proposals. They would choose one of them that they determined would best help their peers.

When You've Been Kicked Down – *Get Up and Keep Going!!!*

I became very excited hearing about this center and the possibilities it could offer for the First Nations' Peoples of Canada. I already knew how successful the first program had been.

I knew it would be a lot of work, so I passed it by Chuck and he said, "Let's do it!" It felt like a 'new beginning.'

I got busy and wrote our proposal under the organization, The Anchorage Counselling & Rehabilitation Center Inc.

This program, a revised version of the first one, was titled: Healing the Nation-One Family At A Time. Naturally, I was concerned that, should our proposal be chosen and Regina Social Services got wind of it, all hell could break loose. They'd conspire once again to undermine and sabotage our efforts.

It was July 25, 2000, and I had just received a phone call from Saskatoon, SK, with the news that we were awarded the opportunity to implement this program. It was a beautiful summer day, and I felt like doing cartwheels as I was so ecstatic. I knew that this target group needed this rehabilitation program, and obviously, this Aboriginal youth panel saw that as well.

Mary, a social worker whom I'd hired to work as a counselor, would be involved in the program should we be awarded the UMAYC. That day, she asked me if I'd like to walk with her to the bank as she had just moved to Regina and had an appointment to transfer her accounts.

I said I'd love to go for a walk. It was a lovely sunny day as we walked to the main branch of the Royal Bank on 11th Avenue. Mary went in for her appointment while I sat by the windows that faced 11th Avenue. I still felt on 'cloud nine' as I sat there waiting for her.

As I sat there, I began to hear music. I thought it was music being pumped into the bank, but I immediately recognized it as Christian music.

I was processing this in a matter of seconds. I thought it quite odd that a bank would play Christian music.

I quickly glanced at the television suspended above me, which was there for clients to watch, and noted that what was on

281

it was a sporting event of dirt bike riding. At this point, I thought I'd try to identify the artist singing, and I became quiet and focused.

Miracle # 12: – The Angels are 'Out of This World!'

As I have shared with you so far, I have had dreams and visions, and smelled the fragrance of the Lord and witnessed Helen being miraculously healed and even Sandra coming alive when I called her forth, but I never expected this.

As I listened, I heard them. They were angels. Yes, you heard me right, angels!

They were singing so melodiously, and the sound was 'out of this world.' I mean 'out of this world' as you'd never hear this on earth.

They were singing notes at a pitch that humanly could not be made on earth! They were singing over and over and over again the same lines so beautifully:

"He's all you need, He's all you need, Jesus is all you need, He's all you need, He's all you need, Jesus is all you need…

I heard this over and over again, and even though the words were repetitive, the sounds changed, and it was incredibly beautiful.

There had to be thousands and thousands of angels singing. I had heard of throngs of angels and thought this is what they must be. Their voices emanated pure joy! I was in a 'Holy presence' and being ministered to, for some reason. After about 15 minutes, I saw Mary coming towards me from her meeting, and when she got to me, I said in a low voice, "Sit down, Mary, and listen to this."

As she and I listened together, there was nothing. I so wanted her to hear what I'd just been listening to, but it was over. She said, "Arlene, that was just meant for you." I thought, 'Why, God, did you want me to be ministered to like this?'

I realized later on why God gave me this experience, and it was because He knew exactly what I was about to face with these government funding agencies, again. He knew how challenging the road ahead would be, and I needed this experience as a comfort. I will always hear them singing in my spirit until I hear them in concert, in person.

I looked up the following scripture that speaks of 'throngs of angels':

> *"The invisible Jerusalem is populated by throngs of festive angels and Christian citizens. It is the city where God is the Judge, with judgments that make us just. You've come to Jesus, who presents us with a new covenant, a fresh charter from God."*
>
> *Hebrews 12:22a MSG*

We Are in the News – *God's Timing!*

The awarding of the UMAYC program to The Anchorage made the news in The Regina Leader Post. I was concerned that when this news reached Regina Social Services, they'd start their nonsense all over again.

There was a time lag for news to get out because the decisions were all made in Saskatoon. We were busy getting staff in place, and I had found a wonderful facility on Broad Street for the UMAYC right across from Regina Social Services. We were interviewing potential participants and admitting them.

Mom Went Through the Tunnel – *And Dad Was There to Meet Her*:

Life continues, and so does death. It had now been 14 years since Dad passed. Mom died peacefully in the nursing home at age 92 years, and Dad was waiting for her to come through that tunnel because the Holy Spirit showed him that before he died.

Gordon knew Lincoln was wonderful with woodwork, and he asked him to make Mom's casket. I was shocked he did that, but Lincoln agreed to do it.

Lincoln found someone to do the upholstery and lining of it. It was absolutely beautiful. He even had a beautiful cross applied to the head of it. I wish I had gotten a photo of it.

Mom's funeral was held at the church we were attending. At the graveside, four-year-old Jonathan said, "Grandma, when is it taking off to go to heaven?"

I may have said that the flight was delayed, but I can't recall for sure exactly how I answered that.

They Know! – *They're the 'Devil in Disguise' –Not Really, They're in the Open!*

At this time, I also bought a home for The Anchorage as a counseling center for our regular counseling services. I had money from my inheritance from my parents, which included Uncle Charlie's money that they held in trust for my brother and me, which enabled me to purchase it.

I purchased it from a woman by way of a back-up mortgage, known as a second mortgage. She believed in our vision for this at-risk group and was prepared to do this. We had determined that this property would prove to be a great investment for The Anchorage.

One would think that the governments involved in aiding the success of this program would not go out of their way to disrupt it, undermine it, and finally destroy it, just because they had a political vendetta against me. They were relentless and vicious and used two of the First Nations' persons whom I'd hired to get their dirty work done. It is known as a conspiracy.

I have no intention in the writing of this book to tell you of all the incidents that were occurring. Some of the same antics were going on with social workers telling the participants, their clients, to 'pull out' of the program or risk losing their financial support.

Yet, to the dozen or so Social Workers who signed a joint letter of support for their clients to take this program, noting that it was benefiting them, I thank you!

This group of Social Workers dared to support their clients against possible political backlash. Some participants who had their financial support threatened did exit the program. Others dug their heels in and stayed. They said if they got cut off from their financial support, they'd go to news outlets to tell them what happened. It is pretty sad that they even had to consider this.

We all have heard that politics can be dirty, and it sure was here! I had visits from persons from the Aboriginal Healing Foundation and Canadian Heritage. Regina Social Services had their own way of undermining the program by ensuring one of their own got hired to do their dirty work.

They had a mission to accomplish—get rid of The Anchorage at any cost! Their joint mission should have been to assist in every way possible to rehabilitate this target group, since it was they and the organized churches that were responsible for the historical generational traumas that they had inflicted on the First Nations peoples through the implementation of the Residential School System.

Yet, they were bent on undermining this program that was deemed by some of their Social Workers as doing their clients much good.

Shame on those who did this! Hopefully for you who participated in this and to those who never saw fit to provide these participants and me justice through the courts, I hope you feel shame and repent to God, your Creator, who saw it all!

Yet, He gets the last word. Yes, He always does!' I know He'll still get 'the last word' on this one, and I am excited to see it unfold.

Grafted-in x 2 – *Confirmed! – You're 'one of us!'*

The Anchorage, as a non-profit organization, had a Board of Directors who were mostly First Nations people.

As events were unfolding and we all could see what was going on, realizing that this program and center would be over with before it barely even began, Erick, one of our Directors, said to me, "Arlene, you're one of us, because they're treating you like us!"

That surprised me, and I said, "How's that?" He indicated that their treatment of me and The Anchorage happens to us over and over again. When we get something really good happening for our people, they undermine us and find a reason 'to shut us down.'

I asked, "What about the First Nations peoples in government that are aligned with the government to undermine your efforts?"

He said, "We call them Apples, because they're red on the outside but white on the inside!"

I'd never heard this analogy before, but it made sense. It was this day, when Erick said, "Arlene, you're one of us!" that I had an epiphany, and said, "Yes, you're right, Erick, I am one of you!" That day, I realized for myself that I'd been 'grafted-in' into a very small portion of their historical trauma, which I have come to name as Historical Post-traumatic Familial Devastation (HPFD).

There didn't need to be anything official to be 'grafted-in' because for me, like with Erick, it just was!

White on the Outside – *But Red on the Inside!*

When we adopted Lin, it seemed she was more 'grafted in' to our family and our culture than we were to hers. Yet, this experience solidified that I was 'grafted-in' to her people, culture, and in part, able to experience their historical pain.

I thought of Lin's Auntie Emma, her dad's sister, whom I'd met. She had taken into her care children of her family members to raise them, just as I did with Lin's children. When I met her, she thanked me and shook my hand. She was happy that I brought

Lin back to meet her dad, who was on his deathbed. I felt a deep connection to this woman.

We All Have Trauma!

A good friend of mine who is a psychologist said, "Arlene, we all have trauma!" I never stopped to recognize that, but I totally agreed. We all come by it differently, and we should not compare the severity of our trauma with anyone else's. Yet, we need to heal enough so we don't cause trauma to others in our family. The cycle must be broken, or we all stay broken.

I was proud to have been recognized as 'one of them!' I didn't feel alone, but somehow connected in their plight to receive equitable treatment and to heal from their historical trauma and racism. It was not exactly the same, of course, but it felt somewhat similar.

In reading my memoir, which may end up being an autobiography, you can see that I, too, had my own traumas. There's transference of trauma when we've not entered into our own 'healing journey.' Those in the caring professions, like medical personnel, psychologists, and psychotherapists, need to heal enough from their own traumas in order to help others.

Healing from deep traumas will go on for our lifetime, yet the journey is liberating, just as forgiveness is.

The details of what occurred with The Anchorage, including my getting a police escort out of the building, followed by a hostile takeover of the home I purchased for the organization, are on my legal documents on Google and on my website: www.anchorinn-hope.com.

My inheritance from my parents and Uncle Charlie was never recovered. I obtained a lawyer who told me what was happening was a hostile takeover. When my lawyer realized it was orchestrated by the Saskatchewan Ministry of Social Services, he said to me, "This is huge!"

It was too big for him and his law firm because it involved the government, a major client of theirs. So he dragged his heels and took my money, and he made sure it didn't go anywhere.

My internal motto was 'keep going' because if I didn't, I would have mentally collapsed.

After this, I applied for funding from the United Church of Canada to do a survey and study on the impact of historical trauma from the residential schools.

My special friend, Lavina Bitternose, a Social Worker, did this short project with me. It was implemented during the June 21, 2003, National Indigenous Peoples Day. Lavina and I are of the same vintage. We still stay connected on Facebook. I love her profile picture where she's holding a sign that says: "Y'all Need Jesus!"

Yes, Lavina, we all do!

Chapter 24
Playing Russian Roulette – Kayla's Safety is Compromised!

During the operation of this program, 2000-2002, and all that was on our plate, we as a family never forgot about Kayla, who was going to be a year old. She was still in foster care.

During Kayla's first year of life, her dad would go to the Regina Social Services office to have visits with her. It was reported that he never missed any of his visits and that he was a loving and kind young man. Sadly, he lost his life when he was murdered by someone who hit him over the head with a baseball bat.

Her dad's older brother, Kayla's uncle, had done a lot of time in the penitentiary. He belonged to the Native Syndicate Killers' Gang. I was told by one Child Protection Worker that this family was the most violent one in Regina. Now that he was out of the penitentiary, Lin married him.

In December 2000, Regina Child Protection Services, knowing that Lin's now husband was extremely dangerous, hadn't been rehabilitated, still used drugs, and was still violent, decided to go ahead and set up overnight visitations for Kayla with them. As with Charlene, they likely were just wanting to see how it goes. Their plan was to give Kayla to them.

This plan was totally, and I mean totally, unprofessional, irresponsible, unethical, incompetent, and ludicrous. Most people without any education as a Child Protection Worker, whose role is to protect children, would never have allowed this.

They had all of the history on Lin's and her husband's files. To take the risk of something happening to Kayla was huge, but they didn't give a damn! If she'd been related to them, they'd never have allowed it.

Yet, they did allow it, and why did they? Was it racism? Did they really not give a damn? Or were they simply incompetent? Or were they lacking training? What it was was absolutely NUTS! Child Protection Services and this Worker must have missed taking the prerequisite free course, Common Sense 101, on how to keep children protected and safe, before being admitted to a university to study Social Work.

Earlier, Mama Judy had reported to me and Kayla's Worker that when she'd come to pick her up, Lin would take quite a while to bring Kayla to the door, leaving her to wait outside.

Then, when Lin brought Kayla to the door, she was crying and hard for Judy to settle her. Child Protection Services didn't care, and they kept up with these visits until this critical incident.

The incident occurred just before Christmas, 2000, and Kayla's first birthday.

Here's What Happened

Lin's husband, under the influence of alcohol and drugs, went over to the next apartment in the fourplex apartment where they lived, stabbed his brother, and then came after Lin with the knife.

Thankfully, Lin grabbed a door that was off its hinges and shoved it towards him, giving her enough time to run for her life in the dead of winter. She ran to a neighbor's house, and the police were called.

Lin was transported to the hospital to be checked out. The next day, the police dropped her off at Lincoln and his partner's home. While the officers sat warm in their car. Lin walked through the snow in paper slippers up to their home.

At least if my son and his partner had known that she had no shoes or boots, they'd have brought them out to her. This may seem like a minor point, but it speaks volumes about the lack of care and racist attitudes that the public and some of the public servants still have.

Thank God that Kayla's angel was watching over her, as hours earlier, she was picked up by Mama Judy before this violence broke out at their home. This night could have been one of their overnight visits with Kayla, and that could have been tragic for Kayla.

Where to Place Kayla? – *Exploring the Possibilities, But For One!*

Child Protection Services decided that they had to place or adopt Kayla out. They went to Lincoln and his partner, as they were already having visits with Kayla. They asked them if they wanted to take her. His partner told them that she belonged with her grandparents and her other two siblings, and to place her with us.

Child Protection Services couldn't figure that out on their own that Kayla would be best with Chuck, me, and her siblings. They must have considered our ages, being in our early fifties, and hence, didn't approach us. Still, that didn't make sense since we had Kayla's siblings. The possibility of our taking Kayla should have been discussed. Why wasn't it?

If you read the tab entitled **The Demands of Justice** under my website, www.anchorinn-hope.com, you will understand why they did not approach us.

They were also busy, for the second time, of upending a second rehabilitation program designed to help at-risk First Nations' peoples like my daughter. Shame on them!-but they had no shame! They had no intentions of coming to us.

Finally, a Social Worker contacted us because Lin wanted Kayla to come to us. Then we began weekend visits with her in 2001.

October 08, 2001 – *Kayla Comes Home*

It was hard for Kayla to be away from us because she knew where she belonged, and it was with us and her siblings. She had been living in a foster home in a small village a short distance from Regina. When we'd come to pick her up, she'd have her coat on and stand by the door ready to go while we chatted with Mama Judy.

When we first had weekend visits with Kayla, she had a very 'flat effect' and rarely smiled. She was like 'a tiny robot' as we buckled her up in her seat belt for the ride home. You could see she was content to be with us, and soon began to smile more. She had also been put through trauma, like Charlene and Jonathan had been, and she needed to heal.

When she came for her visits and it was bedtime, I'd give her a bottle, and she knew where her crib was, and without a murmur, headed for it.

I realized right away that she lacked what is known as 'critical stimulation' where an infant requires to be held to bond to their caregiver. When she came for her weekend visits, I purposely rocked her in our rocking chair with her blanket and sang to her. She wasn't relaxed at first since she wasn't used to it, but she soon became relaxed and enjoyed it.

Mama Judy did her best with Kayla, and she was blessed to have had her, but she had her own children as well as other foster children, so she was 'maxed out.' One evening, during one of Kayla's visits, Chuck took the three kids to church for a potluck supper. I wasn't feeling well, so I stayed home.

He told me that Kayla kept pulling on his pant leg and said that when he looked down at her, he thought she needed to come home with us now, for good! Of course, that's what we all wanted, but these visits kept up and kept up.

Finally, Mama Judy told Kayla's Worker to not drag this out any longer but to give Kayla to us. Lin signed the papers to have her placed with us, as it was obvious that Social Services did not want to support us. If they had wanted to, they could have done that on their own a long time ago. It was finally getting done, and Kayla would be coming to us!

On October 08, 2001, Kayla was home with her family for good.

Chapter 25
2002 – Life Continues to be Eventful

By March 2002, the woman that Regina Social Services put in place to bring down The Anchorage completed her diabolical assignment to destroy the non-profit organization I began. Social services and this woman acting on their behalf cared nothing for the participants or us, and this was the second program they sabotaged.

Growing up, Mom used to say to me, "Arlene, you never accept 'No' for an answer!" I guess Mom was right again because that tenacity kept me forging forward.

So, Chuck and I decided to take the name Anchor from The Anchorage, and we called our now 'for-profit' counseling business Anchor Inn Rehabilitation & Counselling Center.

We registered it as a joint partnership. Then we found a very nice office space downtown across from the Saskatchewan Provincial Court House. Here we began to heal and to help and heal others.

Even though there was all of this heartache and tragedy over Lin losing her children and what she'd gotten into, she would on occasion send Chuck and me cards, like the two below:

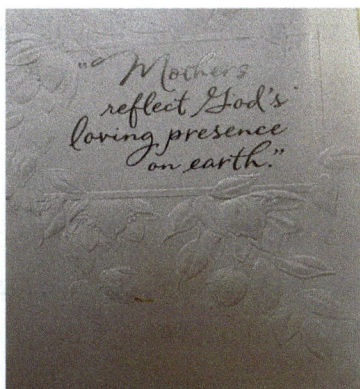

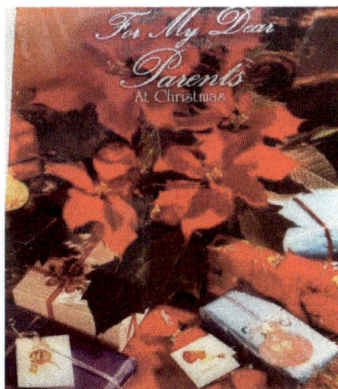

Lin has Baby # 4 – *Lance, Born August 31, 2002*

Here we go again! What does Child Protection do again? You likely guessed it; they put him with Mom and her violent husband, who is the father of Lance. They did this knowing all about him, and even after the episode that Kayla was saved from.

In the spring of 2003, the next plan of Social Services was to put Lin in a woman's shelter at Sophia House, away from her husband, just to see how she could parent Lance in the absence of his father.

I spoke to Lin on occasion. I said to her that it was good she was away from Lance's dad and at Sophia House for women who'd suffered domestic violence.

She proudly told me she could go anywhere she wanted to with Lance and that she was still connecting with his dad, her husband. She disclosed that when she was allowed to have Lance for a couple of days at a time while still in foster care, she continued to connect with his Dad.

Shortly after this, I received a phone call from a staff member at Sophia House. She was calling me on behalf of Lin.

The message that Lin wanted to get to me was that there is something 'big in the works' for Lance and Kayla to be taken to Lin's reserve.

She wanted me to know that Social Services had arranged for Lin's sister and family to come to Regina to meet Lance and Kayla and that they'd take them back to the reserve to raise them. Jonathan and Charlene would be next to join them. We never did adopt the children, but had an agreement between Lin and Social Services and ourselves to keep them.

Charlene would not be able to cope with being displaced from me at that time. I had become her lifeline, and to take any of her siblings now would traumatize her. Charlene had stopped seeing Lin as she could not handle connecting with her without regressing. We did agree to have Kayla visit her mom to connect with her baby brother, Lance. Chuck took Kayla for the visits with Mom and Lance.

At the time, we had no idea about the 'political diabolical plan' to put all the children on Lin's reserve with her, whereby her siblings would oversee their upbringing.

We adopted Lin through the Adopt Indian Métis (AIM) program, and now they would take her children from us with not a word or any regard for us, or for what's best for the children.

After all, they'd just finished undermining a second rehabilitation program for this 'target group' that Lin represented and completed a hostile takeover of the home I had purchased to run our business out of. Now, they were planning a hostile takeover of Lin's children, our grandchildren, to return them to her reservation like we were nothing.

Lin didn't want that to happen. I am not going to guess her motives for not wanting that. I would like to think she felt that her children were safe and well cared for with us.

It may have been more self-serving in that she didn't want to be shipped up north to the reserve to try and parent her children, whom she never wanted to parent. I knew that she'd never stay there.

Of course, receiving this message was unsettling. I was glad that I had never seen Lance because if I had, I would have bonded with him, and I was now 56 years old, and so was Chuck. We just finished going through hell with their government antics, and I was not even going to approach them. My energy reserve was almost empty.

Miracle #13: – 'A Heavenly Intervention'

I have not documented every intervention that God has done in my life by calling them miracles because I usually think of miracles as healings or, for sure, 'raising the dead.' Still, some dreams are definitely miraculous in that I am shown what is about to happen or needs to happen. In those dreams, the Holy Spirit gives me direction and encouragement, and I am eternally grateful for this. Yet, this particular dream troubled me.

Here it is

The setting for this dream was in a place near Valeport, SK, that is just a few miles from Craven, SK. My dad used to take me fishing there as a young child.

299

It was a beautiful summer evening, and the sun had almost set. There was a rosy hue against the backdrop of the evening sky.

A dear friend of mine, Nita, who was 20 years my senior, was with me. We were sitting by the water's edge on the grass, a short distance apart from one another. We were not visiting with one another, and it was very quiet. We were enjoying the evening and the tranquility around us. The lake was like a sheet of glass with not a ripple on it.

Then I noticed one ripple appear just a short distance from me. It continued to move towards me until it stopped just a few yards from me. Then a fish's head came out of the water, looking straight at me. This fish seemed very pleasant and even happy, appearing like a cartoon caricature of a fish. He had a message to deliver to me and did so in a pleasant but emphatic tone:

"Now, Arlene, what about Lance? You are to bring him 'under your covering' and he will be a blessing to you! This will be the last time that I will ask you to do this."

With that, I was now wide awake. I knew without a doubt that this was one of those God dreams. There was no second-guessing. I looked over at Chuck sleeping, and I thought what a great grandpa and dad he'd become to these three grandchildren of ours.

I thought, 'Chuck, you have been through a lot in marrying me, going through all of these traumas and challenges with me.'

I became disturbed in my spirit, so I got up and walked around, talking to God or that Fish!

On occasion, I tell God what He has to do, if you can imagine! I said, "Alright, God, you spoke to me and I am not telling Chuck about this dream, but You will need to speak to Chuck for me to agree to what you have asked me to do, and if You do and he comes to me and says we are to take Lance, then I will do it."

Basically, I was saying to God, "You do this for me and then I will obey You." That may seem pretty brave or stupid to do this, after all, this is God. Yet I've come to recognize that He enjoys having a personal and intimate relationship with us, and He looks at our hearts and our motives.

Three days later, Chuck walked into the house and said, "Arlene, we're to get Lance!"

I asked him how he'd arrived at that revelation. He said, "I was just walking down the street and I heard God clearly say (which was an inner voice), 'Chuck, you are to get Lance!'"

Then I shared my dream with him, and we knew what we needed to do.

My Letter to Lin – *One Last Time!*

Lin was still in Sophia House, and I decided to put in writing what Chuck and I were prepared to do concerning Lance. My motive in writing this letter was twofold. One, she could read it over and again if need be, so she'd know what we were and weren't prepared to do.

Secondly, she could use the letter to share with whoever she needed to, such as her Child Protection Worker, and lastly, nothing would get lost or misinterpreted by Lin relaying a verbal message to them.

Shortly after this, I received a phone call from Lin's Child Protection Worker who informed me that Lin wanted Lance to be placed with us and have him grow up with his siblings, and so the department would start with weekend visits with us as they did with Kayla.

Meeting Lance – *For the First Time!*

What an absolute sweetheart! He came with lots of smiles and was very social and interactive. Charlene was also seeing him for the first time. She said she knew he was going to look just like that.

I taught pediatrics in nursing and in seeing him, I thought he may have Fetal Alcohol Affect (FAA) or Fetal Alcohol Syndrome (FAS) as Lin had, but I put this in the back of my mind, realizing that if that was the case we'd deal with it as he grew up.

Alarm Bells Going Off – *Again!*

During the couple of days we had Lance, he was waking up crying, seemingly having a nightmare. What was more alarming than that was when I was changing his diaper, I noticed that there was a tear running outward from his anus and that his anus was slightly lax.

Of course, that was very alarming to me. I recognized that this tear could not have occurred from him simply being constipated. It could only have occurred by blunt force impact.

It was now Sunday morning, and I spoke to Chuck about it and decided there was no way that Lance was returning to this new foster parent until I had him medically checked out.

The Blame Game – *That Gig is Up!*

The reason that I needed to do this was to sound the alarm that Lance was being sexually abused, and secondly, to protect Chuck and me.

If my readers take the time to read the tabs entitled The Demands of Justice on my website: www.anchorin-hope.com, they will know that the other three children had also been sexually abused.

Charlene was examined by a Children's Justice doctor, not a pediatrician. This doctor in determining the healing timeline of Charlene's burn injuries, implicated Chuck and I, as she'd be in our care at that time these burns occurred. Yet Charlene told this doctor, "Mommy burnt me with a knife and it was a very hot knife," which this doctor also documented in this same report.

The ligature marks that I told you about earlier were, according to Charlene, when her mom tied her and Jonathan up, leaving them alone. Those markings also had to have occurred while the children were in our care.

I had also taken Charlene to the Regina City Police upon their request to have photos taken of her injuries. When I asked to see those photos, they said they did not exist. How convenient!

What happened to Chuck and me up to that time was more than concerning. Therefore, should Lance return to this foster mother with these injuries, the likelihood of them occurring while he was in our care would have been very high.

I called the medical clinic where our doctor practiced and found that he was in that afternoon. When our doctor looked at Lance's injury to his anus, he confirmed that Lance had been sexually abused, and this tear had to have occurred from blunt force trauma.

Confronting the Foster Mom – *She Tried Her Best!*

When the foster mother came to our home to pick up Lance, I asked her to sit down because I needed to talk to her. I relayed to her what I found and what the doctor had to say about Lance being sexually abused.

With that revelation, the foster mother broke down crying. She indicated that when Lance returned to her from the visits with Lin, she would find blood in his diaper, and she was concerned that something wasn't right. She had called the worker, and she did nothing.

She also indicated that when Lance returned to her, there was still milk in his bottles and that they smelled off. She was sure something was in them that should not have been there and requested that they come and get one of these bottles and test it to see what was in them.

The same Child Protection Worker told the foster mom not to worry about it, but to just clean the bottles very well. This was upsetting to the foster mom because she was sure something was put in those bottles that should have been identified.

Child Protection Services – *Now in Damage Control!*

The foster mother certainly had relayed what we had talked about to the Child Protection Worker as they took Lance to be examined, minimized the findings, and moved him to Mama Judy's home. It is possible that she no longer wanted to continue to provide foster care to Lance, or they didn't want her involved.

This now former foster parent to Lance was so brave in being that transparent with me about her concerns. She was putting Lance's safety and well-being as a priority, as they should have done. She reported her concerns, but the information was not taken seriously, and the concerns for Lance fell on Regina Child Protection Services' deaf ears.

If this foster mother ever reads my book, please know that you did the right thing, as they should have, and I am very grateful to you, and thank you.

To refute or downplay our doctor's findings of Lance, they had a Children's Justice doctor examine him for what looked like a 'cover-up.' They also used the same doctor as before. Do these doctors get extra money to do this? As a former Pediatric Nursing Instructor, I knew what I was seeing with Lance, and I only needed that confirmed by our doctor, which it was.

This is how Regina Child Protection Services and Children's Justice actually operate when they need to cover up. Yet, this is not to say that all of these doctors and Child Protection workers operate like this, but those involved with us who knew they'd 'messed up' again did. Their unprofessional and unethical practices were legally a 'breach of their fiduciary duty' to protect babies at-risk.

We, as a family, already had a good rapport with foster mom Mama Judy. When Mama Judy had Kayla, she was also relaying her concerns to the Protection Worker, but as you know now, they kept putting Kayla in harm's way, and they'd done the same with Lance.

Our visits continued with Lance. We would pick him up from Mama Judy's home, and then she'd come to pick him up at our home after his weekend visit.

Child Protection Services – *Dragging Their Heels.*

The visits happened every weekend, the same way. Mama Judy said that when she got Lance into the car to go home and he realized he was separated from us, he'd start crying and do so all the way home. Then it took at least a day to settle him down.

Child Protection Services dragged their heels in placing Lance with us, just like they did with Kayla. It made me wonder why. It seemed that they wanted something 'not to work out.' I absolutely did not trust them after all that happened.

After this had been going on for a couple of months, and Lance being upset each time he went back with Mama Judy, she told them to give him to us, because that's where he belonged!

Finally, Lance came under our covering as God wanted it to be—and oh, what a blessing he was and continues to be!

The day he came for his first visit with us in July 2003, we stopped to get a picture of the four children together. I am sure he knew he was with his siblings and family,-and you can see the look of joy on his face and all of their faces.

Lance is almost 11 months old here, Kayla is three and a half years old, Jonathan is coming seven years old, and Charlene is nine and a half years old.

Chapter 26
2004 to 2005 – What are They Cooking up Next?

I need to tell you about the issues with the children since this consumed most of our lives between trying to make a living and coping with their needs.

In 2004, Lin was pregnant again. We heard that Lin gave birth to a baby girl while in the hospital. Her baby was 30 weeks along when she delivered her in the hospital. Her name was Summer, and she did not live.

Various other occurrences were going on. Charlene continued to have problems at school due to her severe anxiety and PTSD. Charlene would tell me that she saw her aunt, Donny's sister, in the school hallway, and it freaked her out.

She said her dad would also be outside the school fence watching her, and when she moved to a different area in the schoolyard, he'd follow her along the fence. This freaked her out. There were times when we had to pick her up from school in a hysterical state.

Chuck and I knew that the school was informed to watch us and to report to Social Services if they found anything was 'a miss.'

Ms. Lewis, Charlene's grade 5 teacher, had terminal cancer. She knew what Social Services were doing, and she provided

Chuck and me with a letter of support. This letter was unsolicited. She told us that if we needed to, we could use this letter to show support for our love and care with Charlene. Ms. Lewis passed away soon afterwards.

Time To Get Pro-Active – *Enough is Enough!*

The lawsuit that my lawyer took on in 2002 was over with. He and his firm did nothing except take my money and look after their own interests.

I was not going to any lawyer after this bad experience, but it was time I had to get proactive before they tried anything more to ruin our lives and the lives of our grandchildren.

They'd ruined our business, The Anchorage. They undermined two rehabilitation programs that I wrote and found funding to implement; they were working at ruining our reputations; they orchestrated a hostile takeover of the counseling center I purchased with my inheritance from my parents; they supported Lin and Donny to get Charlene back with them; they denied that Lin had a mental illness, DID, and they weren't done yet, but I was DONE! Done with all of their criminal acts, incompetence, and dysfunction!

I had to get my 'ducks in a row' by getting psychological assessments done on Charlene and ourselves to counter all their accusations. I had to hire Dr. Colin Clay, Chaplain and a professor in Theology, at the University of Saskatchewan in Saskatoon, SK.

He had expertise in Satanic Ritual Abuse (SRA) and had counseled clients who were recovering from leaving these cults. He also wrote a book on this. He agreed to meet with Charlene.

I brought Dr. J. Cleland, a Clinical Psychologist, with me to be a part of Dr. Clay's assessment in determining if Charlene had been exposed to SRA. All of the findings were in the affirmative.

I had to be with Charlene during these interactions with these two men, who were strangers to her. She would have panicked if I had left her. I heard new things I'd never heard before, and I witnessed her traumatic reactions. It was immensely painful for her and me.

Lawsuit QBG 1306 of 2005 as a Self-Litigant

On July 25, 2005, I filed the above lawsuit against the Saskatchewan Government (Minister of Social Services) and all of the Defendants that are listed on the legal documents. After filing it, I stood on the steps of the Court of Queen's Bench in Regina, SK, and I said a prayer for God to help me. I thought of my dad, who had died on this day, eighteen years earlier.

I felt both of my daddies looking down on me, my Abba Father and my earthly dad. I knew I'd need the Great and Holy Spirit to guide me through this process since I hadn't a clue how to do this and navigate the justice system.

I figured I had the best lawyer possible, Jesus, but I wasn't sure about these earthly judges. Yet there were the 'halls of justice' in heaven, but I felt I needed justice now to put a stop to their nonsense.

Chuck and I were barely making it financially as we went along. Having put my savings into our education, and the home I'd purchased for the business being taken by a hostile eviction and takeover, I had lost everything.

My programs were shut down, and I was paying a lawyer who did very little for us. And now, raising our four grandchildren, we were very strapped financially.

We didn't want to ask for financial support. I am remembering when Charlene and Jonathan reminded me that they remember when grandpa put only one dollar in the gas tank. We had a good laugh, but at least we had a little more than fumes.

This lawsuit would need to be done one step at a time, having just enough money to be able to file a document at a time as I went along. This way, I was able to afford to proceed with this lawsuit.

Certainly, if I lost this lawsuit, I would need to pay the defendants. That was a risk I was willing to take because I thought that any reasonable Court would be able to see what went on here and come to the same conclusion I had come to and deliver all of us justice. This would be simple to see as long as I laid out the facts of my case.

I was suing them for the grandchildren whom they left in harm's way when they knew better or should have known better, as well as the hell they'd put Chuck and me through, and surely award us the collective damages.

Lin Just Had Another Baby – *Autumn*

Lin gave birth to Autumn Starr L on August 31, 2005. The four grandchildren wanted us to take Autumn into our care, and Chuck and I felt no resistance to not take her as we knew that eventually she'd be put in harm's way.

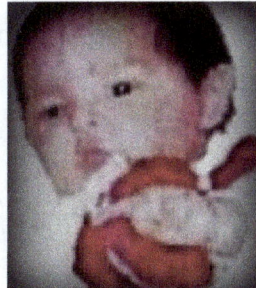

311

We let Lin know this, and Social Services set us up for visits to begin at the end of October 2005. Our first visit was for a weekend, and Chuck and I picked up Autumn from a Regina Social Services office.

The Protection Worker gave us instructions from the foster mom as to Autumn's needs, one of which was to be sure to put her to sleep on her tummy. She said if we needed to, we could call the foster mom, as she left her phone number in the diaper bag.

I told the Protection Worker that we would not be sleeping Autumn like that, as she'd be a higher risk for SIDS (Sudden Infant Death Syndrome) and that Autumn was being weaned off of the street drugs that Lin had been using and was on Phenobarbital to prevent seizures. I emphasized to the social worker that the foster mom should not be doing that. The Protection Worker became irritated with me and said, "Do what you want, Arlene!"

Over the weekend, I observed Autumn closely because I was concerned about her vulnerability. She was around eight pounds when she was born at full term, and she was a beautiful baby girl.

Nevertheless, due to Lin's usage of street drugs, she would be in a vulnerable state. My vocation in the past had been as a nursing instructor on a hospital pediatric ward. During this time, when holding Autumn, I thought that I noticed a very brief apnea spell where she stopped breathing.

It was a millisecond and very, very brief. I was hoping my mind was playing tricks on me. I was concerned enough that I called her foster mother and reported that I had concerns about her sleeping her on her tummy and why.

The foster mother told me, "Oh, it's no problem sleeping her on her tummy, that's how she loves to sleep."

I tried to impress on her the importance of not doing that, but she wouldn't listen. Then I thought I'd try to impress her with my educational background as a pediatric nursing instructor, hoping she'd listen, but she was not listening at all.

During our conversation, she told me that Autumn was the first baby that she'd had in a year. When I asked her why that was, she told me that the last baby she had died in her care. She said that the baby vomited and choked on their vomit. Well, it was a huge concern hearing this.

This foster mother was not very concerned about Autumn, nor was the Child Protection Worker, who said, "Do what you want, Arlene!" I felt there was nothing more that I could do to convince her to take special precautions, and the Child Protection Worker was not any better.

The Worst Possible Outcome – *Autumn dies.*

The last Monday of October 2005, Autumn went back to her foster mother. On the Friday of that same week, Lin called me crying hysterically that Autumn had died.

Our family was thrown into grief again. Charlene had become very attached to Autumn over that weekend visit, and because of her abuse while being exposed to the horrific acts that her mom and others did while she was in Lin's care, she freaked out and regressed in her healing journey.

Death Notice: Autumn Starr L.- passed away suddenly at the age of 8 weeks and 2 days. She is lovingly remembered and missed by her mother, Melinda (John); grandparents Charles and Arlene Lowery; her older siblings Charlene, Jonathan, Kayla, and Lance...

What was left out in this notice was that Autumn Starr L died suddenly on October 28, 2005, while in the care of the Ministry of Saskatchewan Social Services (Child Protection).

After Autumn's death, I took time away from work and let the defendants' lawyers know that I would not be in court at the beginning of November 2005 as planned due to 'grief and loss.'

Autumn Starr's Funeral and Burial – *November 04th, 2005*

There were lots of people at the funeral that I did not know. Kayla was hiding behind me, not wanting to be seen. Charlene was watching her mom and being triggered, but we managed to get through it. We were not taking the children to the interment as that would have been too much for Charlene. I promised Charlene that we could visit the gravesite as a family later on.

The Wheels of Justice Suddenly Come to a Screeching Halt!

I filed a Motion to Amend my Statement of Claim since I thought my first Statement of Claim had been written like a narrative, and that it would be more manageable to organize it in three parts to have it adjudicated.

Further, I wanted to add the Government of Canada to it, and the henchwoman that the Saskatchewan Ministry of Social

Services positioned to bring down The Anchorage. Further, I added the Saskatchewan Ministry of Social Services for not protecting Autumn, which resulted in her death.

The first judge on the bench was the Honorable Fred Kovach. It was obvious that he had read all of my documentation that was filed with the court. At this hearing, the judge methodically polled each one of the Defendants' lawyers, asking them, "Did you, Mr. …, read Ms. Lowery's Statement of Claim?" to which they all answered in the affirmative, that they'd read it.

Then Justice Kovach turned to me and said Ms. Lowery, you may add all of the Defendants that you have requested to add, and you may amend your claim as per your request. Then he turned back to the lawyers and said, "You are to respond to Ms. Lowery's amended claim by filing your response, new or amended. And the hearing was adjourned until 2006."

For once, the 'Wheels of Justice' seemed to be moving in our favor.

At the beginning of 2006, the matter was back in court. I had amended my claim and delivered it to all of the Defendants. They never responded to it as they were supposed to do because, as I soon found out, they didn't need to since they'd managed to get a new judge.

The 'wheels of justice' screeched to a halt! Justice Chicoine, who had been sworn in as a judge not long before, was treated to a celebration party in Estevan, SK that was hosted by the New Democratic Party (NDP). I knew this as the announcement was posted on the internet, but I can no longer find it.

Yet, this court managed to haul him up to Regina, to do 'their dirty work' to help these Defendants out, which he did! This is our justice system!

Justice Chicoine came into court stating he'd never read the materials on the file, and yet directed his first remarks to me, stating for me not to keep him and all the lawyers present there until 8:00 p.m. The writing was on the wall that justice would be denied.

Of course, this judge threw the lawsuit out as frivolous, and he likely never did read it.

Does this court think that babies and the children in the care of this ministry do not deserve justice when they are left in harm's way and die in their so-called protection? These are Indigenous infants and children, so are they disregarded more than affluent or white children? Surely this is not racism, or is it?

The system will remain broken, and babies and children will continue to be put in harm's way and die, unless the court stops throwing cases like mine out as frivolous. Accountability is necessary.

Autumn's Autopsy

I requested a copy of the autopsy, and a good person there provided it to me. Guess what! The Phenobarbital drug that Autumn was supposed to be taking was not provided to her, as this foster mother admitted that she ran out of it and that she had not gotten around to refilling it. Therefore, Autumn had not received it.

The prescription was filled, but I did not think to look at the date when it was filled. What was in the bottle that she sent in the diaper bag labeled as this medication, which I gave Autumn while we had her? Was it water? This would be important information to acquire if there had been a Public Inquiry. She died with a low therapeutic dose of this drug in her bloodstream.

Autumn should NEVER have died!!! The conclusion of the autopsy was that the cause of her death was undetermined. No, it was not! Yet, labeling it like this was deceptive.

I am certain the autopsy report should have read like this: It was determined in the blood analysis that she had a low therapeutic dose of Phenobarbital, which precipitated a seizure while she was in the prone position, and she died of suffocation.

Chapter 27
2007 – 2008
All Hell's Coming against Us!– Again!

2006 was bad enough, but 2007 was very hard. Chuck and I were very busy raising four children with various special needs, like Charlene.

Charlene was often up in the night, having had a nightmare and reliving the trauma she'd been put through. She and I were often too tired for her to get to school and for me to go to work.

I had to decide whether to let Justice Chicoine's decision stand or appeal it. I knew that this ministry would keep up their dishonest and unethical acts if they were not 'held in check.'

Therefore, I needed to keep going as I wanted Charlene to be old enough that her voice would count and she could say where she wanted to live, just in case the Saskatchewan Ministry of Social Services had any more intentions of taking the children to Lin's reserve.

Saskatchewan Court of Appeal – *Here I Come!*

I had filed an appeal to Justice Chicoine's judgment on the basis that the Defendants' lawyers did not file a new or amended defense to my Amended Statement of Claim, as they were ordered to do by Justice Fred Kovach.

My readers need to understand that Justice F. Kovach told them in court with all of us present that these lawyers on behalf of their clients needed to respond to my Amended Statement of Claim either new or amended which meant they had two choices: they could either amend their initial Statement of Defense or they could write a new Statement of Defense.

This was very clear to me and very clear to them, and I am sure my readers can also understand this.

I had added two new Defendants to my Amended Statement of Claim, plus I claimed damages for the death of Autumn, so my original Statement of Claim was null and void.

The Defendants never filed a response to my Amended Statement of Claim to strike it on any grounds *as they were ordered to do.*

Why didn't they? Were all five lawyers simply too lazy to do the work? Or did they know that Justice Chicoine was going to be their Hero in this dysfunctional, toxic court system, rigged against vulnerable babies and children and self-litigants? Of course, they knew!

At this very juncture, *I, on behalf of my four grandchildren, should have won* when **five lawyers did NOTHING!**

Surely this is not too hard to figure out for five learned, seasoned lawyers and a supposed ethical learned unseasoned judge to figure out!

No motion, new or amended, was ever filed, and therefore, they could not strike it. Therefore, my four grandchildren and I would win ALL of the damages, including for Autumn's death, as added to my Amended Statement of Claim.

If I had done what these lawyers did, it would have been the end of the judicial road for me, but not for them! What went on throughout my journey through the court process was shocking to me. I saw things as a novice in the justice system that were unbelievable.

Starting out on my journey, I believed that there would be fairness. I was very naïve to think it would be fair. It was a dog fight and a dog's breakfast, and the dogs won!

Perfect Your Appeal or Else

So after filing this appeal, I did not move it forward. In August 2007, I had an emergency surgery to remove my gallbladder. Then I had complications of a nicked diaphragm that caused a partially collapsed lung, and I needed to be readmitted to the hospital.

After I met with the Appeals Registrar, I made it clear that I was not going to perfect my appeal, as I realized that I did not have a chance to receive justice.

After this, I received a notice from Justice Cameron with the Saskatchewan Appeals Court telling me to perfect my appeal, which is to get the matter back into court, or risk going to jail.

Later on, but still being in a trauma state, I wrote a paper that I entitled: **The Brick Wall of Injustices.**

https://www.scribd.com/document/248679270/Brickwall-of-Injustices

It is filed with Scribd, and I cannot recall why they even have it. Perhaps those details under these tabs may be for another book, or perhaps a documentary, or even a film. Any of those venues would be great to bring light to how First Nations' babies and children are protected by the Saskatchewan Government and how the Government of Canada needs to have a tangible response to their apology.

Lin gives birth to Lily – *Another Precious Baby's Life Cut Short!*

We heard in January 2007 that Lin gave birth to Lily. About mid-March, Lin contacted me and told me that Lily was in the care of one of her friends. I asked her how Lily ever was put in the care of this woman.

Lin told her case worker that Chuck and I couldn't take Lily, and they said it was up to her what she did with her baby, and left her in charge of protecting Lily.

This was another brilliant Care Plan that Child Protection Services came up with! They instructed Lin to do their job, denying what she and the gang members were involved in and did to her other children. Lin was unable to keep her other children safe, and now she was given this mission to find Lily a Caregiver.

So, after Lin found Lily a Caregiver, we heard about what transpired. Lin chose her friend to take care of Lily. We knew about this woman, and she had her own children apprehended at one time, but now she's Lily's caregiver. Totally absurd!

When Lin called, I asked her if she could arrange a visit for her children to see their sister, Lily. I suggested a day and time at our office for this woman to bring Lily.

Lin had it all arranged. The photo below shows the four children, Jonathan, Kayla, and Charlene holding Lily and Lance.

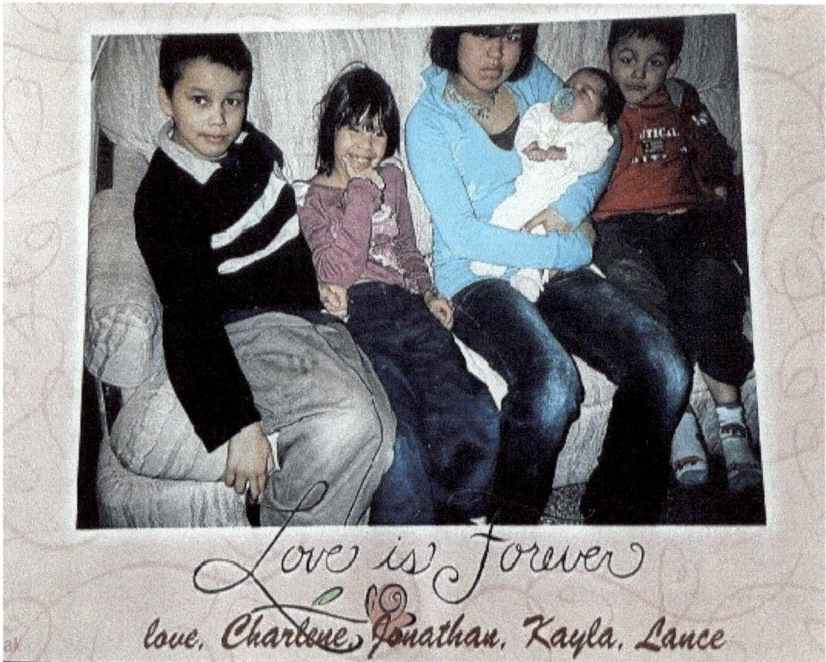

Love is Forever
love, Charlene, Jonathan, Kayla, Lance

When Lily was leaving that day, I leaned over to see her in her stroller. When I looked into her eyes, the strangest feeling came over me because it was like 'looking into the eyes of God.' I heard in my spirit a soft whisper, "Keep going, grandma!"

That experience didn't resonate with me until I received a call a few days later from Lin. She said, "Mom, it happened again! Lily is gone!"

I went into shock, but not like the first time. I think my looking into Lily's eyes and recalling the message—Keep going, grandma!—was as if God had prepared me for this phone call and this tragic outcome.

Of course, I wanted to know what happened, but Lin said she didn't know.

Lily's Funeral: Dobson, Lily Mae Adele, Death was Mar 29, 2007

Lily was buried on April 10, 2007. The above was taken from the web when I looked up her obituary on Google.

Lin gave Lily's middle name after my mom's first name, Mae, along with my middle name, Adele.

When we told our grandchildren that their sister Lily went to be with Jesus, Charlene's immediate reaction was "I knew this would happen!" I could see Charlene going numb.

If you look at Charlene's face in that photo of her holding Lily, you can see the look of dread on her face.

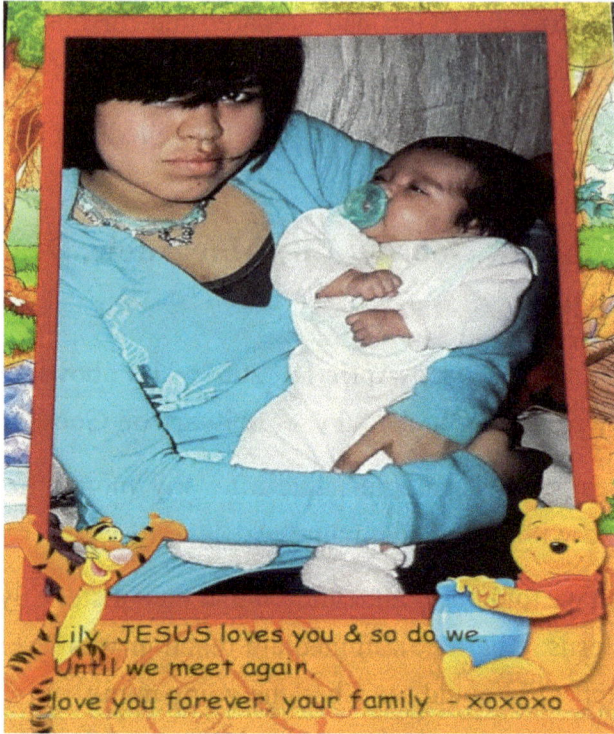

Lily, JESUS loves you & so do we. Until we meet again. I love you forever, your family - xoxoxo

There was no way that Charlene was going to endure another funeral, as the last one was chaotic for her. Charlene was 14 years old at this time, so I presented to her three possible scenarios: one, we could all attend the funeral or two, we could have, as a family, a private viewing of Lily or lastly, we don't need to go at all, as we could remember Lily from having had our visit with her?

Charlene said she wanted to view Lily with only our family, which excluded even her mother. The Funeral Director lived on our street, and I asked her if it was possible for a private viewing of Lily the day before the funeral, and she said it was no problem and she would let Lin know.

I also let Lin know Charlene's wishes and asked her if she was alright with just our family there, which was Chuck and me, and her four children, having a private viewing. She knew it was for Charlene's well-being, and she said she was fine with it.

The day before the funeral, our family arrived at Lee's Funeral Home parking lot at the time we'd arranged. There in the parking lot in a car was Lin and her friend, who was Lily's caregiver at the time of her death. They were waiting in the car for our arrival. Lin knew that this was to be a private viewing, and she wasn't to be there. Well, this showing was anything but private, as the funeral was obviously now called a day early by Lin. An entourage of Lin's 'mob of associates' arrived through the front doors of Lee's Funeral Home.

Charlene did not want to see her mom or this woman. She knew this woman was supposed to care for Lily when she died, and did not like her. Now the entire 'gang' was there. This was Lin being loving and caring towards her daughter, whom she and some of her friends had put through hell.

Lily was in a white casket and dressed in the cutest dress with a matching hat, all likely paid for by the Saskatchewan Ministry of Social Services.

When we were at the casket, Lin brought out sheets of butterfly stickers and began putting them on the inside of the lid of the casket, saying, "Here, Charlie (which was the nickname her dad and mom gave her), you pick what butterflies you want to put on."

Charlene had an aversion to butterflies for some reason. This ritual that her mom was engaging in was extremely troubling for Charlene. She was visibly triggered by it.

Seeing this, I asked her if she wanted to go sit down with grandpa and the kids, and she immediately said yes. Once we were seated, it was obvious that she was very upset. She said, "Grandma, can we go?" I, of course, told her that we'd go and we did.

Lin wanted the babies' plots to be close to where my parents are buried. So the Saskatchewan Ministry of Social Services paid for the funerals and the plots, which were close to my parents. There are still no headstones on Autumn's or Lily's grave sites. Charlene wants headstones placed there and has told her mom this.

One day, I called Sister Margaret from Martha House, where Lin had stayed after Charlene was born. She had told me I'd need to look out for Charlene, as Lin would not be able to parent.

So I shared with her that we now had four of Lin's children, and I told her about the deaths of Autumn and Lily and what Charlene had been through. I told her that Autumn died just before Halloween, and Lily just before Easter, and did she think that this was strange, considering it appeared that Charlene had been exposed to Satanic Ritual Abuse. Her response was "No, it is not strange at all for you to wonder that." Sister Margaret knew more than I knew.

She then told me that she was now retiring and moving back to Montreal, Quebec. We never spoke again, but I was always grateful to her and Martha House.

A few years ago, Lin thanked me for keeping her children safe from 'all the bad people,' but she didn't seem to recognize that she was immersed with them.

An Opportunity to Become Clergy – *With the Anglican Church*

Chuck had wanted to preach one day. Since he had accepted the Lord as His Savior in the Anglican Church, and that church was looking for a priest, he applied for it.

The church we were attending, where the children went to school, had ordained Chuck, but never asked him to participate in any official or unofficial duties.

Chuck was offered that opportunity with the Anglican Church and accepted their offer. This, of course, meant we would need to attend that church. The day he accepted this offer, we attended a couple's banquet at the church where we were attending,

At the end of the meal, there was a raffle for a pink and white Afghan throw. The Lord whispered to me in my spirit, "Arlene, you will win this," and I did win it.

That night, Chuck had a massive heart attack. It was the beginning of November 2007.

The surgeons thought of doing a heart transplant since his left ventricle was so badly damaged that it was 'like a piece of cheese.' They told us they could not stitch anything into it. They had to leave his surgery for three months for healing to take place, so they could do it.

327

In February 2008, they put in a Teflon patch in his left ventricle and performed five bypasses.

Another Answer to Prayer

After his surgery, his heart was not going into normal sinus rhythm, and late in the evening, the nurse called me to say that at 8:00 a.m. the next morning, the cardiac team was going to shock his heart to see if it would go into normal sinus rhythm.

She told me that I could be there if needed because we all knew that his heart may stop and not be able to start up again.

Miracle # 14 – 'Please get his heart beating in rhythm!'

I spoke with Helen, my biological mother, and she said she'd pray. I begged the Lord to not let this shock happen! I kept praying, and about 3:00 a.m. I received a peace and a message, 'It is done, he'll be alright.' I then fell asleep.

Just after 6:00 a.m., the phone rang. It was a nurse telling me that Chuck's heart had gone into normal sinus rhythm and there was no need to come to the hospital for 8:00 a.m. Thank you, Lord!

In speaking with Helen, she told me that she was praying at her kitchen table, and about the same time, she got the same message that all would be well, and she also went to bed.

After the surgery, the heart surgeon told me that if Chuck looked after himself and did not smoke again (as he was a smoker before we met and had the odd relapse), he should be able to live another 11 years.

Eleven years was an odd number. I was not going to tell him what the surgeon told me, not ever! The way I dealt with that news is to say to God, whose report am I going to believe? Well, I will believe the report of the Lord! I just wasn't sure if that was the report of the Lord.

Chuck never complained or acted like a cardiac invalid. I sometimes came to the office and walked in to find him sleeping in the chair, and I recognized that I often looked at him to see if he was still with me/us.

The pink and white Afghan throw that I won at the church the evening before he had a heart attack became like a 'healing blanket.' From that night onwards, we slept with it over us. There were heart shapes crocheted throughout the pattern, reassuring us that God was with us.

Chuck was in a vulnerable state after his surgery. It took months before he was strong enough to resume his counseling. We began to attend the Anglican Church on the promise that Chuck would be able to preach sometime.

The children were growing up, and time was marching on.

Chuck always gave me the most beautiful cards and would buy me flowers whenever. He was kind, and the grandkids overlooked the times that he'd be short with them because they got a lot of excellent mentoring from him and lots of hugs and encouragement.

The participants in our programs saw that, too. If you think about it, as I have, just how many men would have taken on four grandchildren who were all wonderful children but who had their own 'special needs.' There are not many men like Chuck. The grandkids and I were so fortunate to have him.

I am so thankful to God that He led me in the right direction when I think of the times I almost 'threw in the towel' when things were tough in the beginning. If anyone is reading this now and you feel like you need to end your marriage, please get in a quiet place and talk to God, because He may want you to walk away, and He may not. As Mary said to the servants at the wedding at Cana, "Do whatever he tells you."

The Wedding at Cana

On the third day, there was a wedding at Cana in Galilee, and the mother of Jesus was there. 2Jesus also was invited to the wedding with his disciples. 3When the wine ran out, the mother of Jesus said to him, "They have no wine." 4And Jesus said to her, "Woman, what does this have to do with me? My hour has not yet come." 5His mother said to the servants, "Do whatever he tells you."

John 2:1-5 ESV

Chapter 28
Wayne's Brother Jim Died – Where is he, Lord?

After Wayne's mom died, Jim came to live with us for a time. He was going through a lot, as I described earlier. Jim had just died in his late forties of lung cancer.

Wayne had died a few years earlier, so I did not want to go and visit because of his sisters.

What I did do was write Jim a letter and had it delivered to his hospital room. The gist of the letter was to let him know that I loved him.

I told him that the fighting over land and money was not important in this life. What was important was that we love and forgive one another and believe in Jesus Christ, who came and died on a cross for our sins. I told him that this is God's gift to us, His Son, and no one can earn it, but if we accept Jesus as the Son of God and sincerely confess our sins and ask for forgiveness, we'll go to heaven.

I told Jim that Wayne had accepted Jesus Christ as His Lord and Savior and that he's in heaven, and that when I get there, I want him to be there too. I referenced this scripture,

"And He will wipe away every tear from their eyes; and there will no longer be death; there will no longer be sorrow and anguish, or crying, or pain; for the former order of things has passed away."

331

Revelation 21:4: - Amplified Bible

I had no way of knowing if Jim had accepted Jesus as His Lord and Savior. I could only hope and pray that he had. I was troubled in not knowing this, and so it was the middle of summer, late in the evening, when Chuck and the children were asleep, that I sat up in bed ready to do business with the Almighty.

As I sat there, I was recalling this scripture from The Book of Acts, where Jesus told the disciples that after He went to be with His Father, He would send a Comforter, the Holy Spirit, to be with them. The day that happened became known as Pentecost, since it happened 50 days after Jesus ascended into heaven:

1 When the day of Pentecost came, they were all together in one place.
2 Suddenly, a sound like the blowing of a violent wind came from heaven and filled the whole house where they were sitting."

Acts 2:1-2

It was one of those lovely summer evenings, not a breeze, and it was very still when I began praying, well, actually simply talking to God.

I was determined to do business with Him. I said, "God, You sent the Holy Spirit back then like a mighty, violent wind, and I have all the faith in the world that you can do that tonight for me as a confirmation that you have Jim with You."

Further, I said, "I am wide awake and I will sit up all night until You come like a mighty, violent rushing wind into this bedroom like You did on Pentecost!"

I was not tired at all, and I was determined to be up all night waiting for this mighty rushing wind to appear in our bedroom to confirm to me that Jim was with Him.

What I was doing was putting out a fleece. This was done in the Bible by others seeking an answer from God!

Well, I don't know when this happened as I wasn't looking at a clock, but I woke up in the morning and of course realized I blew it because I fell asleep.

Miracle # 15: – 'A Mighty Wind of His Spirit' – Acts 2:2.

In the morning, Chuck was making us coffee when he said to me, "Arlene, I can't believe that you slept through that!" because Chuck would sleep through anything, unlike me.

"Slept through what?" I asked.

"Well, there was such a loud wind that blew through our bedroom, and it was so forceful that it woke me up. It just came through our room, and then it was gone, but it was so loud and powerful!"

I was so thrilled to learn this. I shared with Chuck about the fleece I put out and that God had His own way of responding. Why did He knock me out cold? Normally, I am a very light sleeper, particularly with children around, who could wake me up crying or calling me.

The Lord wanted a witness to what He was doing, and He also showed me that Chuck and I were one with Him, which was confirmation of our marriage and His watching over us.

If you are not a believer reading this, I urge you to please believe, because Jesus is real; He came as God with us, the only

Son of God, Jesus Christ of Nazareth, and left us His Spirit, known as the Comforter. *He answers prayers*!

He came to die for your sins. If you sincerely confess your sins to Him, you have a ticket to heaven. It is that easy! And yet, it is that hard because of our pride:

16 For God so loved the world that he gave his one and only Son, that whoever believes in him shall not perish but have eternal life.

John 3:16 NIV

As His Spirit Moves – *So be it.*

After five years of being in the Anglican Church, Chuck never got to preach once. From the start, I knew it was not God's will for us to be there or for Chuck to preach there, but God would need to speak to him on that.

One day after church, Chuck told me that he needed to drop the kids and me off at home, saying that he just needed to go for a drive. I knew that God was ministering to him.

When he came home, he said, "Arlene, we need to leave the Anglican Church." I asked him how he came to that conclusion, and he said that the Lord directed him to this scripture in Revelations 3:15, 16, *The Berean Bible*:

To the Church in Laodicea…15 I know your deeds; you are neither cold nor hot. How I wish you were one or the other! 16 So because you are lukewarm—neither hot nor cold— I am about to vomit you out of My mouth!"

It was certainly verse 16 that stood out, and that was how it felt to him and had been for me. We are not in any position to judge any church, as only the Lord will do that, as it says in The Book of Revelation, but when you hear Him that clearly, then you need to obey, as He doesn't want you there. We met some very lovely people there and visited even after we left.

We went back to the evangelical church that ordained Chuck, as we had been connected with them, and we felt at the time that the Lord wanted us to return there. We let the leadership know of our decision. Staying there was short-lived. We also left after returning for a few weeks.

The church was supporting the Options Pregnancy Center, where I was told that they participated in doing funerals to honor the aborted fetuses and babies as part of their post-abortion support for the moms. That was not the issue, but stating three Options was.

Certainly, there are three Options in a democracy for those in the world, and we have 'free choice.' However, we didn't think that a Christian organization should support an organization that presents abortion as an option.

The church did not advocate for mom to have an abortion, but clearly presented the three options available to her in their brochure and in their counseling as an Option. There are times when medically an abortion may be needed, but the woman and her doctor need to determine this.

Otherwise, hopefully with God's help, the woman will choose to have her baby. As Christians, we need to support only two Options: to support mom through her pregnancy and assist her to come to a decision to keep her baby or to adopt her baby to a family seeking adoption.

If a mom has an abortion, certainly there needs to be love and support ministered to her as she has experienced trauma.

So we left there and finally ended up at another evangelical church that we thought had to be 'hot' in addition to being Biblically sound.

Rejection Sucks! – *But This is What Happens as a Disciple of Jesus Christ!*

We were like wandering sheep, but we still had the Master Shepherd, Jesus. We felt rejection like Jesus felt when the people in the synagogues in Nazareth, where he grew up, recognized Him as a wise Teacher, yet rejected Him.

They would not allow Him to preach, and so He did not perform many miracles there:

> 56"Where then did this man get all these things?" 57And they took offense at Him. But Jesus said to
> them, "Only in his hometown and in his own household is a prophet without honor."
> 58 And He did not do many miracles there, because of their unbelief."

Therefore, we knew that this was our reality too. Chuck had the gift of prophecy, and I, a Seer, which is similar to the gift of prophecy, but different. We wanted to find a church we'd feel comfortable in and where we could be used, but that wasn't happening.

Writing this book is my way of processing all of this, and I am gaining insights along with you. The following post I came across explains how it felt for me, although Chuck and I never discussed this:

Prophets – The Uncomfortables.

Posted on 2018-07-09 Author Glenn Loughrey

"They (seers and prophets) are to experience, fully for themselves, the cost of being faithful to the prophetic ministry. They will make others uncomfortable and will be made to feel uncomfortable as a result."

To fulfill our calling, we are to develop a unity with God through word and sacrament, contemplation, and prayer. Here we will let go of ideas, positions, and ideologies and begin to become one with God."

We had no intention of being uncomfortable or making anyone else feel that, but this was happening. We were always pleasant and forthcoming, but underneath, we felt rejected.

When we were in need, we were helped, which we were grateful for, but it was a deep spiritual connection we were looking for. We wanted to fit in, but didn't or couldn't.

Sadly, we see churches are more and more taking up degrees of political positions, engaging in back-biting, gossiping, and in all forms of manipulation, and are ignoring the 'heart of Jesus.' Churches will not survive as a church that God approves of if they continue to do this. Many will become discouraged, and that is a shame.

15 It is true that some preach Christ out of envy and rivalry, but others out of goodwill. 16 The latter do so out of love, knowing that I am put here for the defense of the gospel.
Philippians 1:15,16

Perhaps that's why many have not become believers, and others have left the church, yet still believe. Currently, I am not regularly attending any church, non-denominational or denominational. Instead, I am taking time to write this book and a possible blueprint for a 'healing program' as a response to the Government of Canada's apology to the First Nations' peoples.

The historical trauma that both the government and religious organizations imposed on them, through the Residential School System, needed more than a verbal apology or monetary compensation.

Chapter 29
2013 to 2019 – 'Birth and Death' and More Miracles!

Lily's Autopsy Report – *The Shocking Details*

Again, I asked the Coroner's Office for a copy of Lily's autopsy report, and once again, they sent it to me. Actually, I had no legal right to have it, but someone there thought I should see it. It was not opened until 2013, which was almost seven years after her death.

The reason for this was that I could not take any more bad news and grief, as I was exhausted, and I knew it likely would be bad. I had to do self-care and guard my own mental health.

Charlene was helping Chuck and me pack up our downtown office as we were downsizing our business for financial reasons when she found the sealed envelope holding Lily's autopsy report.

Charlene was grown up now, and she asked me if she could read it.

"If you think you can handle that, then you can," I replied. She read it and came to me to tell me that they found ethyl alcohol in Lily's blood, and she wanted to know what that was. I knew what it was, but I read it off of Google: Ethyl alcohol is the type of alcohol people consume in alcoholic beverages.

Lily had died in March 2007, and the cause of her death was undetermined. After reading this, I know that she was murdered.

Who poisoned Lily? They did so by having her ingest alcohol. I am now sure that this was also in Lance's bottles. That is why they stunk so badly. You may recall that the foster mother called the Child Protection Worker, requesting that she please come get one of the bottles and test it. This worker and the ministry she's employed with 'didn't give a damn!'

I am glad I found this out seven years later, or I don't know how I'd have reacted.

There are other interesting descriptions of what the First Responders noted in the home where Lily died, which is documented in that Coroner's Report. This would be of interest if there had been a Public Inquiry. The evidence of alcohol in Lily's blood was SHOCKING!

Autumn's and Lily's deaths both needed Public Inquiries. I believe the Coroner's Office knew this also, or I'd never have received these reports. Their precious lives should have accounted for something!

More Grief, Trauma, and Miracles!

Teen years are often tumultuous years for them and their parents. Charlene was now in high school and from her diagnosis of Post-traumatic Stress Disorder and losing her two sisters and grandpa getting sick, she had crippling anxiety and panic attacks and began missing a lot of high-school. She had to take summer school to catch up.

We had the children enrolled in a Christian school because we needed support. This school was considering putting Charlene with one of their church families because she was acting out at home and missing school. That was shocking to Chuck and me, because they didn't even consult with us that they were considering this, and we found this out from Charlene. Naturally, that didn't happen, and she wanted to go to another school in grade 11. We supported her. Chuck and I had a contract with her to respect our boundaries, but that was difficult to monitor.

At 18 years of age, she received money that was held in trust for her from her First Nations' Band. Due to her impulsivity, she spent it in less than a week.

I was still close with Charlene during her teen years, but due to her trauma and the special needs she presented, I felt like I was on a roller coaster with her. She wanted me close to her, never wanting me to leave her, acting like a frightened child, to switching and acting out, and then I was her worst enemy.

This is normal for teens to some extent, but for those who have experienced the degree of trauma she had, it can be very exaggerated. It had to have been draining for her, as it certainly was for me.

She was put on medications for her mental health issues, but was not taking them. After a while, she realized she needed to take them.

Charlene graduated from grade 12, and that spring she applied to go to university at the First Nations' University of Canada (FNUC). She was accepted to begin that fall.

Miracle # 16 – A Warning and an Intervention by God

We were in a low-rental home from the Saskatchewan Housing Authority. We still worked some, but raising four children and being now in our early sixties, we didn't work much.

My savings had gone on putting Chuck and me through university and seminary, and the rest went into the home I purchased as an investment for our business, which was stolen by a hostile takeover.

In the summer of 2012, Charlene seemed to be stable and doing better. She was excited about going to university in the fall. She had a car now and was socializing with her friends.

Jonathan had just finished grade nine. Kayla and Lance were still in elementary school, attending a Catholic school close to where we rented.

That summer, on a Wednesday night, I had a 'God dream.' In the dream, I was shown Charlene connected to a male and saw that they had a definite connection, but it was concerning. This male was someone I did not know.

It seemed that Charlene didn't know this person very well either. It was not clear to me what that connection was, but it was unsettling, and it was a warning. The dream was that short.

So I prayed about it, and three days after having the dream and it not going away, I decided I needed to talk with Charlene.

Now, on Saturdays, the motto at our house was 'work before play!' Chuck would do some counseling while the kids and I would get our chores done so we could have the rest of the day to ourselves. So I decided to talk with her before we all had our usual Saturday morning 'check-in' before chores.

I asked Charlene to come into the living room and sit with me on the couch, as I wanted to talk with her. I asked her how things were going, as we had that contract with her. She reported that everything was going great. I then told her I had a dream about her, and in it, she had a connection to a man, and it was unsettling.

Then I said, "So, Charlene, I am going to ask you again, how is everything going?"

She turned away from me and responded indignantly, "Well, you should know, shouldn't you!? You had a dream, didn't you!?"

I said that I wasn't shown everything, but there was a definite connection to this man, and then I spontaneously asked her if she was pregnant. She said she was not going through with it, and she had gone to Planned Parenthood and had another appointment that afternoon. Further, she was getting an abortion that coming week.

So, what happens to me in crisis situations is that I go into overdrive to get through them. That's neither 'good nor bad,' it is just me. I called the other three grandkids into the living room for our usual check-in before Saturday chores.

I started out by telling them that Charlene was going to have a baby, to which Kayla said, "Oh, that's different!" I said we were going to support her and the baby.

Then I told them the story in the Bible where Jesus came across a woman who had been caught in a sexual sin, and they were going to stone her to death. Jesus said to the crowd that anyone who had not sinned was to cast the first stone.

Then everyone put their stones down and walked away because they knew that each of them had sinned and done wrong. Then I told them that Jesus did one more thing: He went to the woman and said, "Neither do I condemn you, now go and sin no more." So I told Charlene that we, as a family, were all there to support her and none of us was condemning her. I told them that the one scripture that I have always stood on was Romans 8:28 NIV:

28 "And we know that in all things God works for the good of those who love him, who have been called according to his purpose."

I said that God would take this situation and make it a blessing for Charlene and our family.

Then the kids left to start their chores, and Charlene said to me that she was still going ahead with the abortion, and she didn't care what I thought. She said that she'd just gotten accepted into university, and this isn't happening.

I told her that it is happening, meaning you are pregnant. Further, I told her that she needed to understand that there'd be no abortion happening under our roof (Chuck's and mine), but we would support her if she had her baby.

She asked, "What does that mean? Do I need to get out?"

I said that if she was going to have an abortion, it was her decision, but she would need to move out before that happened.

She panicked and said, "Can't I ever come back here?"

"You cannot live here, but you can come and go and visit, and the love we have for you will never change that. What you do about your baby is on you because you are 18 years old," I replied.

Charlene had been through hell with the loss of her baby sisters, and the childhood abuse she suffered was more than tragic, but she still had to face this as an adult.

She said, "Well, I am going to have an abortion."

With that, she packed up clothing and toiletries, and off she went. She became connected to the Youth Pastor at the church that supported the Options Pregnancy Center.

The Youth Pastor called me to remind me that it was Charlene's decision as to whether she had an abortion or not. I was reminded that they even have funerals at this center if they do abort their baby, so they can help the mom bring closure to their experience.

I told this Youth Pastor, "This all sounds great, but what would Jesus do?" I emphasized that no one was taking away 'her right to choose' because she had a 'free will' to do whatever she wanted to do, but under 'our roof' she didn't have three Options, only two: one is 'to keep' her baby or two 'to adopt' her baby to another family. His response was that he burst out laughing. Jesus said,

"Your boasting is not good. Don't you know that a little yeast leavens the whole batch of dough?"
1 Corinthians 5:6NIV.

Here, Jesus was talking about sin and the religious teachings of the Pharisees and Sadducees of that day, which are still evident in too many churches today.

Charlene's Decision – *God Was With Her!*

"Teach children how they should live, and they will remember it all their lives."
Proverbs 22:6. Good News Translation

Children can go their own way and rebel and use drugs and alcohol, but when, as a parent or guardian, you have planted the 'Word of God' in them as a child, it will not return void.

They can be in the worst mess of their lives, but they know He's there for them to reach out or call out to and that He'll respond. He never left them; they left Him.

I had faith she'd make her own decision and the right one.

Fear is Awful – *'Trust and Obey for There's No Other Way!'*

As a child, I heard my mom singing this around our house, 'Trust and obey for there's no other way to be happy in Jesus, but to trust and obey.'

Mom was not a good singer, but she tried. However, it was those words in this song that she sang over and over again on any given day that remained in my spirit and heart.

Charlene had her own experiences with God and visions and dreams. One such time was when Chuck was in the girls' bedroom saying bedtime prayers with them. I had just come out of the bathroom, and at the end of the hallway, I heard a male's voice clearly and emphatically but rather annoyingly say, "Heh! You're not paying attention to me!"

The voice was elevated at the end of the hallway outside the girls' bedroom. Jonathan and Lance's bedroom was across from their room, and both were sleeping with their door closed.

I immediately recognized this disembodied voice as an entity that was not welcome here. I went down to the girls' room. Kayla was asleep, but Charlene was awake, and I asked Chuck and her, "Did you hear that?"

They both said they did. Chuck responded that he heard it, but it was likely that Ernie doll that Jonathan had that says "I'm so tired!" I assured Chuck it wasn't the doll talking. Charlene, who was around nine years old, stated exactly what I heard, "Heh! You're not paying attention to me!"

That same evening, after the children were all asleep, Chuck was downstairs, and I was in the living room reading, this entity spoke again, "Heh! You're not paying attention to me!" This time, the voice was just inside the front door in our living room, and it was clearly directed at me.

This time, I addressed it and said, "No, I am not paying attention to you, and you are to leave our home right now in Jesus' name!" I couldn't be sure that worked, but I was hopeful.

Three days later, this entity woke Charlene up. She felt a hand on her shoulder waking her up, and it said the same thing to her, "Heh! You're not paying attention to me!"

Normally, she'd come running to get me and be frightened, but she didn't. So I asked her why she didn't come to get me. She told me that she was so scared that she called for Jesus to help her, and that the room filled with a bright light and she fell back to sleep.

We never experienced that entity again. Another encounter she had was when she was 11 years old. She was in the living room and yelling for us to come quickly, saying, "Jesus is outside our house. He's standing at the end of our driveway."

I heard her from my bedroom, and by the time I got there, she said, "Grandma, I really did see Jesus. He was there, and He just disappeared when you came." That was like when I heard the angels singing in the Royal Bank, and when Mary got there, it all stopped.

Of course, I wanted to know what Jesus looked like. She told me that He had such a kind face and was smiling at her and waved to her. She said, "Grandma, I waved back to Him." She was so excited and so happy that I knew that He'd come to her for such a time as this.

I asked her what He was wearing, and she said He was in a white gown with a red scarf across Him, and she showed me that it was diagonally across Him.

Another experience she had was when we were visiting the gravesites of her infant sisters. She was sitting on the ground between two tombstones, where they were buried. She said, "Grandma, I just saw a lady's feet walk by and she had sandals on." She felt comforted and felt those feet belonged to an angel connected to her sisters and her. She saw this reflection like in a mirror that appeared on the shiny black onyx headstone across from her. So I never worried that Charlene would go through with an abortion because she knew the Lord and He was with her through the 'hell' she'd been through as a child, and He was with her now.

She knew that God had given me this dream about this man and her, and even though she had been rebellious, He'd never left her and never would.

On the Sunday of that same weekend, I turned my laptop on, around midnight, and I saw that Charlene had emailed me, "Grandma, please come and get me in the morning because I am going to have my baby."

That day, we went to the doctor so she could begin her prenatal care. Thank you so very much, Jesus!

February 11, 2013 – *Charlene's Healthy Baby Boy!*

Charlene named her precious son Noah Peter Lee. What a beautiful baby he was, and what a wonderful boy and blessing that he has been to Charlene and our family. God is so good!

We had to move from our rental home with the Saskatchewan Housing Authority because we were making enough money by now to have to pay the increase in their rent, which was over $1,600 plus utilities, which we could not manage, with office expenses and raising our grandchildren and helping Charlene. We could not manage financially, so Chuck bought us a mobile home in Glen Elm Trailer Court.

Charlene, now an adult, was able to sign a contract with the Saskatchewan Housing Authority, and she and Jonathan were able to stay in the house. We did not want to rent as the prices were very high, and to buy a home, the prices were also at an all-time high.

I didn't want to be on the title for the mobile home, as I never knew if the Saskatchewan Government would attempt to collect on their invoice for me to pay up. I didn't accept their offer to waive their bill if I promised not to bring this matter forward ever again. I never received invoices from the other four lawyers on behalf of their defendants.

A Change of Venue – *And the Grandkids are Growing Up*

After leaving our downtown office after renting there for 12 years, we now had two spots to counsel from at a Baptist Church, not too far from us. We continued to see clients while raising Kayla and Lance.

We were still very involved with Jonathan, Charlene, and baby Noah, who was growing and such a blessing. We were still attending the same evangelical church, which, sadly, Charlene felt that some now treated her differently after she had Noah. Yet, there were others like Geraldine who emanated Christ-like values and loved her.

I told Charlene that I knew she had asked for forgiveness and that God had turned her sin, like He does all of our sins, into something beautiful if we allow Him to work in our lives.

Both Charlene and Jonathan were baptized in this church, which was a water baptism by immersion. After the Pastor had lowered Jonathan into the baptismal waters, and he came up, the Pastor turned to the congregation, and with a smirk said, "Well, we'll see how long that lasts!"

I couldn't believe that, but there was more to come of this leadership's mindset and attitude.

Charlene and Jonathan left the Saskatchewan Housing Authority and rented a home. Both had jobs for a time. Kayla was turning into a rebellious teenager who was becoming difficult to manage.

Kayla began using alcohol and drugs to cope with what I suspected to be Attention Deficit Disorder (ADD). I took her to an addiction counselor who apparently told her that she didn't have a problem.

Of course, she did have a problem. One evening with friends, under the influence, she decided to jump out of a moving car. When the police came, she ran from them, and when one caught her, she slugged him, all 110 pounds of her. She was put in jail for a night and most of a day. She was feisty, and we hoped this experience would turn things around. We thanked the Lord that she wasn't gravely hurt or had died.

Thank God, Kayla graduated from grade 12. By the end of grade 12, she was out of control, and for Chuck's and my sanity, I urged her to move out. She did, but we still stayed connected.

Helen is Dying of Cancer – *There'll Be No Miracle for Healing This Time*

Helen would have been 87 years old in four months when she went to be with the Lord on August 28, 2013.

A Recap of Helen's Miracle:

I feel led to refer you back to Helen's miracle when she was 59 years old. It is at 11.6.

Saying Good Bye – *Thank You, God, and Thank You, Helen!*

This time, she was diagnosed with cancer of the pancreas, and she did not feel led to call for the Elders of the church. Her husband, Emil, was not a believer, yet he wondered how this first healing was possible.

The last time I went to see Helen, it was in the hospital at Central Butte, SK. Chuck and I could see she was very low. She said she would not be getting well this time. Before Chuck and I left her, I thanked Helen for having me and told her that I loved her.

She said she was glad she'd had me, and that she loved me too. Of course, we'd said these things on other occasions through the years, but this would be our last time here on planet Earth.

Emil and their daughter arrived just as we finished our visit. Emil said rather sarcastically, "Well, Jesus better come soon!" Of course, he was losing his wife, and it was a very trying time.

At suppertime, three days after our visit, I received a call from Helen's daughter to let me know that she had passed. Before hanging up, I asked to speak to Emil.

He said, "Arlene, Jesus did show up!" I was about to ask how so, but he went on to explain, "I was sitting beside Helen right by the window and all of a sudden it got dark outside and then there was a big flash of lightning right outside of the window and the lights went out and Helen was gone, just like that!"

Somehow, that experience shook him to his core, and I believe his cynicism left and made a believer out of him.

The funeral was held in Moose Jaw, SK. Their daughter asked me to speak, and Lincoln was a pallbearer. I never wanted to see Helen in her casket and didn't.

Miracle #17: – The Angels are Singing Again

Raising four grandchildren, I became a night hawk. This was the time when the house was quiet and the kids and Chuck were asleep. The Lord and I could have our time, or I could do some administration work for our counselling business.

It was after midnight on 9/11 (September 11th, 2013), exactly two weeks after Helen's funeral, when I turned on my laptop and the screen said 'Locked out.' That never happened before.

Then I heard music coming from it. As I listened, I immediately recognized that it was those angels again, and there were 'throngs of angels,' singing at octaves that no human could ever begin to produce or reach. There could be no doubt that I was listening to angels.

There was one disappointment. There was no message like before. They were praising God and in a language totally foreign to me. So I didn't want to yell for anyone to come to hear it because, like with Mary, it might just stop. Everyone was asleep anyway.

It was celestial and gorgeous, and I could hardly believe that I was hearing this. I knew exactly what I was hearing and what was coming through my laptop, as it was as clear as it could be.

As I sat there listening, I became excited and thought about how I could record it. I had just gotten my first cell phone, and I didn't know how to record on it. So I checked how to do it, and I got the steps down and then tried to record it.

Wow! It worked! I had recorded it on my phone, and now I could play it for my family and anyone else. I put a long recording on it. Then I continued to listen to them on my laptop and was getting very tired. I didn't want to turn my laptop off, but I had to, and so I did and went to bed.

The next day, I played the recording on my phone for Chuck and the grandkids. Charlene had grown close to Helen during her illness after Noah was born. When she heard this recording, she said that she prayed, asking God to give her a sign that Helen was with Him, and as she was listening to this singing, she said she knew this was an answer to her prayer.

I played the recording for the Pastor's wife, where Jonathan and Charlene were baptized. I thought she'd be excited to hear this, but she showed no excitement. Her only comment was, "Arlene, why do you think only you heard this?"

I wasn't sure why such a question was even being asked, but my answer was, "I think the Lord wanted to minister to me." For about three months, I played that recording to various people, and it ministered to them also.

One day, I was in Moose Jaw, SK with Lance, and he asked to take a video of the planes flying in an air show going on from the Air Force base. Sadly, I didn't think that Lance's videotaping would go over my recording, but it did, and it was lost. I wanted to get upset with him, but then I knew not to because it was accidental. It was as the Lord wanted it to be.

I wanted to take it to the university, to the linguistics department, to see if they could decipher the words that were being sung. Yet, I was thankful to God for this experience.

I never saw Emil after the funeral, as his daughter had no love for me, and she would not want me showing up to visit her dad.

After a few years had passed, I heard from one of Helen's relatives that Emil was in the nursing home at Central Butte, SK. I inquired about him, but a staff person told me he had recently passed away. I believe he is with the Lord and with Helen, too.

2015 to 2019 – *Graduations and Grief*

Reflections on Our Family Times – Memories!

As a family, we always made it to various Bible Camps during the summer months and on certain occasions like Thanksgiving and Christmas. There were three main family Bible camps we'd go to, and we'd also send the kids to Bible camps for their age groups during the summer months. These camps were always a blessing for us, as we did not have much extra money to go on holidays with four children.

We had lots of trips to beaches and had picnics and barbeques. Chuck did get the boys into baseball and floor hockey, and all four grandkids were into soccer. We tried to provide as normal a childhood for them as possible.

Chuck and I were hoping to move out of the mobile home into a condo, leaving Charlene to rent it with Noah. We had an offer on a condo in the middle of

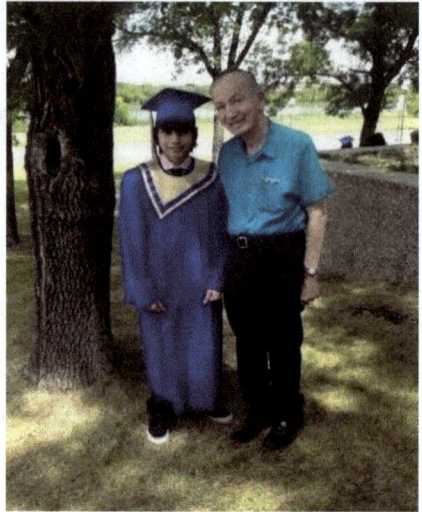

Photo of Jonathan's Grade 12 graduation with Chuck

March 2019. Right at that time, the doctor had found a spot on his lung that they weren't sure what it was.

The photo below is a collage that the children did for their Mom for her birthday, June 25, 2017.

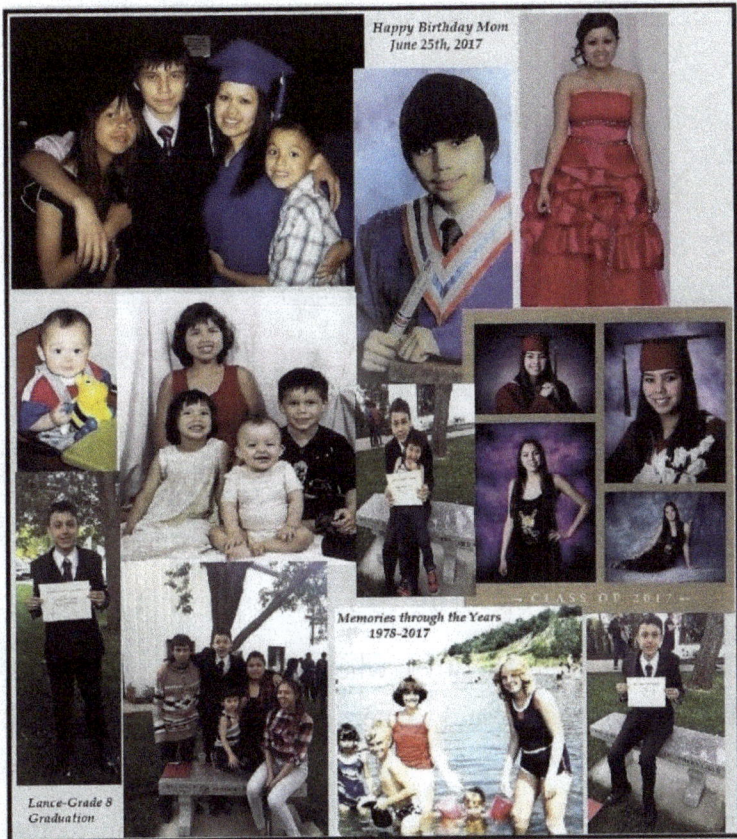

Happy Birthday Mom
June 25th, 2017

Memories through the Years
1978-2017

CLASS OF 2017

Lance-Grade 8
Graduation

The top left of the above photo is all four children at Charlene's graduation. Next to her photo is Jonathan's grade 12 graduation photo. Top right is Charlene in her grade 12 grad dress, below her are Kayla's graduation photos. The little guy in the highchair is Lance.

Below is Lance's grade eight graduation with his siblings and Noah. The photo at the bottom center is of Lincoln, Lin, and Caine with me and my friend's daughter, Debbie. We are at the lake enjoying a swim.

Soon after Jonathan's grade 12 graduation, he joined the army. In the beginning of March 2019, Chuck went to Jonathan's acceptance ceremony into the army along with Charlene.

Later that day, we had a send-off supper at home.

"Arlene, You are Going to Live Longer Than Me."

It was on March 16, 2019, when Chuck and I were sitting in the living room and he said to me, "Arlene, you are going to live longer than me."

"Why are you saying that?" I asked. "Are you ready for takeoff? I thought we were going to go together in the rapture."

The Rapture, of course, is prophesied in the Bible, how the Christians will be raptured as Christ is to return for His Bride, which is His church.

He said, "I was talking about ten years from now." I wanted to believe that. I didn't want to think about what he said to me. I had seen him becoming frailer in the past couple of months. Chuck never complained about his health and just kept going.

Earlier on the evening of March 19, 2019, I had been to a friend's place for supper, but when I came home, Chuck had a cough like he'd get from time to time. I went to the drug store and got him cough syrup with codeine, as that would settle it down.

He took that and went off to bed, and I said I'd be there shortly. He kept coughing, and when I came to bed, he said to me, "The cough syrup is not working this time."

I said, "Chuck, I think we should go to the hospital and have you checked out."

He emphatically said, "No!" Then I said that I'd call the paramedics to come and check him out, and if they thought he should go into the hospital, then we'll go in.

With that, he insisted, "Arlene, turn the lamp off and lie beside me." I did what he asked me to do, I turned the light out and laid beside him.

As I lay there, I asked, "Can I pray for you, for us?"

"Yes," he replied.

I took his hand and I prayed, "Lord Jesus, you see Chuck and he needs to get well and I ask you, Lord, to give him a 'healing touch' and a good rest tonight." Then, I added, "Lord, please send your angels tonight because we can use them." We said goodnight to one another and that we loved one another.

It was approximately 3:00 a.m. when Chuck called me asking for help to go to the bathroom. He was so weak that he could not walk. I settled him in bed in a sitting position when Charlene happened to come out of her bedroom.

I asked her to come to the living room and told her that grandpa wasn't doing well. Before I could say it, she said we needed to call the ambulance. She called 911 and said she'd wait outside for them and asked them not to put the sirens on.

The paramedics arrived, a man and a woman. The woman was asking Chuck a lot of questions, which he tried to answer. Chuck was able to tell them it hurt when they took his blood pressure. She began an intravenous after hearing this.

Charlene held the intravenous bag as the woman took his vitals. I sat on the bed near Chuck. As I looked at Charlene standing at the end of the bed holding the intravenous bag, she mouthed the words, "he's dying," and the fear in her eyes was palpable.

I knew he was dying. The woman paramedic said, "Mr. Lowery, you are very ill and we need to take you to the hospital."

I'm Not Going to Any Hospital! – *I am Going Home to be with the Lord!*

That was the very last place that he wanted to go, and in fact, he decided right then, or God did, that he was not going anywhere. With that, he called out my name and reached for my hand, and I took it. As he leaned towards me, his face went bright red, and the sound he made was like a woman giving her last push to birth her baby, and he was gone!

I sensed his spirit leave the room, and I said, "He has stopped breathing."

The paramedic said, "Get off the bed! We need to shock him."

"Grandpa, you can't die, you can't!" Charlene cried out.

They were not able to bring him back. The paramedics asked, "Should we keep trying?" Charlene was so traumatized, she said, "Keep trying! He can't die, he can't!"

I went to the living room and called my son Caine, who lived only eight blocks from me. Lance got up, and soon Noah was up too. The police arrived, and so did the fire department.

Soon, Caine was there. The paramedics told him that they managed to get a heartbeat, but I knew that Chuck's heart with that Teflon patch had finally given out. They continued to try for 40 minutes, and there was nothing more they could do. I am sure they did this for Charlene.

Our Grief – *Our Memories!*

Kayla soon arrived, and she was devastated. Her grandpa had a very special place in his heart for her, and she had a very special place in her heart for him.

I felt numb and cried a little, but I was more in shock. My helpmate was gone. Chuck loved me unconditionally. He went through all of those difficult times with me when I was busy with a lawsuit against these defendants, and he never complained once.

Sure, he did say once in a while it would be nice if we had alone time or went on a vacation just us, but that was about it.

Early on, in raising the kids, he'd get frustrated with them acting out at the table, and he let them know he was upset and went into our bedroom, hollered, and slammed the door.

I was the enforcer, and I had a talk with him about slamming doors. I reasoned that his frustration was understandable as he had not brought up children, and here we had four. Yet, he needed more emotional regulation, and I told him that if he got frustrated, he could go for a walk or take a drive and come back later, and we'd talk about it. I said you'll not slam doors!

So we had that understanding. When he became frustrated in the child-rearing of four kids, he was off to Bingo, and there were quite a few Bingo dabbers in his car.

In the week before he died, he said to me, "Arlene, do you remember when I'd get frustrated with the kids and you'd point to the door and I knew to leave?"

I said, "I sure do!" and we both laughed. In fact, that was the same time he told me I'd live longer than him.

If I forgot my glasses at the office, Chuck would go and get them. He always made sure I had lunch when we were working. I could go on and on in the little ways he spoiled and loved me. If we hadn't had Jesus at the center of our lives, we would never have made it.

He always picked each card that he bought me and for the kids with a lot of thought and love behind them. You could be sure he'd carefully read the words so they matched his heart.

After Chuck passed, Kayla was looking through the cards we'd bought each other, and she found one card that I'd given Chuck where it said how patient he was 'all of the time,' and I crossed out the word 'all' and put 'most' of the time. We had a good laugh.

Chuck was the best husband I could have had. At the same time, he thought he was fortunate and blessed to have married me.

We counseled together, shared our love for the Lord and our faith together, and we learned how to give each other grace, at times lots of grace. We were married just short of 25 years.

March 20, 2019 – *I am a Widow Now and the Children are Fatherless.*

It was getting light outside, and the coroner had just left. The hearse had taken Chuck away. As one of the police officers was going to leave, he came by and gave each of us a hug and said to all of us, "Tonight, I saw so much love in this family."

There was, and there is. We have our strained moments on occasion, but the love of our family underpinned it all.

When we went to Lee's Funeral Home, the Funeral Director told us that they had Chuck on a gurney just behind the wall of the office that we were meeting in. She asked if we would like to go around and view him. She said that he was not embalmed, but we were welcome to see him.

This was something that I did not want to do, but the three grandchildren wanted to. We came around the wall separating the office from where Chuck was lying, and Lance draped himself over Chuck's body and just wept and wept. It was a deeply touching moment.

I noticed that Chuck had a big smile on his face. The funeral director said, "Yes, that is how he came." She went on to say that she'd seen a lot of corpses in her day, but never one who came with a big smile on his face. That'd be Chuck!

Jonathan was not there as he was in Quebec, just starting his course for the army, and he decided he wasn't going to come home. He soon called back crying to say he had to come home for grandpa's funeral and arrived the next day.

I had no inclination to call Chuck back to life like the time I did with Sandra, and I will tell you why.

The Lord Prepared Me – *Yet Held Me In the Dark*

Around mid-December in 2018, three months before Chuck's passing, I had three dreams in succession.

The first dream was seeing children grief-stricken and crying because it was like their parent had died, and it was very 'heart-wrenching' and disturbing. Then, I saw an angel sitting on a large rock and bent over, carving a cross to go on to something, perhaps like a casket. This cross was connected to whoever these children were crying over, as it seemed someone close to these children had died.

The next day, I told Chuck about the dream, thinking that the Lord may be bringing some children to me for 'grief counseling' who had lost their parents.

The second dream I had was where I was in the church we were attending, and I was shown that there was no room for me there, and they, the Pastor and a few parishioners, wanted me to pack up and leave, as there was no ministry there for me. The scenes were descriptive.

The third dream I had was in this same church. There was a celebration that was to take place at the end of December to commemorate a 'crossing over' to the new church building they'd acquired. As I was waking up from this dream, I heard the Lord speak to me, "You will not be crossing over!" That dream was a confirmation of the previous dream.

Often, that's how God does things: He provides a confirmation so there's no doubt about what you are to do, or how you are to do it, or how He is leading you. I also told Chuck about the other two dreams.

In the past few months, we considered leaving this church, but Chuck was still, on occasion, giving messages on a Sunday at a Seniors Care Home as a representative of this church.

I noted that the last two times Chuck preached there, two different Elders from the church sat in on his messages and were taking notes, which seemed odd to me.

In the last message Chuck gave, he mentioned Ash Wednesday and talked about a CNN commentator commemorating Lent by having ashes on his face and what that meant to some Christians about Ash Wednesday.

A few days before the next Sunday, when Chuck was to give a message again, he was told that they had found someone else to do it. That was odd to me. Perhaps he was let go. Yet, we did attend this church's service.

On our way to church that Sunday, Chuck said to me, "Arlene, I am surprised that you still want to go to this church," referring to my dream about 'my not crossing over to this new church building.' I told him, "I'm taking your lead and not leaving unless you hear from God and say we are to go." Three days later, God had Chuck leave that church, and he 'crossed over' into heaven.

The Funeral Service – *"Keep it Short!"*

After Chuck died, I did not call this Pastor as I was grieving, planning his funeral and being there for our grandchildren. About two days after he'd passed, the Pastor had heard about Chuck's passing and called me to ask me where the funeral was going to be held. I said it would be a small one, and perhaps we could do it in the chapel at Lee's Funeral Home.

He said we could have it at the church, and so I accepted his offer. Charlene, Kayla, and I met with the Pastor and his wife at the church office to plan the funeral.

The Pastor said that since the service was going to be mid-week, some people would be coming from work and may need to get back to work again; therefore, it was best to keep the service short, about twenty minutes.

The funeral came, and it was a nice send-off for Chuck, although he'd already been sent off. Jesus didn't have a funeral, and we really didn't need one, but tradition says we should.

We picked Lin up for the funeral from a hotel, but she'd been drinking. She sobered up enough and was given some breath spray and took the service in. I was glad she came and showed her respect for Chuck, and she was a support for me, along with my son, Caine, other family members, and friends.

The head Pastor and his assistant briefly spoke at the service, and the Pastor's wife videotaped it. A few of Chuck's friends and a past participant from one of our rehabilitation programs spoke about Chuck. I did the obituary, and I took at least fifteen minutes to talk about my husband and our life together.

Charlene, Jonathan, and Lance spoke about their love for their grandpa, too. Kayla didn't speak but stood there with her siblings. I'm sure she'd have broken down crying.

At the end of the service, the Pastor made a point of saying to the attendees that at funerals, you always hear the nice things that are said about the person (which implies that if only you really knew the other things). I wondered why that needed to be said at all. There was a luncheon after, and it was a lovely service. Actually, the service went well over an hour.

After the funeral, I apologized to the Pastor for going over the twenty minutes, but it was a very insincere apology. God forgive me! He told me that they'd planned to move furniture that afternoon from the old church into the new one, where the service was being held, and that was the reason he wanted to keep it short.

I took note that he lied the first time, stating that the service should be kept short as attendees may want to get back to work and certainly took note of his priorities.

After Chuck's death, neither the Pastor nor his wife bothered to call me to ask how I was doing, but of course, I never did crossover to their new church just as God had instructed me.

A few months later, I sent a check for the service. This prompted his wife to call me to thank me for the money and to say that they'd use the money to startup an addiction program in

Chuck's memory, and asked me what my future plans would now be.

Since their previous Youth Pastor had relapsed in his addiction and died of an overdose, I suggested they perhaps do their addiction program in his name also.

The grandkids honored their grandpa! Besides Chuck being a great grandpa, he was also the best dad that our grandchildren could have had. He loved each and every one of them unconditionally, and I know they loved him.

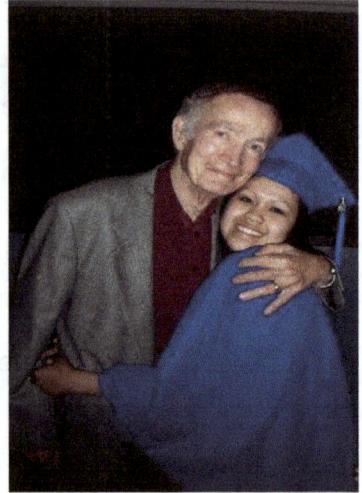

The following is what Charlene wrote as a Memoriam to her grandpa on Lee's Funeral Home's Website on April 10, 2019:

'Grandpa was the kindest man I knew, you could always go to him for a simple hug, and be able to feel safe and loved in his arms. Grandpa was the best dad a girl could ask for.

He loved all four of us so much. I will cherish my memories and love you always.'

Charlene Dobson

This year, on the sixth anniversary of Chuck's death, March 20, 2025, Kayla also posted her memory of grandpa. She posted this on Facebook with a photo of Chuck and me at her grade 12 graduation and left this message:

"6 years without you and not a day goes by where I don't miss you."

Chapter 30
A New Beginning – What Will That Look Like, Lord?

Being a widow was a new experience. At first, I wanted to be gone and be with Chuck. Although divorce was devastating for me and my children, and Wayne's death was hard, this felt somewhat different.

Financially, as well as emotionally, I was on my own. The grandchildren were feeling the loss, and I was more fully aware of the meaning of this scripture: James 1:26-27 (ESV)

If anyone thinks he is religious and does not bridle his tongue but deceives his heart, this person's religion is worthless. Religion that is pure and undefiled before God the Father is this: to visit orphans and widows in their affliction, and to keep oneself unstained from the world.

James 1:26-27 (ESV- 2016)

I had not saved any RRSPs for retirement as I had nothing much to save. I left the nursing field early, and I didn't have a working pension. My savings from the money inherited from my parents and Uncle Charlie were invested into the property for The Anchorage and were stolen when the government pulled off a hostile takeover of it. I had also spent the remainder of my savings on our education. So now I am self-employed and I live in a mobile home with Lance, Charlene, and Noah.

I found out that Chuck had a $3,500.00 life insurance policy, which was used to help bury him. I am not complaining, but this was my reality.

The condo Chuck and I were going to buy fell through. With the cost of living and needing to finish raising Lance and helping out Charlene with Noah, I had to work, and I was now in my early seventies.

One thing I was sure of was that I had a Father whom I called Abba Father, who would now be a husband to me. I had the Holy Spirit, the Comforter, whom Jesus Christ had sent once He went back to His Father. I had to roll my grief onto my Father because He asks us to, as He knows it is too much for us to carry:

"For my yoke is easy and my burden is light."

Matthew 11:30

Moved Our Counseling Business – *Needing Only One Office*

By June 01, 2019, I had moved our office to a nice facility on Victoria Avenue. The kids and I had church on Sundays in our living room until the late fall, and then we began attending a small church that was trying to become planted in Regina.

I was working extra hard and too hard for the first while, wondering how I was going to financially make out. The Lord has recently slowed me down. I am blessed to be able to still work part-time, but I sense God has something new for me, and I will fully retire very soon from my counseling business.

371

Charlene's Unraveling – *'The Toll of Grief'*

With her grief over her grandpa's death and having witnessed him dying, she relapsed with her PTSD and panic attacks. Emotional regulation was often difficult for her. She couldn't work during that time, and she had a very good job as an assistant administrator with the Saskatchewan Government.

She didn't give up her job but was forced to. She was to go on 'short-term disability.' Instead, her employer sent her a letter stating that she had abandoned her job, when they knew the truth since she–had given them doctors' reports. She kept leaving messages at the psychiatrist's office to get a report to her employer, but that never happened.

The psychiatrist blamed his secretary for not getting his report to them on time. Charlene had no reserves to fight this, as her physical health was suffering from diabetes, and she was sick.

They legally could not release her from her job 'for cause' because she was a model employee and had excellent reviews, so they came up with a lame excuse that she simply wasn't showing up and had abandoned her job. COVID had just started, Her employer knew better than to do this to her, and even though she was unable to get the psychiatrist's report, they had other medical reports, and they knew she was having difficulty getting the psychiatrist's report. Was she experiencing racism? It sure seemed like it.

The World is Unraveling – *The COVID-Effect!*

By the beginning of 2020, COVID was on the march, and people were panicking, stocking up on toilet paper and so on.

Controversy and conspiracies were flying around. Addictions were increasing, and the mental health of people was on the decline.

Chuck's friend who spoke at his funeral, Rev. Murray Logan, died of COVID ten months after Chuck passed. They prayed together every Friday. Likely, they're still doing that.

Churches and families were splitting over what to do about COVID-19. Don't take the vaccine or take it, mask up, don't mask up. Poor Dr. Fauci was either a villain or a hero. The far-right political groups, including churches aligned with Trump and his dysfunction, spewed out their collective nonsense. Chaos abounded.

People, including me, began working from home and isolating, and Lance was doing his grade 11 and 12 classes online. As a family, we celebrated Lance's achievement of graduating from Grade 12. I am sure Chuck saw it all and celebrated too.

Kayla with Lance   *Lance with Jonathan*

373

Lance was even considering getting into politics and becoming Prime Minister to ensure that all the First Nations reservations had clean drinking water and other things that they needed.

One of his grade 12 teachers told him that if he ever ran for Prime Minister, he'd get her vote for sure!

Somehow, we got through COVID, and Lance graduated in the spring of 2021. Lin and I were able to attend his graduation ceremony. Lance soon had a job at Brandt Industries doing welding, and I was so happy for him.

Lance was a very sweet and caring boy, and he is the same now as a young man. He did not bend the rules too often. If he came home and found that I'd fallen asleep on the couch, he'd go and get a blanket to cover me. I tell you that to let you know he has a kind heart, and I know it'll remain so. On all of his report cards in elementary school, the teachers would say something like this, 'Lance is a wonderful boy!' He absolutely was. Even to this day, he's a blessing to me, just as that Fish (God) told me in that dream, that he'd be a blessing to me.

Charlene started going back to University in 2023. Kayla got clean and sober and married a wonderful man. They recently had their second daughter.

Jonathan left the Army a few years ago for the Navy, and he is stationed in Victoria, BC, studying to become a Marine Technician.

My life was so taken up with Lin and her children and our work that my two sons and their children never received much of my time.

Lincoln has a successful business at Regina Beach and has a grown daughter, Sophia, who is a wonderful young woman. Caine is married to Crystal, and they have two young boys who are sweethearts and keep them very busy. I am fortunate that both my sons and their families live close by.

What Do You Have For Me Now, Lord? – *There Must be More!*

After one year, I was sitting in my living room and thinking about how far I'd come with my grieving and stabilizing the counseling business since Chuck's passing.

I heard the Lord say to me, "Chuck is with Me, Arlene, and you are no longer married, you are Mine. I have work for you to do for Me before you 'cross over,' so follow my leading in everything."

There was a release in my spirit after that and a peace that came from Him.

Truth and Reconciliation – *A Response to the Verbal Apology.*

I know that the Lord wanted the program, that the Indigenous Youth chose, 'to rise from the ashes,' to be implemented. The program Healing the Nation-One Family At A Time was submitted to Canadian Heritage along with an evaluation of the program.

Once they'd shut The Anchorage down, another Indigenous organization asked Canadian Heritage if they could have a copy of this program to implement it, knowing it was such a great program for their people, but they were denied access to it.

Currently, I am writing a simple approach to addressing addictions with a focus on preventing suicides. It is to be uplifting and can be further developed by First Nations' leadership if they see the value in it. The portion I am writing is a vision that I received from the Creator, which is called: The Potter's Wheel-His Hands Only!

I will complete it after this book goes to print and provide it to the wonderful Indigenous peoples that the Creator has connected me with, in one way or another, as well as some of the past participants who took one of these rehabilitation programs.

Indigenous leaders need to embrace 'the vision' and develop it and run with it, for it to become a viable path to Truth and Reconciliation from 'coast to coast to coast to heal their people across Canada, connecting them on their terms.

Chapter 31
The Trappings of Trauma – When to Let Go...

Most of us have had to apologize for something in our lives. While counseling clients, and I am included here, too, we apologize for things we never should have to apologize for.

We do that because we are carrying the shame of others' actions and taking responsibility for them, even protecting them in some cases. We need a filter to determine what we legitimately are responsible for and sorry for, and what we're not!

The book called *Kids Who Carry Our Pain – Breaking the Cycle of Codependency for the Next Generation,* by authors Dr. Paul Warren and Dr. Robert Hemfelt, is exceptional in describing this. One or more family members can carry the pain for the family. They carry not only the trauma for the family but also the toxic shame.

Healing from past traumas also means breaking unhealthy cycles of codependency for you. Hopefully, others will also benefit from it.

Many of us have experienced some type of trauma and unresolved grief. Left untreated, itoften leads to mental health issues, like Post Traumatic Stress Disorder, Anxiety disorders, Borderline Personality, DID, and the list goes on and on. Yet, they are all linked to trauma.

Even though we do have a predisposition to getting these mental illnesses following traumas, two people exposed to the same trauma and circumstances will react differently, since it has to do with such areas as our genetics, temperaments, past and current life experiences.

The severity depends on the support and intervention that are available to each individual at the time. With so many variables, one thing remains constant: trauma and grief require healing, since if we don't heal, other people around us are the recipients of our acting out, addictions, and narcissism.

Today, there is a lot said about narcissism and its various forms. Basically, narcissism is self-centeredness, which accompanies an elevated pseudo-ego. It is not pleasurable to be around people who display these behaviors and manipulate you to have their own needs met.

Empathy and even sympathy are necessary attributes for us to have when dealing with family members who have not healed from their traumas, but this validation will not heal them.

As a non-Indigenous person, I have had to ask myself, "Arlene, are you responsible for the historical trauma that my daughter and grandchildren have experienced?"

I have lived over seven decades, and that time has gone fast, and much of what happened was long before I walked this earth. Yet, I am responsible for my own actions.

We all have a destiny with the hope of leaving this world a little better than when we found it. We must heal ourselves and extend healing to our family members, and help them in their own journey. At times, it requires tough love or even letting go.

If a family member refuses to help themselves, then you must walk away and let them wallow in their self-pity and pray for them to get help. Their unresolved trauma is like a landmine.

It is hard to let go when you see that the loved one is not stable and you worry that they may take their life, but God, your Creator, will lead you in your journey, and you can trust Him.

Next, I share about a personal struggle with codependency and trauma within my own family.

The Very Thing I Knew I Should Do – *I Couldn't Do!*

After Chuck died, I was still living with Charlene, Noah, and Lance. I now wanted a place of my own.

Through Charlene's teens and twenties, there were happy highlights, trips, and good times. We were really good or we were really bad. At times, it felt like co-dependency on steroids. When this was in play, it caused considerable stress between us.

I bought Charlene a trailer across the street from me so Noah and she could have their own place and to help create some distance between us. The trailer needed lots of repairs.

Charlene also helped me in many ways as I did her, but we needed healthier boundaries, and I wasn't sure how we'd get there. There was no doubt that we loved each other very much. She gave me beautiful cards, too. Still, my helping her with her childhood traumas, and her now being an adult, a change was needed.

I am unable to change anyone. That is a hard lesson for any parent and every therapist to learn, since we wish we had a 'magic wand' to make everything better.

I tell my clients that I am not a fixer, but I am a facilitator. I am there to listen to your story and respond to it by helping you find ways to deal with your losses and your reactions to your issues and traumas.

Yet, when it came to helping Charlene in her teens and early adulthood, it felt like I was teaching her to ride a bike. Whenever I would help her gain balance and let go and say, "Now just keep pedaling, you can do it!" there would be another crisis of either health or death or some other traumatizing event.

Panic and anger were too often directed towards me. Their fear of being abandoned or letting go of that bike is very real to the one coping with unhealed trauma, and it is very real for the parent. Trauma in a family creates codependency as a means of coping.

Charlene needed to know she could pedal on her own and balance. I had to ask myself if I was ready to let go of propping her up. I had been overdoing it for too long. I was also being too dependent on her for certain things, which I could still do on my own. The trade-off wasn't healthy,

I had to let go for good and say, "Pedal! Keep your balance! YOU CAN MAKE IT!"

Online-Dating – *Looking for Mr. Right*

Perhaps the way to get out of this mobile home and on my own would be to find my Prince in Shining Armor! At times, I felt I needed someone to rescue me.

It was 2022, and Chuck had now been gone for over three years. I began to wonder if God has someone for me. No one had come along, and I hadn't really been looking.

I reasoned that God designed us to be in a meaningful relationship and marriage, and so having this desire wasn't wrong.

Then I thought, 'Lord, You are now 'my husbandman' as it says in the Bible, but You could find someone for me, though, and give me away.' I reasoned that He knew the desires of my heart, which were to have another helpmate. Not just any helpmate, but I wanted it all this time: he needed to be a Christian and have You as first in his life; I need to be attracted to him in every way and of course that meant even sexually. And oh God! It would be great if he were 'good-looking' and loved me unconditionally. Oh, and one more thing, Lord, I don't want him to be poor (like Chuck was), and you know I don't have much money. Money was just an asset for comfort.

Co-dependents also try to tell God what to do and how to do it. Guess what? He doesn't like that. Yet, He understands our 'human side' and works with us, and He may even give us the desires of our hearts. It says in the Bible that He will do that – if it's good for us.

Just so everyone knows, besides God, I am in no way a 'gold-digger.' I would contribute to expenses and extras, but I don't want to financially support a man, just as he would not want to fully support me. At this stage of one's life, a prenuptial arrangement is prudent. Of course, I will need one of those for sure, after I sell at least a million copies of this book! – Right?

So I asked, "Lord, who is he and where is he???" Thank God, His mercies are new every morning. He will not give us enough rope to hang ourselves, as a parent would do, but in the process, He teaches us. Hopefully, we learn.

I decided to help God out, so I paid to go on an 'online dating site.' I found one guy who met the criteria listed above. Bingo! I got lucky! At the time, I shared with my Pastor what I'd done. He warned me about catfishers, and by now, I'd heard about them.

Further, he told me that he noticed when we laid Chuck to rest that he saw my emotion and how much I'd cared for Chuck, so I should likely not seek a man and marriage but stay single.

I thought about my age and the saying, 'age is just a number,' but maybe he was right. Yet I thought, 'Am I to be like a nun?' That didn't seem right.

After about three days of connecting with this man, he started 'love bombing' me, which was a red flag. I let it go on since I needed my ego stroked a bit.

Perhaps this is not a miracle, but it is definitely one of those God-dreams—His intervention:

"I was driving, and there was just a little snow covering the ground. It was dusk out. For some reason, I drove off the road, driving in a field. I didn't know where I was going, but I recall I felt happy and content. Then, I heard a loud voice yell, STOP! I slammed on the brakes. Then, I was shown the front tires of my car precariously hanging halfway over the edge of a cliff. If I had gone one inch further, I would have plunged into the ravine below. I then slowly backed up, turned my car around, and got back on the road, heading back from where I'd come."

It was clear that the Lord was warning me not to go any further with this guy, but I decided to play along with him for a few more days. I signed up for a website that identifies these catfishers, and there he was.

When he'd told me he loved me and was about to send me flowers and a teddy bear, I blew his cover, sending him what I'd discovered. Of course, he said, "I do really love you, Arlene!" then switching to say, "I knew I couldn't trust you!"

Lesson learned?

Well, hopefully.

Spiritual Oppression – *What Would Jesus Say and Do?*

In November 2022, Charlene had her gallbladder removed and was very ill. She phoned the Pastor and his wife from the hospital, asking for prayer as she was very sick in medical intensive care.

In March 2023, the Pastor and his wife wondered why Charlene wasn't attending there anymore. I told them that she was attending another church, which had a lot more people her age, as she wanted to meet someone. I explained that Charlene didn't go to bars and lounges and did not like online dating, so it was understandable that she'd want to mix with more people around her age. Most who attended this church were seniors like me.

Upon hearing the reason, they became very indignant, saying that she should not do that because it would be in this church that God would bring her someone to marry.

They went on to remind me that when she was in intensive care last November, Charlene had phoned them asking for prayer, and they fasted and prayed for her. They exclaimed, "Now that she was well again, she did this!" Then I was asked, "What do we get out of it?"

I didn't say anything, but I thought, 'Well, your reward is in heaven, so says the Bible. ' That was one too many insensitive remarks. I still love and care about them, but church leaders need to stop this type of control, as parishioners will end up leaving. Later that week, I decided I had to leave this church, as this kind of control was stifling the Holy Spirit at work in me.

Making A Deal With God – *Would He Listen or Would He Answer!*

It was July 22, 2023, Saturday evening, and I was talking to God. He, of course, knows the number of hairs on our head, so He already knows how I am feeling.

It had now been over four years since Chuck had passed. I said to Him, "Lord I know the last Pastor said to not go on dating websites and that likely I should just remain single until I go to be with You, but I am not under his covering, in fact I am not under any earthy Pastor's covering, but I am under Yours, You alone!

I said, "Lord, You are my Shepherd and I am Your child, so I'll tell You what (can you believe I talk to God like that?) I am going to do. I will go on the Facebook Dating Site. Further, I promise that this will be the last time I'll go on any dating site. If You have someone there for me, please reveal that to me, and if not, then I'm done with online dating."

So I put my photo and information out there, and I went to bed. After being up and having a coffee, I remembered that I had put myself out there on Facebook, and I was also recalling a dream that I had in the night, which I knew was from the Lord.

Anyway, I was anxious to see if anyone had put any likes on my Facebook profile and went there first. I saw there were about a dozen or more likes.

Now for 'the process of elimination,' which sounds rather cold, but now I had to decide if I like him or not, and if I don't sense a connection, then I get to send him to the Recycle Bin. This sounds like going to a buffet and deciding what you like there.

So there was one left out of all of the likes, and I went back and looked again at him. He was four years younger than I, but we were both in our seventies, and he liked me first, so it must not be an issue for him.

So shortly after, I sent him a short text, and he responded. After a few days of being on this Facebook site and texting, I didn't want to be on it anymore, as I am still a businesswoman, and others can see I would be on there, and I thought that may look rather tacky.

So I asked him if we could text by using our phone numbers, and if we could even talk soon. He showed some reluctance to do this and then said, "Sure, it'll be fine."

In the meantime, I went back to the dream I had from the Lord, early Sunday morning on July 23, 2023, and wrote it out.

Here is the dream:

The time of day is dusk, and it is cloudy out. I am standing in a stubble field. I'm looking straight ahead, but I now notice something moving to my right, and I look and see it is a man.

He was about 25 feet from me, which was a significant distance. He was walking perpendicular to me, heading east, and I was standing facing south. When he got in line with me, he stopped and turned his head to the left, and we looked at one another.

He never turned his body towards me, only his head, and never made an effort to walk towards me. He just stood there looking at me. He seemed to want to walk on past me, but for some reason, he was unable to.

What I noticed when I looked at his face was a lot of sorrow, and he seemed weighted down with a lot on his mind. Then, I woke up.

When I looked back at his three photos, he had on Facebook Dating Site, one of them was just like the man that I saw in the dream. Of course, I wasn't going to tell him about this dream and his photo that matched up to what I saw in the dream.

We began to chat, and the conversations were enjoyable. He had his own 'disappointed longings' in life. He was a proud family man.

After talking with me for two days, I could see he was trying to move on, saying things like, "Are you really four years older than me? Do you think about dying? Are you really a great-grandma?" and "I'm not your man if you want this or that."

It was obvious he was trying to discourage me or convince himself that we wouldn't work out and move on. In fact, he called me to say I just want to take you out for supper and to a show, and then quickly said, "I don't know what I want!" I certainly knew that even before he told me this.

So, did I know what I wanted? Well, I knew the kind of man I wanted, if you can recall from the first guy who was a catfisher.

I had mentioned to him that my faith was very important to me and that I love Jesus and have a relationship with Him. He was concerned and said, "Oh, yeah!" I think he may have been wondering if I was one of those 'far-right fundamentalist evangelicals.' As we spoke further, he learned that I was brought up in the United Church, as he was.

Currently, he was attending an Apostolic Church. He seemed to be curious about me, but not wanting to talk much, keeping himself at a definite arm's length.

The following Sunday, from when we first connected, I saw that he had called me in the afternoon, and so I called him back and we talked well over an hour. We learned more about one another, our joys and our losses in life, our grief. This exchange was encouraging, and I was hopeful that I might get to meet him.

That week, he knew and everyone around me knew that I had an infected tooth and would need a root canal, and that I was in a lot of pain.

Three days before I was to get the dental work done, he called me. He was on his way home to his farm and mentioned he'd spent about $23,000 on repairs for his semi and then laughingly added that this money would be enough to fix my teeth because he knew I needed even more work.

I said it's all relative, and he agreed. He said we'd meet soon, perhaps for a coffee at a Tim Hortons. I asked him to give me a heads up so I could free up my schedule. He said he would. Anyway, it did not happen.

He's A Player – *Don't Bother with Him.*

Since we were having our last nurses' reunion, and for me it was a bit of nostalgia, I posted my nurse's grad photo on Facebook (the one in this book). His Facebook photo showed up on my page, and I thought it was a friend request from him, so I responded, but it was only that we just had a mutual friend.

He noticed this on the day I had the dental work done, and well after 9:00 p.m., he responded to my friend request. He gave me the exact same spiel that he had posted on the Facebook Online Dating Site. Now, I'm in pain and on painkillers and am irritable.

I knew he didn't catch my name. Certainly, my nursing photo, when I was 21 years old, looked much different from the photo posted on the dating site. So he ended his text spiel by saying, "The picture, you are a very beautiful lady.'

389

I should have been flattered, but I was irritated because he likely copied and pasted what he had on the Facebook dating site. I first apologized for imposing on him, thinking he'd sent me a friend request, and then I said, "We have never met, but I can see you don't know who I am. It's me, Arlene."

He responded with a thumbs-up emoji and just asked, "How's the tooth?"

He was in his seventies and engaging with my 21-year-old self and flattering me. I was processing some thoughts and emotions, and decided that this guy is a player, and if he had been interested in how it went with the dentist, he would have called me.

Of course, I was expecting too much considering we hadn't even met, but being tired and in pain, I concluded he was a player, and so it was best to not say anything to him and just forget him. After all, he said he didn't know what he wanted.

After a week had gone by, I told my girlfriend what happened, and she said, "Arlene, you should have responded to him because guys don't like that." I thought that I was too touchy and began regretting my reaction.

So, eleven days after that exchange, I texted him and told him I was not in the habit of ignoring anyone by not responding to them, but I gave him a couple of reasons why I hadn't. It may have seemed like excuses, but it was definitely short of my saying "I'm sorry."

He immediately responded to my text. We had a short text exchange, and he said he had been processing a lot of thoughts. I said that was good and that "God was with us." I know he was raised in the church and attended church, so I just wanted to encourage him that whatever you are processing or concerned about, God was with us and will give us the answers.

Why That Dream? – *God, Did You Bring Him Into My Life?*

So I wanted the answer to the significance of this dream and an answer as to what God wanted or what, if anything, I should do.

At this time, I attended a new church as I did on the odd Sunday. I was enjoying this Pastor's messages and the praise and worship. I felt he flowed in the gifts of the Holy Spirit and had the gift of discernment. He shared about his mother being healed of cancer, and so we had that in common with Helen being healed of cancer.

On this Sunday, the Pastor was praying over people who wanted a fresh anointing of His Holy Spirit. When he went to pray over me, he hesitated and said, "The Lord wants you to know that He is cancelling those lies that others have said about you and is releasing you from them!" Then he prayed for me to receive a fresh anointing of His Holy Spirit since I'd been wounded by this.

Well, I wasn't surprised by this revelation that others may not like me and likely said some unkind things about me, but the most important thing for me was that I was in God's will and that He was pleased with me. When I was in error, I wanted His correction.

After this tooth incident with this man, whom I will call Jacob (not his real name), I wanted peace about this dream and this man. I wanted guidance from above.

He's More Than A Player! – *Run the Other Way as Fast As You Can!*

On another Sunday at this same church, I went for prayer. A woman who was at the front of the church, who was assigned to pray for people, came to pray with me.

I indicated that I needed prayer for two things: one, to ask God to give me wisdom and energy to complete the portion of the rehabilitation healing program, 'The Potter's Wheel – His Hands Only.' The second thing I wanted prayer for was to do with Jacob.

I shared with her that I had gone on the Facebook Dating Site and connected with this man, and I asked for prayer for him and for God's will to happen in our lives, whatever that was. I was not led to share about the dream I had before connecting with him.

She asked me where he was from, and I told her the area. Then she asked his name, and I did not think to say I'd rather not say, but I told her his real name. With that, she had an immediate visceral reaction and said, "Oh, this is God dear! You run the other way as fast as you can. He's a Player, a Womanizer! A really bad man!"

She re-emphasized, "This is God!" I understood that what she was meaning was that this is God's intervention and God just used her to save me from the 'big, bad wolf!' She then walked back to her seat, leaving me there, and I could see that she was visibly shaken.

I had been walking with God long enough to know her reaction was not so Godly. I momentarily stood there thinking, "Did this just happen?" I was deeply troubled, not from hearing that she thought that he was a player and her telling me to run the other way, but that she would not pray for him, and her reaction.

So I went over and sat down beside her and asked her for her name and phone number, as I told her that I might want to call her to discuss what she'd told me.

She provided that information to me, and she said a few more derogatory things about him.

I said to her, "He is a family man and is very dedicated to them."

She said, "I have nothing bad to say about his family, only him!"

I said. "If he is that bad, then why isn't he in jail?"

She then responded, 'That's a very good question!"

I asked her if we could pray for him anyway. She was resistant as she did not respond to my suggestion.

So, I went on to give her some Biblical rationale: "You know the Bible has many different people in it who were outcasts and rebels, like Mary Magdalene and then there was Saul who murdered Christians and God got a hold of him on the road to Damascus and blinded him and dealt with him and he became converted and followed Christ. You and I know that Saul changed his name to Paul and wrote most of the New Testament. So I would really like to pray for him since God can change him too."

That never moved her to pray with me for him, but that was between her and God. I knew in my spirit I'd not call her. Anyway, I prayed for Jacob that day, and I continue to do so to this day because God has led me to do so.

Spiritual Oppression – *Do Not Quench the Great and Holy Spirit.*

So this experience was like many other experiences I have had, which had me leave churches in the past. If His Spirit is being quenched in me by leadership, then I can't hear God. Some leaders do that so they can be the Holy Spirit for you.

My ears weren't ringing in my knowing that certain people were saying 'not nice things about me' as I'd sensed that. I was secure in His love for me, the love of family, along with a few others. What I wanted for myself was what He wanted for me, to fulfill my destiny.

What quickly quenches the Holy Spirit is gossiping, judging, and backbiting, and going around thinking you are the only one who has the Great and Holy Spirit living in you.

Shepherds are to guide, encourage, and nurture their flock and not try to be the Holy Spirit for their sheep because they're not. Certainly, there should be prayer, discernment, and wisdom. The response by this woman was very troubling, and the Holy Spirit definitely wanted her and me to pray for Jacob.

I decided to look up what it says about quenching the Holy Spirit. I came across an article by Sam Storms, a Pastor from Oklahoma City, Oklahoma. I'll quote an excerpt to explain:

"Paul says in 1 Thessalonians 5 that God has granted to Christians the ability either to restrict or release what the Spirit does in the life of the local church.

The Holy Spirit wants to intensify the heat of his presence among us, to inflame our hearts and fill us with the warmth of his indwelling power.

And Paul's exhortation is a warning to all of us lest we become part of the contemporary bucket brigade that stands ready to douse his activity with the water of legalism, fear, and a flawed theology that, without biblical warrant, claims that his gifts have ceased and been withdrawn."

He goes on to say, "We quench the Spirit whenever we despise prophetic utterances (1 Thessalonians 5:20). Certainly, one should have discernment, but we need to appreciate how the Holy Spirit is working in each person's life."

The author goes on to give Seven Ways We Quench the Holy Spirit. The link to the whole article is:

https://www.desiringgod.org/articles/seven-ways-to-quench-the-spirit.

He Will Have the Last Word – *After All, He is the Great I AM!*

I didn't know if I'd ever hear from Jacob again, but I definitely wanted to. On August 31, 2023, I was driving to Red

Lobster to celebrate Lance's 21st birthday, and my cellphone rang. Lance grabbed it and said, "Who do you know from this place?" And of course it was him.

I pulled the car over, called him right back, and got his voicemail. I excitedly told him I'd call him back once I got back from our outing. Perhaps I sounded too happy or excited.

I obviously was not turning and running the other way as that 'sister-in-the Lord' told me to do, because I needed to directly hear from Him. After all, He had given me that dream, and it was Jacob. In the dream, he was unable to move past me, and I didn't want him to.

Of course, I called him when I got home, but it went to voicemail. I told him he could call me back if he wished. He must not have wished to, as I never heard from him. I only noticed that he was looking at what I posted on Facebook, and I could see what he'd posted. I started to even look when he was online, connecting with others, and it bothered me that I was even doing this.

I Know the Plans I Have For You – *Says The Lord: Jeremiah 29:11*

In the middle of September, my granddaughter, Kayla, and her husband had their first baby. They were living in a small town not too far from where Jacob's farm was.

So when they came home with their baby girl, I went to their home on a Monday morning, September 18th, 2023, to stay and help her. I had plans to leave on the Friday of the same week.

Early Thursday morning, September 21st, I woke up having had a vivid dream from God. It was in three consecutive parts, like three scenes, but I knew that they were all connected somehow.

First, I will describe the three parts and then provide you with the interpretation I received:

The Dream:

Part One:

It was evening, and it was dusk. In front of me was a man, and with him were around three others. I cannot be exact about how many were with this man, as my attention was drawn to my left, where a tigress and her cub were lying in the grass.

I noticed that the tigress was on high alert and she could 'spring out' at anyone if she saw or heard anything because she was guarding her cub. I knew I had to be very quiet, in fact, extra quiet.

Now, the man in front of me was there to guide me to safety, as well as the others who were with him. I knew I was to follow them. There was a door ahead of me that I knew I needed to go through to get to safety from the Tigress. What was on the other side of that door was not revealed.

I began motioning with my hands to communicate to these people in front of me to be very quiet, pointing to the tigress and her cub, and then pointing to the door in front of us, as I walked behind them. The great news was that we all got through the door, and I was safe, well, we were all safe.

Part Two:

There was a man in this part of the same dream. He was very gregarious, and there were lots of women around, and he enjoyed or loved women. There were no other men in this scenario, and it was like he had a smorgasbord of women.

I was observing him and his interactions with these women. He would go up to each one of them, briefly admire them, and then would squeeze one or both of their breasts in a flirtatious and teasing manner, and then move on to the next one.

I was amused by this and a little disgusted until I was startled because he was right in front of me, and he just finished squeezing my breast. I stepped back from him, and before I could say anything, he said to me with a big grin on his face, "I like yours too, they are smaller, but very nice!"

That scene ended when a woman came up to me to tell me about this man because somehow she knew him very well. She showed me that as a young boy, he'd experienced trauma, and he had been emotionally wounded. Due to this trauma, he was never able to fully bond with a woman.

This behavior that I was observing in him was a result of these emotional wounds. She knew him intimately, and I wasn't sure at the time how it was that she knew him so well.

Part Three:

When this scene ended, I was now in a home, and I didn't know whose home it was, as it wasn't familiar. There were others in the home, and they all likely lived there. No one there was aware of my presence. I was simply observing this. I was a bit elevated simply observing, like from a balcony of a theater. The scene was taking place in their kitchen.

Someone had given birth to a pair of identical twins. There was a lot of commotion in their kitchen. I could not see who had birthed these twins, but that didn't seem important because the focus was on these twins, particularly the one twin.

Although the healthy twin was not seen, someone was holding the second twin, who was not doing well at all and who was having breathing issues. Two respiratory paramedics came into the room to get him breathing, but he was too weak and he died.

There was a time lapse, like an intermission. Then, I saw a man enter the kitchen. He was a little under six feet tall and of a darker complexion with dark hair. I noted that he was serious-looking, as if he were there on a mission.

He asked, "Where is the baby?" Everyone knew he was referring to the twin who didn't live. Someone said, "That baby died." This man then said, "Bring him here."

That same person said again, "The baby has been dead for about a week now and we haven't yet buried him." This time, the man spoke in a very firm voice, like delivering an order as one being in charge. "Bring the infant here!" This person obeyed and went to get the baby. From where I was observing, I saw him go through a set of French doors leading to a family room or den. He came back into the kitchen carrying the dead infant.

As he entered the kitchen, I could see that there was an umbilical cord lying on the floor. It was in the shape of a Y, but it seemed crumpled. I knew that it had been connected to the identical twins at birth, and, of course, had been joined to whomever had given birth to them.

The man handed the deceased infant to this man. Everyone could see that the baby was grayish blue and definitely dead. This man cradled the baby in his hands, holding his head in the palm of one hand with the baby facing upwards towards him.

He then began to gently blow on his face. He did this a few times. Then, he turned him over, placing his one hand under his body and positioning him face-down over the sink.

Then, he began gently patting his back with his other hand. I could see lots of fluids draining from the baby. When the fluids finally stopped draining, he turned him back over towards him as before. Again, he began gently blowing on his face, and a pink color began to come into the baby's face and his frail body. He let out a cry and began to breathe. Everyone there, including me, was ecstatic, clapping their hands and in awe of what they'd just witnessed.

The final scene was like an encore, where the curtains open at the end of a performance. The place was not revealed, but it was not the home or the kitchen that I was shown. It was revealed that this sickly twin was now fully grown, and he looked identical in every way to his other twin. I recall feeling very happy to know this. The End.

Then I woke up.

The Interpretation

I knew that this entire dream was prophetic and that it would come to pass, but I didn't know when it would all come to pass or how.

The first part was clear to me, except for knowing who the four people were who led me to a door that I needed to go through. Later, it was clear that the man was Jesus and the others were angels on assignment and on a mission. The tigress was Charlene, and her cub was Noah.

As for the second part of that dream, the individual at the end of the dream, who shared with me about this man, was his angel, who knew everything about him. I knew that the Lord was definitely on assignment for this man and wanted to heal him. I knew this man was Jacob.

The man in the third part who had resuscitated the dead twin was Jesus. It was revealed that the infant's death was not physical but spiritual. He had died due to emotional and spiritual wounds. I knew that he was also the same man in the second dream, Jacob.

Jesus came into the last scene and drained from him all the dross that the enemy had deposited in him, which were the byproducts of trauma, anger, confusion and heartbreak, and he breathed 'new life' into him. Jacob was now set free and 'born again.'

I wondered what the significance of the Y-shaped umbilical cord was that lay crumpled on the floor. I knew that Jesus, the Giver of life, and the twins were all connected. The twins were now 'born again' and both had spiritually matured, becoming

401

identical and now all three were connected again, and their connection was sustainable.

His Ways are Higher Than Mine

God gave me a desire to pray for this man, which I do. Would our lives be connected here on earth? I was hoping so, but I was not going to do anything to make that happen, as God didn't need my help.

Yet, my flesh got in the way. I thought I'd give Jesus a hand to hurry this along, which was becoming connected to this man. So on September 28th, 2023, I sent Jacob a message through Messenger saying, "Hello, how are you? I hope you are doing well. The harvest must be nearly done." I ended it by saying I miss connecting with you.'

Without praying about this, I decided to give him 48 hours to respond to my message, and if he didn't respond, I would block him as my friend.

When I did not hear back, I blocked him. I did this more to protect myself because I was now becoming a little 'obsessive-compulsive' about him, looking to see when he was online, when he posted something, or if he looked at my story that I'd put up. Rejection never feels good, so I needed to self-protect.

I decided that God will make a way, if we are to be together, as He always has the Last Word.'

Chapter 32
Your Name Shall Be Montana –
What's That All About?

About seven years before Chuck's passing, I had a dream, and I never wrote the date down, but the dream was sealed on my heart.

In this dream, like in many dreams I have had from the Lord, the time of day was in the evening when the sun is about to set, and it is dusk. Perhaps it has to do with my age or when these events will occur.

The Dream

Again, I was in a field, but not a grain or stubble field, but in the country. The ground seemed rugged and a bit stony. In the distance, I could see mountains.

Then I noticed a man walking towards me, and I just stood there until he came directly in front of me. He had in his hands what appeared to be a scarf or shawl folded up. He proceeded to unfold it, and then he draped it around my shoulders and looked at me and with no expression, firmly said to me, "Your name will now be Montana."

Then, I woke up.

Looking back on the dream in three parts, I realized that this man was the same man, Jesus. He never smiled but looked serious, like he was on a mission. This scripture now took on more meaning for me:

"He had no beauty or majesty to attract us to him, nothing in his appearance that we should desire him."
(Isaiah 53:2).

Also, I couldn't recall the name for a Hebrew or a Jewish prayer shawl, so I looked it up. One of them is called a tallit, but there are different prayer shawls. I only knew that it was a Jewish prayer shawl.

Why did I need a new name? I didn't know, but I liked that name. I wondered why that name and if it had any significance. Well, it must have significance if Jesus gave it to me. I went to Professor Google to see what the word Montana meant.

"Montana is a word derived from the Spanish word meaning 'mountainous.'

Throughout Scripture, we find Bible verses about mountains used as symbolic elements to describe steadfastness, trustworthiness, immovability, strength, and faith.

It's a name that parents may choose with the hope that their child will embody these characteristics and lead a life filled with courage and divine blessings."

In Hebrews 12, we find a fascinating passage that uses two specific mountains as symbolism and a summary of God's covenant plan.

So I looked up Hebrews 12, verses 22 to 25, and they spoke to me:

"22But you have come to Mount Zion, to the city of the living God, the heavenly Jerusalem. You have come to thousands upon thousands of angels in joyful assembly, 23to the church of the firstborn, whose names are written in heaven.
You have come to God, the Judge of all, to the spirits of the righteous made perfect,
24to Jesus the mediator of a new covenant, and to the sprinkled blood that speaks a better word than the blood of Abel. 25See to it that you do not refuse him who speaks."

I heard those 'throngs of angels' twice, and I have witnessed His power 'to raise the dead.' His redemptive message is in the above scripture, where we are under a new covenant because of Jesus, whose blood was shed for our sins, so we can be written in His Book called The Lamb's Book of Life as one who has been redeemed by Jesus, the Lamb of God.

You and I have been chosen, and our sins have been forgiven. That is worth praising God, the Creator, who gave us His One and Only Son, Jesus.

God provided a way, the Only Way, for us to enter the 'Holy of Holies' and spend eternity with our loved ones. Our acceptance of God's Son and confessing that we are sinners in need of His forgiveness will release us from the penalty of our sins, which is darkness and eternal separation from God. Our PRIDE is what will take us to HELL, therefore:

25 "See to it that you do not refuse him who speaks."

January 2024 – *Grief and Joy in Life*:

At the time of my writing this book, it is November 2024. I hope to have it go to publication as soon as possible. Yet, there have been a few significant happenings that I do want to share with you that have slowed this down.

In 2023, we had a very lovely Christmas and the start of our New Year 2024. The grandkids were all home through the holidays, and Jonathan camped out with Charlene, Lance, and me before going back to Victoria, BC, to the Navy.

The First Week of January – *Our Pets are Precious*

Dave was Chuck's cat that we got as a birthday present for him about 10 years earlier. He was two years old at the time, and we got him from the Used Regina website. He was a fearful, skittish cat, but after a year, he'd stop hiding when strangers came. He was such a sweetheart.

In 2020, about a year after Chuck had died, we were having supper at the home of the new Pastor and his family. When the Pastor asked how I was managing with grieving the loss of Chuck, Lance spoke up and said, "Oh, Grandma is doing great because she sleeps with Dave every night!" It was one of those 'Oh My Gosh' moments as the Pastor and his family went into shock, and I burst out laughing and explained that Dave was our cat.

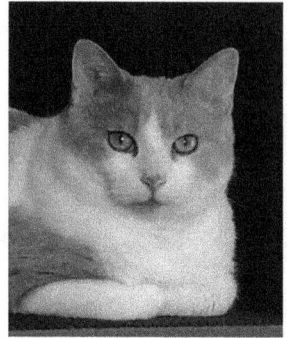

Dave

Well, Dave took very ill before Jonathan went back to Victoria, BC, from his Christmas break, and we had to put him to sleep. Charlene and Jonathan took him to the vet and brought him back in the pet carrier. He was gone. I bawled and bawled for a couple of days straight.

The Last Week of January on the 27th – *What's Going on, Lord?*

It was Saturday morning, January 27th, my son Caine's birthday. I had just left him my usual Happy Birthday message, which was to sing Happy Birthday to him if he couldn't pick up.

I realized I forgot my briefcase and I needed to get to work as soon as possible, as my client's appointment was for 9:30 a.m. I had mentioned to Lance that he needed to move the extension cord that he was using to plug in the van, because the cord was going across the sidewalk, and someone could trip over it. Instead of my insisting on him doing it right away or my doing it, it did not get done.

I usually look down as I walk because, being older, I don't want to fall, especially not in the winter. That morning, I was 'deep in thought' as I looked across our street, thinking of the man who had just passed away in his mobile home and his wife, who was now in a nursing home because she had an early onset of dementia. I was thinking of my parents and how brief our lives are.

Well, you likely guessed what came next: my foot caught under this extension cord and I face-planted on the concrete sidewalk that had been freshly cleaned off. I had nothing to break my fall because I didn't have my briefcase.

I don't believe that I lost consciousness because I sat up right away, and I thought, 'Oh my goodness, I have fallen.' Then I thought about my client who will be there soon, and I needed to get into my office.

So I picked myself up, went to my car, and realized that I must have dropped my keys. I went back to get them where I'd fallen, and as I picked them up, I saw blood in the snow and decided maybe I might be hurt and should go inside and check it out.

I went into the house and sat in the living room, and by now I realized I must be hurt and hollered for Charlene to come. When she came into the living room, she took one look at me and said, "Grandma, what happened? You are hurt! I need to get you to the hospital!"

I told her that I wasn't going to go to the hospital, but I would go to see a doctor, but first I needed to call my client and let her know that I had an accident.

Once I got in the car, with Charlene driving, of course, she said. "Grandma, I think you broke your arm because I heard it crack when you moved it, and you'll need an X-ray. She convinced me to go to the ER at Regina General Hospital.

I was very pleased with how quickly I got into a room and a bed. I soon needed to go to the washroom, so I made my way there. I never thought to turn on the light, but when I went to wash my hands, I looked in the mirror and said, "Arlene, you have just smashed the left side of your face!"

Yes, I had. I never turned the light on as I'd already seen enough.

To summarize the damage, I had a hairline fracture of the left orbital bone under my left eye, I had chipped teeth and a split lip from my teeth going through it which needed stitches, the CT scan showed that I had two small bleeds between the coverings of my brain, that according to the neurologist would absorb quickly and that there was no need for a follow-up. Thank God that there was no bleeding in the brain.

I felt fortunate that it wasn't worse, although I was bruised and banged up badly. Once home, that same evening, the doctor called me back to report that my left forearm had a green stick fracture, which is like we see in children, and that the bone was not actually broken but bent. So there was nothing to do for that but to keep my arm in a sling. Hence the crack that Charlene heard.

Anyway, I was very banged up, and the ophthalmologist was worried that I might have a retinal detachment. Thank God, I did not. I was not to drive for a couple of weeks, and so Charlene chauffeured me around because I went back to counseling very quickly.

I was feeling pretty sorry for myself, particularly when I looked in the mirror. I thought I would never look the same again. I asked God to help me recover totally and to be able to get my teeth fixed. Perhaps if I could get a facelift, I might look even better than before.

Now that's a whole lot of vanity, and I'm sure I got this from my mother. Remember my favorite story of *The Ugly Duckling Who Turned into the Beautiful Swan*?

More Grief – *And This One is HUGE!!!*

It was the middle of February, on a Friday, and Charlene came to me late in the evening and said, "Don't be alarmed,

Grandma, but an ambulance is coming for Noah because he had a seizure. "She said they were not going to put the sirens on.

She told me that Noah came into her bedroom and said he smelled burnt toast, and then his eyes rolled to the side. She laid him down on her bed. He was alright now, but she wanted to get him checked out nonetheless.

I was concerned, but she ensured that he was alright now. She told me he had not been feeling well and was growing quickly, having just had his 11th birthday.

I called the hospital in the morning, and Charlene wasn't saying much. She was understandably very stressed, but didn't want me at the hospital.

She called after lunch and asked me to come up and told me about his vital signs acting up, and the monitor going off, and the medical team was uncertain what was going on. She said that they were going to be doing a CT scan of his brain.

I was becoming more concerned. This was my first time driving since my accident, but I hurried there.

Once the CT scan was done, a pediatric resident doctor came to the door and motioned for Charlene to leave the room so she could talk with her. I knew that they'd found something, and my heart sank.

About five minutes later, Charlene opened the sliding door a little and frantically motioned for me to come outside to her in the hallway. She was crying and devastated.

"The doctor said they found a mass on the left side of his brain, and we have to go to the Children's Ward in Saskatoon

University Hospital immediately!" she told me. I asked her to sit down as I thought I was going to collapse. Charlene told me that her painful crying almost moved the doctor to tears.

I seemed to snap out of the shock and declared, "We will pray right now, Charlene. He's going to be okay. We'll get through this. It's all about Noah and we must 'keep our spirits up' and not show him how worried we are."

After praying, we went back into the room where Noah was. Of course, he knew that something wasn't right. Every night, he came to me to give me a hug and kiss, and of course, I told him I loved him, and he said this back to me. We were very tight!

Soon, the doctor came in to say that his vitals had been stable for long enough that we didn't need to send him by ambulance and that we could travel by car to Saskatoon. The doctor had called the hospital, and they were expecting him to be there sometime in the evening.

I said quietly to myself, or rather to God, "God, can this really be happening? Please stay close to us, send us Your angels, let me be in Noah's place. You say in the Bible we are allotted a life of three score and ten years, plus you have given me that and more." For anyone who doesn't know what a score is, it equals 20 years and three of them is 60 years+10 equals 70.

I knew that Charlene was up all night, so I offered to drive. We went home and packed some essentials, made coffee, and grabbed some snacks. Lance had work to go to, so there were the three of us to go to Saskatoon. We asked Noah if he wanted to go in the car or the van, and he said the van.

I left the car for Lance. Charlene said she'd drive halfway there and then we'd trade off.

It was dark now, and I asked the Lord to get behind me. I thought of Carrie Underwood's song, Jesus Take the Wheel.

We arrived at the hospital around 10:00 p.m., and as we were waiting for Noah to be admitted, Lance walked in. He couldn't stay at work, as he said he needed to be there with his family. He has such a soft and big heart.

Some Light in the Darkness – *Hope*

Once Noah was settled, Lance drove back home, and I booked a hotel room. When I got to my room, I collapsed on the floor and cried all that was being held back, crying out to God for His intervention. Charlene was able to make a bed in Noah's room and stay with him.

The next day, tests were being done, and the following day, he had an MRI and an EEG.

An MRI is a detailed X-ray using magnets to show what's going on in the brain, and the EEG traces the electrical brain waves and activity to determine if there's a problem in a certain area.

After being there for one day, we didn't know what this mass looked like, whether it was cancer or not, and whether it could even be removed. So many unknowns and fighting off fear.

I was praying without ceasing, and when I got back to my hotel, I'd drop to my knees and pray. I have to admit that I am perhaps a lazy prayer warrior as I do it sitting or lying down, but dropping to my knees meant I was really doing business with God.

That particular night, God met with me in this hotel room, and His comforting presence and peace came over me.

On the third day of being in the hospital, the neurosurgeon met with us. She told us that the tumor was not cancerous and it was operable. Thank God!

She said it was in one area, but harder to get at, and they were uncertain if he'd be left with any deficits. She'd consult with other neurosurgeons as it was a delicate procedure. Since it was slow-growing, they would keep an eye on it and would only tackle it when they had to. This news provided hope and relief.

Grief Boiling Over – *Lookout!*

The morning that we were to go back to Regina, Charlene had a meltdown with me as her target again. The first day Noah was in the hospital, she took a photo of him in bed, and I put it on my Facebook Story as she had. The photo we posted was of Noah smiling and giving the peace sign.

When she saw I'd posted it too, her reaction was 'over the top.' She told me not to post anything and demanded to know who I was talking to. She told me not to tell people about Noah and not even to ask for prayer.

The last two nights in Saskatoon, I spent at The Ronald McDonald's House. It was a lovely place to be in with wonderful meals and people who were volunteers.

It was the first time I had a good sleep and relaxed. As I sat in their lounge, a volunteer came and sat with me. I told her about Noah and dealing with Charlene's demands, and I broke down crying. I realized then that everything had taken a toll on me—this crisis with Noah, and my worry for Charlene—and I was grieving and still healing from my accident.

Of course, I knew she felt helpless about Noah's situation and was very scared and in deep grief. I understood that. I promised her once again that I would not post anything further. I wanted to appease her and bring down the temperature for all of us.

Charlene wanted me to come up to talk with the Hospital Social Worker. I said, "No, I will park in front, and you can come down to the van with Noah." She kept up her demands, and again, for Noah's sake, I agreed to go to his room.

I asked for this conversation to go to a private room, as Noah was right there, but Charlene insisted we stay right there. Then, I told her that if you keep this up, you can do all of this solo, as I am not here for you to do this to me. Her tirade then stopped, and she broke down sobbing. She told the Social Worker that Grandma has always been her rock. She insisted that I not leave her as she needed me.

Like many times before, I reassured her that I was there for her and Noah and loved them and we'd get through everything together.

Descending into Darkness – *When Will This End?*

Once we were home, things settled down. Noah had to be put on a 24-hour blood pressure machine to determine what was causing his blood pressure to elevate.

Baby Picture of Noah with Nonny, His Cat

Charlene kept up her university classes, Lance and I were back working, and we were all taking one day at a time. I continued to be an emotional and financial support. These emotional outbursts towards me were always cyclic. As the saying goes, you are always 'waiting for the other shoe to drop.'

Noah had to return to Saskatoon as an outpatient to get a follow-up MRI on March 28th. The day before, Charlene began acting out again, accusing me of talking to others about Noah. She demanded that I hand over my cell phone to her.

I asked her why she was acting like this and to please stop. She knew that she'd better back up and back off since a couple of years earlier, I had filed a police report on what was going on, and that resulted in a Peace Bond being put in place. She wasn't going to risk that happening again, so she stepped back and walked away. I felt very vulnerable.

The evening before the Saskatoon trip, I extended an 'olive branch' toward Charlene by texting her that I did not want any further confrontations and that if she was able to keep the peace and do it for Noah, I would take the day trip with her to Saskatoon.

I emphasized that we must consistently get along for Noah's sake, as he didn't need that stress. He was not well, and his blood pressure was being monitored. I asked her to let me know in the morning what she'd decided. Noah had to be in Saskatoon the next day at 4:00 p.m.

Noah home from the hospital after the diagnosis

The next day, after lunch, Charlene still hadn't said a word to me about my text. I was not going to ask her anything in case of a blow-up, yet I had not gone into work, and I made myself available for her to speak to me until it was time for her to leave.

I wondered if she'd talked Lance into missing his work, asking him to go with her. After they left, I sat there and thought, 'I have allowed her to use my vehicles, my bank cards and I pay most of the bills including gas because she is going to university and if I continue to cater to her, and accept her terrible outbursts, then I am allowing it to continue.' I knew this situation was not going to get any better, and I'd need to do something.

The Dream – Part One – Fulfilled –*Time to Go Through the Door!*

A Recap of the Dream Part One on September 21, 2023:

The tigress and her cub that were lying in the grass in the early evening were Charlene and her precious cub, Noah. The people leading me towards the door that I needed to go through for safety, to a new beginning, were Jesus and three angelic beings. I had to do this without the tigress (Charlene) or her cub (Noah) being startled.

After they'd left for Saskatoon, I sat on the couch and noted it was about 1:00 in the afternoon. I asked the Lord, "What am I going to do?" He urgently said, "Today is the day that you are to go through that door!" I knew that was right and God had gone ahead of me, but where would I go?

Charlene, Noah, and Lance would be coming home around 7:30 p.m. at the earliest, so I had to get moving quickly.

I began looking for rooms that people wanted to rent. Then, I thought my things were already in the living room since Charlene now had my bedroom, and I had a daybed, a small dresser, and a few other belongings already in boxes, all in the living room of the trailer.

I wanted my photos, pictures, and wall hangings, and I'd leave everything else. Then I called a friend who had offered to move me when I found something to buy to get on my own. So I would see her availability to move my things, and next I'd secure a room to rent.

I called her and told her my situation and asked if she could get her friends to move my things when I found a room to rent. She said, "Arlene, this must be God because I knew someone was stressed and needing help, and I called my parents and grandparents, and the feeling wouldn't leave me until I heard from you!"

She went on to tell me that she had just moved her teenage daughter down to the basement, and her bedroom on the second floor was vacant. I hesitated for a moment and then gladly accepted her offer. When I hung up, I found a small storage area nearby to put boxes and a few other things in so I could go through them later.

By 6:00 p.m. I was moved into her place in the upstairs bedroom that I called The Upper Room. In the Bible, after Jesus was resurrected, He told His disciples to wait for Him in the Upper Room to come to them. I asked Jesus to stay with me in this Upper Room and help me heal.

I did a check-in with myself once my belongings that I needed were in my room. It felt tremendous, like a weight had been lifted off my shoulders. Then, I called another friend to meet her for a late supper and to relax from this ordeal.

419

About 8:00 p.m., my phone blew up. Finally, I answered it. It was Lance. He said, "Where are you? Grandpa would have never done what you did!"

I told him that I had to do this so there could be peace, and said I needed to go and hung up.

As I lay in my bed that evening in The Upper Room, I thought of Noah, sweet Noah, and how I loved him so much. He was going through such a terrible time and would need brain surgery, unless God chose to heal him miraculously.

I was always there for Noah and Charlene, and I knew at this crucial time that with my leaving, they'd feel like I had abandoned them. I was not abandoning them, but I just needed to create distance between us to keep the peace for Noah and finally for myself.

I no longer metaphorically would grab onto Charlene's bike, so she could keep her balance, because she had to do it now, and I knew she could do it now. God knew she could now do it.

My leaving her like this was my way of telling her, "You can do it, Charlene, just keep pedaling, and if you lose your balance, just get back up on your bike and keep pedaling. I know you are stronger emotionally." God knew it was time she relied more on Him as well as others, as I wouldn't always be here.

The Lord saw the 'Big Picture' and went ahead of me/us. He guided me through that door without arousing 'the tigress and her cub.'

That night, I said my prayers and thanked Him and heard in my spirit, "All is well, My daughter!" and fell fast asleep.

Answer to Fervent Prayer – *I Had a Dream From the Lord!*

I was interceding and praying all the time for Noah and Charlene and other family members, too, but Noah was at the very top of the list because of the medical crisis he was facing.

I wanted to know how things were going, but Charlene did not want me to know anything. Although I offered several 'olive branches' to connect with Noah and her, or just Noah if she'd let him come with me, she did not respond and was very bitter.

On May 08th, 2024, I had another dream from the Lord.

This dream was not at dusk but early in the morning. It was just beginning to get light out. In the dream, He took me into the trailer and into the living room. I saw a deep pile of blankets on the couch, and I knew that Noah was under them.

I became aware of Charlene being in the bathroom, and she was having diarrhea. There was a major problem because the water had been turned off in the trailer. I then walked over to the couch as I wanted to see Noah, but I didn't want to wake him up. I carefully peeled back a corner of the blankets just to see him, but this roused him.

He'd been sleeping on his stomach, and he was so happy to see me that he raised himself up. With a huge smile on his face, he excitedly said, "Nana, Dr. Good came to see me last night and he said that tumor in your head (and he held his hand in a fist to demonstrate the tumor), I am going to remove it and it will be gone very soon!"

Noah was so happy, and so was I. I could see he was still sleepy, so I told him I loved him and to go back to sleep, and I placed the blankets back over him.

Charlene came out of the bathroom, and we met in the kitchen. I could see on her face confusion, oppression, and depression. I asked her, "Do you realize that the water has been shut off? I'm very concerned about that."

She seemed to have some awareness about this, and then she said somewhat indignantly, "Yes, I'm aware of that!" acting like she wasn't that surprised. Yet, she was now showing some concern over the water having been turned off. I had considered telling her about my interaction with Noah, but then I woke up.

The Interpretation of This Dream

Before I tell you what the Holy Spirit gave me as the interpretation, I need to point out that the symbols in this dream, like water, blankets, and diarrhea, have Biblical relevance.

Throughout the Bible, dreams have often told a story and had symbols to explain what God wanted to show His people, either to show them what is going on currently, possibly a warning, or what will occur. Dreams like this are revelations, words of knowledge, and prophetic.

The Holy Spirit gives me the interpretations of my dreams by revelation. I don't always get all the details, and He, at times, withholds letting me know, until it is the right time, like about Chuck's death and the children crying. After these dreams, I write them down as I hear Him speak to me.

This is what I wrote:

"My daughter, let us look at the dream I gave you. I had you visit the trailer, and it was early morning, and all was quiet. Charlene was there, but in the bathroom.

My child, I took you to the trailer to visit Noah and see the spiritual condition around him. He is in the living room where my Holy Spirit met with him. All the blankets over him represent my heavy covering over him, protecting him from evil spirits in that trailer.

The visitation that Noah had was from Me. He recognized me as Dr Good, and I used my fist to show him that the tumor would be removed from his brain to prepare him and to encourage him.

Faith is arising within him. He is still a child, My child, and I am his Abba Father. I am his Great Physician. I knew him before he was formed in his mother's womb, and I made sure he came forth and lived, to live an 'Abundant Life.'

Know that the issue of the water being turned off was My Holy Spirit. I did not turn the water off in the trailer, but Satan did, responding to a rebellious spirit that resided there that led to bitterness and wrath.

These were generational spirits that she was exposed to, that continued to interfere with her ability to stay close to Me. Her having diarrhea represented my 'cleansing power' of what the Enemy had left there, going down the sewer.

In prayer, you bound all of this (these evil spirits) on earth, and it was also bound in heaven, and then you loosened it from her, and it was then loosened in heaven. Today, My Holy Spirit, the water, has been turned back on!

You see, My daughter, you had to leave this trailer for Me to get Charlene's attention and even Lance's, who has been oppressed and has had My Holy Spirit quashed, but I am reviving him and maturing him. New Doors and New Beginnings are coming. They'll continue to come for you as well My child. Know that I am with you and I give you My Shalom.

Note from scripture with regards to binding and loosing that was mentioned above:

> *"Whatever you bind on earth will be bound in heaven, and whatever you loose on earth will be loosed in heaven."*
> *Matthew 16:19.*

In this verse, Jesus describes the authority He is giving to His followers as the "keys to the kingdom of heaven."

Symbols in My Dream Related to The Word of God

1. Water here relates to His Holy Spirit

> *"I will pour out water on the thirsty land and streams on the dry ground; I will pour out My Spirit on your offspring."*
> *Isaiah 44:3*

> *Jesus said that He would give life-giving water to those who have believed in Him.*
> *John 7*

The 'layers of blankets' represent God's Covering and Protection, relating to God's covering over Noah:

> *He who dwells in the shelter of the Most High will abide in the shadow of the Almighty.*
> *Psalm 91:1 ESV*

Let all who take refuge in you rejoice; let them ever sing for joy, and spread your protection over them, that those who love your name may exult in you.

Psalm 5:11 ESV

The diarrhea relates to the Spirit of God's cleansing power of the heart.

"What comes out of a person is what defiles them. For it is from within, out of a person's heart, that evil thoughts come – sexual immorality, theft, murder, adultery, greed, malice, deceit, lewdness, envy, slander, arrogance, and folly. All these evils come from inside and defile a person."

(Mark 7:20-23).

Since it is a struggle to remain consistently in God's will, we all need to pray sincerely as King David did.

"Create in me a pure heart, O God, and renew a steadfast spirit within me."

Psalm 51:10.

Chapter 33
To God Be The Glory! – Great Things He Has Done!

After this dream, I was totally certain that God was going to remove Noah's tumor. I knew what he did for Helen when the doctors did the second surgery, because they found no cancer in the biopsies. God gave her 27 years more of life after the Cancer Clinic gave her three months to live, and she never had chemo.

God tells us that here on earth, trying to figure everything out or getting all the answers is like looking through a cloudy or dirty glass, but in heaven, everything will be clear to us:

"Now we see things imperfectly, like puzzling reflections in a mirror, but then we will see everything with perfect clarity. All that I know now is partial and incomplete, but then I will know everything completely, just as God now knows me completely."
1 Corinthians 13:12 New Living Translation (NLT)

I know that God is the Creator and His Great Spirit, Holy Spirit (are two and the same to me), and they can heal miraculously. I prayed that for Noah that he'd not need to have his head touched by instruments.

Yet, I know that God sees the 'big picture' and He works in ways we cannot always understand, but He asks us to trust Him. Is it blind trust? Yes, it is very often. Is it hard? Absolutely!

Can we have enough faith for Him to work? Yes, but only with Him and through Him because on our own, we can't get it done. If someone doesn't get healed or stay alive after you've called them forth after being dead, was it your fault because you never had enough faith? Again, God is in charge, and we need to trust Him.

The Bible states that one day,

"Every knee will bow to the name of Jesus— everyone in heaven, on earth, and under the earth. And everyone will confess that Jesus Christ is Lord and bring glory to God the Father."
Philippians 2:10-11 New Century Version (NCV)

Everyone means even those who chose not to believe, even the proud. Why will they do that if they are that proud? Well, He will reveal Himself even more so that they will be in such awe of Him that they will fall to their knees and confess who He is, even if they are in hell.

For me, I think of how amazing Creation is, the beauty that He created, our solar system, and the balance of keeping us dangling in space, but even more mind-blowing for me is realizing that He created you and me from two cells, one egg and one sperm and brought forth each of us. What a miracle! Each of us is a miracle. Yet, the nonbeliever reduces this to mere science.

Even more 'mind-blowing' is how Jesus was created. He did not come from a sperm because His Father, the Holy Spirit, overshadowed Mary, and that's how Jesus was conceived.

"The Holy Spirit will come upon you, and the power of the Most High will overshadow you; therefore, the child to be born will be called holy—the Son of God."
Luke 1:35 ESV

We created beings are not holy but made righteous and holy only because we have accepted Jesus, who came to take our penalty for sin, by going to the cross, so that we can enter heaven. We have all gone our own way, and so we have all sinned.

Like my late husband Wayne, when he was presented with the Truth of His Word and chose to believe that he was a sinner in need of salvation, said, "It (salvation) sounds good to me. Let's do it!"

My prayer for my readers is that if you have not chosen to believe and follow Jesus, you will say, "It sounds good to me, and so I will do it! Don't leave it for a 'death-bed decision' as many will not get that opportunity like Wayne did. Today is the day!

> *"For he says, 'In the time of my favor I heard you,*
> *and in the day of salvation I helped you.' I tell you,*
> *now is the time of God's favor, now is the day of salvation."*
> 2 Corinthians 6:2

Surgery it Will Be!

So, how would the Great Physician heal Noah? Would it be miraculous? Would He work through a doctor whose destiny He'd ordained to be His hands extended? Would it be all at once or in stages? I didn't know, but I knew that somehow He was going to get it done!

In late September 2024, I was just about to start a counselling session with my client when my phone rang. A family member told me that Noah was scheduled for surgery the next day.

The first report I received was that the surgery went very well and that they had removed 'all of the tumor,' and the second report was that the surgeon left a little of it, as it was in an area that could leave him with a deficit if they took that out. They'd also dealt with the area causing his seizures, so he'd hopefully not be having them anymore. The doctor said they were very happy with the results and would continue to follow Noah.

Lin's family on the reserve had rallied around Charlene and Noah. Jonathan took leave from the Navy in Victoria, BC, and flew to Saskatoon to be with his nephew and his sister. Lance was there, too. Charlene had support. She was still bitter towards me.

So, I said, "If you don't mind me asking, God, why is there a little bit left there?"

Well, I'd get that answer later, but for now, I was rejoicing! Noah never had to have his beautiful hair shaved off. He had a decent-sized scar under his hair, and the bone plate needed to be screwed back on but I was told that he was doing great.

He was only in the hospital for three nights and came home on Friday. We had all been invited for Thanksgiving supper on Sunday to my son Caine's and his wife's home. Charlene and Noah declined to come as he just got home and needed rest, but my daughter-in-law was kind enough to send both of them a Thanksgiving meal. Oh, we all had so much to be thankful for!

I received a report that one would never know that Noah had surgery. He was the same as he was with no deficits, and he was now beaming with happiness. He would be gradually going back to school this month.

An Encounter – *Is Someone Lost?*

On November 03, 2024, I was determined to finally get my memoir ready to be published.

Miracle # 21: – An 'Angelic visitation' – God's Messenger!

Where I was staying, in The Upper Room, as I call it, the woman and her three children who lived here were away in northern Saskatchewan to attend her father's funeral. They were expected to be back around suppertime.

It was around three o'clock in the afternoon when I heard the front door close, and I heard a brief exchange of conversation like two people talking. I just determined that they'd arrived home early.

I was just relaxing on my daybed, leaning up against my pillows, watching television, having cleaned the washroom and my room. Usually, the door to my room is closed, but not this afternoon, as I thought I was home alone, and I didn't get up to close my door, knowing they'd arrived home. I just kept relaxing and watching what was on television.

About 15 minutes after I heard them come home, I noticed a motion outside my door. I saw a young woman gently twirling around, which caught my attention. She was glancing about as though she were looking for someone.

She seemed to be in her early twenties. She had straight reddish hair that looked like it may have been colored and lay partway down her upper back. She was about five feet and eight inches tall. I did not pay attention to her clothes, which was unusual for me, as for some reason, I always notice what people are wearing. I did notice that she had a cell phone in her hand. I couldn't identify her as from a specific ethnic group.

She looked a little perplexed or lost. I asked her if she was looking for Lily, who is my friend's 15-year-old daughter, whose bedroom is across the hall from me. She gently nodded her head sideways. I then asked her, "Who are you looking for?" She said a name, but I couldn't make it out.

As she stood in the doorway, I noted how sweet and somewhat shy or reserved she seemed. For some reason, I never got off my daybed but motioned for her to come into my room, so I could clearly hear her answer to my question. She came into my room and stood several feet from me.

"Who are you looking for?" I asked again. In an almost whisper, I thought I heard "Lad."

Although I couldn't be sure that was the name she was saying, I told her that no one by that name lived here. Then, without a word or an apology for being in someone else's house, wandering around, she turned around and proceeded to go downstairs to leave.

At this point, I got up and followed her. From the top of the stairs, I asked, "How did you get in? The door was locked."

This time she responded in an audible voice, "It was open."

"Please wait!" I said as I hurried to the bottom of the stairs. "I am sorry, but I am hard of hearing, so who is the person you are looking for?"

Again, in a very soft voice, I heard her say Lad."

I said, "Was that Lad?"

She smiled, and I then heard her say very softly, "Lade."

"Is that the letter 'e' at the end of Lad?" With another sweet smile, she nodded yes. I repeated it and spelled it L-a-d-e, saying, "Is that it?" She nodded her head in the affirmative.

I then said, "So did you come into the wrong house?" and she smiled slightly and nodded her head, but it was not a distinct yes or no, and she never spoke or gave any explanation or an apology for this apparent mishap. That in itself was very strange.

Most of us would be aghast if we had accidentally walked into the wrong house, gone upstairs, and finally realized we were in the wrong house. We would definitely apologize, but no apology occurred.

As she opened the door to walk out, I said to her, "I am glad you are a pretty young lady and not a big ugly ol' man or you'd have really scared me!"

With that, she looked back at me and warmly smiled, seeming to be amused by what I had said.

I closed the door behind her and locked it, and immediately went to the kitchen window, which was a few steps away, as I wanted to watch her walk down the sidewalk, but she was nowhere to be seen.

I knew that she'd need to walk past the window to walk down the walkway, which was about 40 feet long to reach the main sidewalk, but there was no sign of her. I waited and waited and became perplexed, knowing that she could only turn to the right of the front doorway to walk away, as turning left there was a high fence and garbage cans. So where was she?

I didn't want to open the door in case she was sitting on the step, looking at her phone. So I continued to watch for her, but after a few more minutes, I went and opened the front door, and no one was there. Where had she gone? She'd disappeared into 'thin air.'

I asked myself what just happened. I wondered what the name Lade meant. I'd never heard that name. Well, there are many names I have not heard of, as some of my clients have unusual names. At some point, I was determined to look up the meaning of Lade.

My friend and her family came home at 5:00 p.m. When I came downstairs, my friend asked me how my weekend went, and I told her about this young woman and my encounter with her, and how she disappeared. I asked if they knew anyone by the name of Lade. She said "No" but added that my experience "sounded spooky!"

I said it wasn't spooky, but I got thinking that maybe I had a visitation, a heavenly one. I was sure the door was locked, and she just showed up in front of my bedroom door, and we had a brief exchange, and then she disappeared into thin air.

My friend told me she had a house monitor on the main floor, so we could see if she was there on the monitor when she came in and what time it was.

We both looked at it, and she said that at 3:14 p.m., the door opened and closed. That would be when she left. Then, for three minutes approximately, I stood at the window waiting for her to walk down the walkway, and she didn't. Then at 3:17 p.m., it showed me on the monitor when I opened the door to see if she was sitting on the steps, and then I closed the door again.

There was no recording on the monitor as to when she came in, but as I mentioned, it would be around 3:00 p.m. when I heard talking.

After supper, I decided to look up the name of Lade as I was still processing 'this Encounter.'

The Name Lade – *Its Meaning*

So I did a Google search and here's what I found:

A user from Ohio, U.S.A., says the name Lade means "Crown." According to a user from Canada, the name Lade is of Nigerian origin and means "God is my crown."

Some references said its origin was unknown. Others said the name was Norwegian in origin and used more as a surname, and was more prevalent in Norway. As a given first name, it was not as common. Also, it's used as a verb.

Lade means 'to put a load or a burden' on or in, to load or burden oppressively, according to the Merriam Webster Dictionary.

So, I looked to see if there was a Biblical reference to this word, and there was. Jesus used this word when he was chastising the religious leaders of His day, the Pharisees, who were not just religious leaders but also lawyers, being experts in the Torah and the law.

To them, Jesus said:

"Woe unto you also, ye lawyers! For ye lade men with burdens too grievous to be borne, and ye yourselves touch not the burdens with one of your fingers.

Luke 11:46NKJ.

Jesus was warning them of their hypocrisy, telling them that unless they repent and change, they'll not go to heaven.

A Message for Me in the Name Lade

Jesus chastising the lawyers in scripture felt good, like somehow God was letting me know there'd still be justice for the grandchildren and our family.

Now, the name Lade means burden, a heavy load. It is very interesting to note that my maiden name was Burden. I found this significant and a connection.

Over a year ago, my son, Caine, said to me about my last name being Burden, "Mom, you didn't have to live up to that name," to imply that I'd had a lot of burdens in my life.

In my memoir, I've described a significant number of burdens in my life, and sometimes they felt like too much. Grief is a very heavy burden. We all have burdens, and it is a part of life.

A heavy burden that I've described in my memoir is about the legal system, those lawyers and justices, who, like the Pharisees, bullied and ridiculed me and administered absolutely no justice. I had to bear the burden of loss of time with my family, financial loss, legal costs, loss of my inheritance, and losing The Anchorage, its program, and losing Autumn and Lily.

435

When I think of it, I feel sad that I have nothing much materially to leave my children and my grandchildren, from my parents' and my Uncle Charlie's hard-earned money or even mine.

As Jesus said to the Pharisees, about the legal system of that day, that they did not lift a finger to ease our burdens, but added to them. I felt that burden—the heavy load they laid on me/us.

*Then Jesus said to the crowds and to his disciples, 2"The scribes and the Pharisees sit on Moses' seat, 3so do and observe whatever they tell you, but not the works they do. For they preach, but do not practice. 4They tie up heavy **burdens**, hard to bear,[a] and lay them on people's shoulders, but they themselves are not willing to move them with their finger."*
Matthew 23:1-4 ESV

When I went to court, I saw lawyers address the Justices on the Bench as Lord and bow down to them. Even though it is intended to show respect, birthed in English tradition, for me, it is disrespectful towards my Lord, and I have also experienced their hypocrisy and cheating.

I know this woman was an angel. Perhaps I prayed for an angel to visit me and did not know it because I did it in the Spirit, which as I mentioned in a prayer language called 'speaking in tongues,' where I do not know what I am praying, but God knows, and fortunately, the devil doesn't know.

I do know that I was praying for relief from my **burdens**, telling Him that I am getting physically and emotionally very tired and discouraged, and wanting my own place to call home. I wanted to retire, and I still wanted justice, but I realized that it may not come in my lifetime.

The Lord reminded me of a vision He gave me in 2005, when I first began this lawsuit. While standing in my kitchen, He gave me this vision:

I was standing in an arena. Again, it was dusk. I sensed there may be spectators, but that seemed irrelevant. Surrounding me were wolverines. They were snarling, showing their teeth, and voracious.

They were unable to advance to take me down. They wanted to, but were being held back. They wanted to tear me apart. Yet, I had no fear.

The next scene I was shown was where they were all fast asleep.

Then the Lord said, "I have now made them as sleeping dogs!" Then I was told to simply walk away, and I did.

In writing my memoir I finally realized that the weight of my trying to receive justice was over with and the 'burden' had finally lifted and that God was now giving me beauty for those ashes for the 'spirit of heaviness,' the burden of it all and He has declared over me, "You are free!"

Understanding This Encounter:

I looked up what it means when angels visit you, asking God why he'd send me an angel.

I knew that angels are Messengers from God. I began to read what others had to say about angels visiting us, earthlings. Here are a few excerpts from one such write-up:

Angelic Visitations: by Teresa Seputis, writes:

437

"The word angel is a transliteration of the Greek word, "Anglos," which means "Messenger." An angel is one of God's messengers, or one who God sends with his message.

That role is to watch over and protect God's people. Psalm 91: verses 11-12 say,

"For He shall give His angels charge over you, to keep you in all your ways. In their hands they shall bear you up, lest you dash your foot against a stone."

People have been known to hear and see angels in visions. It is also possible to have a real physical visit from an angel. When this occurs, you are not having a vision "in the spirit," you are having a direct encounter with one of God's messengers. They come to where you are physically, and they manifest to you and they interact with you. It is sometimes a frightening experience. There is often a sense of God's glory or of His holiness in the visitation. Hebrews 13:2 says,

"Do not forget to entertain strangers, for by so doing some people have entertained angels without knowing it. Most of the time, you will know it if you are visited by an angel."

Even though she looked somewhat unassuming, it was her countenance and her demeanor that provided me a sense of God's glory or of His holiness in this visitation. If she had shown herself with a set of wings, I'd not want her to leave and I may have still been asking her questions.

Answers to My Prayers – *Burden – A 'heavy Load is Not Here!*

Prior to this visitation, I asked three things of Jesus while praying:

Should I revise portions of my memoir, as I have been very transparent, and it is not my intent to embarrass or chastise anyone. I asked Him for His 'seal of approval.'

I also asked Him for a meaningful ending to my memoir for His glory. I told Him that I wanted to find my own place to live in and retire so I can enjoy what time I have left here, relatively free of troubles (burdens) – and to bring me the helpmate He'd chosen.

This angelic visitation confirmed three things for me: Lade (burden) is not here, and I am free as God is my 'burden bearer. So I needed to stop worrying! In my spirit, I heard,

"You, Arlene, are not to be burdened about whether your memoir will be accepted or not, because it is your testimony of My working in your life, and others will be blessed by it."

I had received His 'seal of approval.' He had angels assigned to me to assist me to fulfill my destiny, and again, He would ensure justice prevails in His time, and I was no longer to carry that burden.

Forgiveness is in Order – *Whether You Receive An Apology or Not.*

Forgiveness is a strange 'state of the mind' and 'a matter of the heart.' It is hard for us humans to forgive when others have hurt our hearts. Jesus called us to forgive. An apology is not necessary for us to receive forgiveness from someone. When we forgive, we release bitterness that we've been holding towards that person or persons. Respect and love may be rekindled.

439

When Jesus forgives us, it is complete, once and for all. Imagine God has no memory of our sins, when He has forgiven you and me.

10 God, (the Creator) he does not treat us as our sins deserve or repay us according to our iniquities. 11 For as high as the heavens are above the earth, so great is his love for those who fear him; 12 as far as the east is from the west, so far has he removed our transgressions from us. 13 As a father has compassion on his children, so the Lord has compassion on those who fear him.

Psalm 103

When Jesus' disciples asked Him how they should pray, He gave them this profound prayer known as The Lord's Prayer:

9 "This, then, is how you should pray: "Our Father in heaven, hallowed be your name, 10 your kingdom come, your will be done, on earth as it is in heaven. 11 Give us today our daily bread. 12 And forgive us our debts, as we also have forgiven our debtors. 13 And lead us not into temptation,[a] but deliver us from the evil one.[b]"

Matthew 6:9-13

'Risen from the Ashes'

Miracle # 22: – 'Freedom from Lade' – 'Risen from the Ashes.'

When I realized that God had delivered me from Lade, I could now exchange 'ashes for beauty' as it speaks about in the Bible.

Writing my memoir has allowed me to come to terms with all of this and to give my 'burdens' over to my 'burden-bearer, Jesus Christ. I am FREE!

36So if the Son sets you free, you will be free indeed.

John 8:36

Freedom does not mean that we are free from all difficulties in this life, but we can be assured that He will make ALL things work together for good if we love and honor our Creator, who is the Great I Am!

You, too, can allow Him to give you 'beauty for your ashes, 'like He's done with me. Talk to Him (pray) and ask His Great and Holy Spirit to reveal Himself to you and come into your heart. He will answer you and will never leave you.

Isaiah 61:3 CEB says:

To provide for Zion's mourners,(which refers to ALL who are laden down with burdens)to give them a crown in place of ashes, oil of joy in place of mourning, a mantle of praise in place of discouragement. They will be called Oaks of Righteousness, planted by the Lord to glorify himself.

My prayer is that if you haven't yet found Him, that you will, for He loves you, created you, and saved you from your sins.

He is saddened by the hypocrisy of religion, which has deeply wounded so many by misrepresenting Him. Toxic misrepresentation of Him in churches and elsewhere should not deter you from finding Jesus Christ and walking with Him.

You Deserve to be Loved!

I have learnt through my personal and professional experiences that when you are not told that you are special and loved, you acquire insecurities and low self-esteem. Do not stifle a child's self-worth and their ability to love themselves and others by withholding your love.

If saying "I love you" is difficult because you did not hear it growing up, practice it, and soon it will feel normal and natural.

Every time you tell someone you love them, it creates a circuit, and you receive love and warmth back from them, even if they do not realize it.

When your 'life script' has been devoid of love, the 'good news' is that you can be empowered, with the Creator's guidance and love, to rewrite your script.

Remember that when a child is not told that he is loved, it is like when you stop giving a beautiful plant light and sunshine. Even if you feed and water it, without light, it will still shrivel up and die. We need His Love and His Truth and His Light!

God, the Creator, is Love. Therefore, let His love in, so you are empowered to love others.

How beautiful it is when we invite Him into our cultural ways, in the dance, in feasting and fasting and praying, watching Him work powerfully in our lives, to experience His freedom.

The Blessing

I am thankful for the journey God has had me on. As 'burdensome' as it has been, it has been one of learning from Him and leaning on Him. Perhaps the 'old lady' I met at age four was also an angel. I am sure she knew I'd need Jesus in my journey through life.

Being **Grafted-in** into the First Nations' world and sharing some of their historical trauma provided me the opportunity to see beyond myself, helping me to appreciate more fully their plight. This greater awareness has been devastating and humbling.

Would I have changed my 'life-script' if I could have? On one hand, I can briefly say yes, I'd want it to be more problem-free and blissful, but the answer is "No." God, the Creator, knew through all the 'burdens' of my life, the wrong choices I would make, which were sins, and how it would go until I found Him.

I pray that you'll also seek and find The Pearl of Great Price and Jesus Christ, as your Lord and Savior.

As you read the 'priestly prayer' below, I release over you, in Jesus' name, blessings of love, faith, and healing from your diseases, traumas, and addictions; and may His angels always protect you and deliver you from lade, and the schemes of Satan.

The Blessing
(The Rabbinical Prayer) – Numbers 6:24-26 ESV

The Lord bless you and keep you; the Lord make his face to shine upon you and be gracious to you; the Lord lift up his countenance upon you and give you peace.

Forever and ever, Amen

With much love,
Montana.